D0203675

DATE			

BAKER & TAYLOR

Privatization, Conversion, and Enterprise Reform in Russia

Published in cooperation with the
Center for International Security and Arms Control,
Stanford University

Privatization, Conversion, and Enterprise Reform in Russia

EDITED BY

Michael McFaul and
Tova Perlmutter

with a foreword by
Kenneth J. Arrow

Westview Press

BOULDER • SAN FRANCISCO • OXFORD

Published in 1995 in the United States of America by Westview Press, Inc., 5500 Central Avenue, Boulder, Colorado 80301-2877, and in the United Kingdom by Westview Press, 36 Lonsdale Road, Summertown, Oxford OX2 7EW

Library of Congress Cataloging-in-Publication Data
Privatization, conversion, and enterprise reform in Russia / edited by
    Michael McFaul and Tova Perlmutter with a foreword by Kenneth J.
    Arrow.
        p.   cm.
    "Published in cooperation with the Center for International
Security and Arms Control at Stanford University"—Cip's pub. info.
    Includes bibliographical references.
    ISBN 0-8133-2548-X
    1. Russia (Federation)—Economic policy—1991–   . 2. Privatization—
Russia (Federation)   3. Economic conversion—Russia (Federation)
4. Post-communism—Economic aspects—Russia (Federation)
I. McFaul, Michael, 1963–   . II. Perlmutter, Tova.   III. Stanford
University. Center for International Security and Arms Control.
HC340.12.P75   1995
338.947—dc20
                                                                                                    94-24412
                                                                                                    CIP

Printed and bound in the United States of America

 The paper used in this publication meets the requirements
of the American National Standard for Permanence of Paper
for Printed Library Materials Z39.48-1984.

10   9   8   7   6   5   4   3   2   1

Contents

Part III: Regional Analysis of Defense Industry Issues

Part IV: Transition to the Market at the Enterprise Level

Foreword

These papers examine a transformation whose rapidity is rare in world history. Only once before have countries tried to change their economic systems so completely in so short a time. The emergence of capitalism was measured by centuries, not by years or decades. The transition from capitalism to socialism is the only change comparable in speed. Even so, when we look back at the experience of the Former Soviet Union, the process was fairly lengthy, with errors, reversals, and recommencements. In fact, it was more than a decade from the initial Bolshevik takeover to the real movement toward the classical form of Communist control. The change in Eastern Europe was swifter because of the massive military power of the Soviet Union and the by-then well-developed example it furnished of state socialism.

We are observing then one of the most interesting economic experiments in history. The papers in this workshop are an ongoing record of observations and data that are the basis of our current policy analyses and will be essential raw material for the more scholarly and less engaged historical analyses of the next twenty years. Economic theory supplies a set of demonstrations that a free enterprise system operating under a somewhat hypothetical set of conditions will lead to an efficient allocation of resources. But these conditions are rather stringent. In particular, they require that the future be well predicted by those currently in the market. It appears that precisely during rapid transitions expectations are most likely to be vague, uncertain, and contradictory. Much of the behavior in formerly socialist economies that does not fit the predictions of economic theory is a reaction to these surprises and doubts.

In general, in times of uncertainty, human beings, whether in the market or elsewhere, try to stabilize their environment. In market conditions, this often leads to interference with the free market through guarantees or cartels, to give two examples. This reaction is classic even in much milder crisis conditions in a capitalist system. The term "rationalization" may be unfamiliar now, but it was common currency in periods such as the 1920s in Germany. Similar motivations at the end of the nineteenth century in the United States led to the formation of trusts, not a state interference but an illustration of what is called "corporatism" in one of the papers here. Investment bankers considered unrestrained competition to be anarchy, so they created a whole series of monopolies in the United States. This tendency contradicted the basic interests and traditions of the country, with its reliance on small business and individual initiative, and so led to a political reaction around 1900 against the tendency to monopoly.

Thus it is not surprising that in a period of uncertainty, there is a demand for security. In the Russian case, history suggests the state as a potential source. That the state will play an important role seems to be inevitable. The question is whether its role will be to freeze the status quo and prevent the emergence of a reasonably competitive system or, on the contrary, to stimulate such a system.

Russia today can be compared with developing countries. None has succeeded or even tried to succeed without considerable state interference. In some countries, such as India and Latin America, state intervention encouraged inefficiency and slowed progress to almost a halt (at least until the last few years). In others, however, such as Korea, Taiwan, and Chile and Argentina in the last five to ten years, the state has nurtured industries capable of competing in the world market.

The Russian state will have to play a significant role in large-scale industry for some time to come. I am not optimistic about creating efficiency by rapidly privatizing large firms. In Russia, "privatization" by worker ownership is creating a very rich managerial class that will need large subsidies to keep the workers content. (Of course, there will be many exceptions to this general rule.) This is no incentive for efficiency. In the long run, the entry of new, small firms will be the basis of the future industrial system. The aim of the state should be to operate the large firms while gradually letting them be replaced by new entrants.

It must be emphasized that the state has other functions of the greatest importance. Above all, it must create macroeconomic stability, a requirement which itself will serve to harden budget constraints and improve efficiency. To counter the turmoil of transition, it must create a comprehensive social security system to provide for the victims of restructuring for greater efficiency. A reliable social welfare system will obviate the otherwise inevitable and justifiable demands for worker security. Finally, the state must create the legal and financial framework needed for a modern free enterprise economy.

The papers that follow show clearly the current situation and offer recommendations for the future. A consistent, state-led program that encourages entry of new firms—a program that can be relied upon to last at least a decade or more—is needed to let the highly educated Russian people earn the steadily increasing incomes they deserve. Whether the political struggle will permit this, however, remains to be seen.

KENNETH J. ARROW

PROFESSOR EMERITUS OF ECONOMICS
STANFORD UNIVERSITY

Preface

The papers in this volume are revised versions of presentations made by the authors at a conference on economic reform in Russia, which was held at Stanford University on November 22 and 23, 1993. Professor Kenneth Arrow from Stanford chaired the conference, which was sponsored by the university's Center for International Security and Arms Control (CISAC), under the auspices of its project on Russian defense conversion, and by the Moscow-based Institute for the Economy in Transition. Speakers included all the authors in this volume, as well as other representatives of the Institute for the Economy in Transition, the World Bank, and the European Bank for Reconstruction and Development (EBRD).

As presented here, the papers fall into four groups. Part I of this volume, "State Policies and the Context for Enterprise Reform," offers a broad outline of the Yeltsin government's economic policies for 1992 and 1993. The papers in this section are by two economists from the Institute for the Economy in Transition who are also advisors to Yegor Gaidar, the former Deputy Prime Minister responsible for the most aggressive economic reform policies yet implemented in Russia. The book begins with an overview by Alexander Radygin of the privatization process in Russia through the end of 1993, including an assessment of the program's results so far and a discussion of regulations on foreign investment in privatizing enterprises. Following Radygin's discussion of privatization policy, Sergei Sinelnikov reviews governmental finance and budget policy more broadly, with specific figures on revenues and expenditures, as well as remarks on how tax policies have affected the budget.

From this general discussion of state policy, Part II moves to "Management, Corporate Governance and Enterprise Directors," to consider more concretely how government action has affected the directors and managers of enterprises, and how these people have reacted to preserve their own resources. To open the section, Michael McFaul of CISAC provides a brief history of government-enterprise relations during and after the Soviet era, and describes how directors of state-owned enterprises were able to shape the government's privatization program to benefit themselves. McFaul argues that the Russian government has been too weak to resist the efforts of this firmly entrenched interest group, which gained substantial property rights over enterprises during the last two decades of Soviet rule. He also describes the weak, unstructured securities market and lack of corporate governance norms, and explains how these prevent outside shareholders from monitoring manager performance.

While McFaul's paper introduces issues of managerial power and resistance to change using the historical and larger political context, the next two authors explore these issues through empirical studies. Irina Starodubrovskaya of the World Bank and Katharina Pistor of Harvard University conducted surveys of directors to identify their attitudes toward economic reform. Their findings were slightly different. Starodubrovskaya found moderate optimism among the directors, and she claims that the main shock of economic reform for them is now past. Pistor, on the other hand, interprets her own results to suggest directors need more time to adjust to the changes taking place and to comprehend the free market. She also addresses the importance of strong corporate governance laws in implementing real change.

The last paper in Part II is by Mari Kuraishi Horne of the World Bank. Horne's paper discusses corporatism, a special relationship between the state and society in which the state grants privileges to non-state intermediaries, such as political or industrial organizations, in order to facilitate implementation of state policies. Horne argues that the Russian government's weakness and managers' undue leverage over the state have led to ineffective, unhealthy corporatist arrangements in Russia. She claims that "The only effective prophylactic against the development of an unhealthy set of relations between the state and the enterprise sector is the creation of an environment in which a critical mass of enterprises will be able to succeed without recourse to the state."

With the general environment for enterprise reform established, Part III of the book, "Regional Analysis of Defense Industry Issues," introduces issues concerning the defense industry in particular. In this section, Clifford Gaddy of the Brookings Institution and Jacques Sapir of the Paris-based Centre d'Etudes des Modes d'Industrialisation assess Russian economic change at the macro- and regional level. Gaddy performs a statistical analysis of oblast-level data to test the claims that regions with a high concentration of defense industry enjoyed higher standards of living than other industrial regions under the Soviet regime, and that these regions are more strongly opposed to reform than others. His findings overall are that defense employees probably lived no better, and perhaps slightly less well, than other urban industrial workers, and that "areas of defense industrialization appeared as of mid-1992 to be no more or no less 'anti-reform' than other areas in Russia." Gaddy also uses data from the April, 1993 referendum to show that defense regions tended to have higher pro-Yeltsin votes in the referendum than other areas, and offers potential explanations for this finding.

Sapir discusses the macroeconomic context of conversion, with particular attention to the increasing differentiation of economic trends between regions. His paper claims that "the supply-side approach to industrial restructuring that has been implicitly or explicitly the basis of...'shock therapy' strategies is not well-founded....Some form of coordination between demand and supply policies has to be achieved." Sapir argues that a gradual approach to market reform would have been more realistic and would have enjoyed more popular support and legitimacy.

Part IV, "Transition to the Market at the Enterprise Level," addresses many of the questions raised in Parts I, II, and III by considering conversion, privatization and market transition in terms of the experiences of several specific enterprises. First, John Battilega of

Science Applications International Corporation presents a case study of the Saratov Aviation Plant, one of the first enterprises to privatize in 1991. Battilega suggests that the Saratov plant's experience offers valuable lessons for other Russian companies, such as the benefits of employee ownership as an incentive to productivity.

Tarja Cronberg of the Technical University of Denmark then examines enterprises' conversion strategies in the context of industry in a single geographical area, discussing how, and to what extent, the Perm region is converting its defense industry. She finds that the most common approaches to conversion rely on dual-use technology and other products based on enterprises' existing capabilities rather than responding to market demand, and that managers have little idea of how to establish new networks or how to cope with competition.

Finally, David Bernstein of CISAC discusses the formation of new, small high-technology spin-offs and start-ups, and their role in the growth of the private sector as well as the restructuring of state-owned industry. He suggests that such small companies can provide necessary flexibility for industry as a whole, while also putting to optimal use the entrepreneurial skills of many young, creative scientists. Bernstein also identifies legal obstacles to the development of this sector and recommends that the state provide a more nurturing environment for it.

We would like to thank several people who helped to put this book together. David Bernstein and Elaine Naugle both helped organize the November conference and assisted in the early stages of editing. Flavia Pellegrini also helped organize the conference, helped edit several papers and put together the glossary, the summary of the Russian privatization program, and the list of relevant legislation. Susan Gates was our authority on economics. CISAC editor Megan Palmer scrutinized every page with an eagle eye and made sure we knew when ideas were unclear to a reader not saturated in the minutiae of Russian privatization.

We are grateful to the Carnegie Corporation of New York for funding the conference, this volume, and the project on defense conversion in Russia.

Michael McFaul

Tova Perlmutter

Part I

State Policies and the Context for Enterprise Reform

1

The Russian Model of Mass Privatization: Governmental Policy and First Results

Alexander Radygin

"And it should be known that there is no affair the settlement of which could be more difficult, the conduct more dangerous and the success more doubtful than the replacement of the old order with a new one."

Machiavelli, *The Prince*

Introduction

The wave of privatization that flooded the world in the 1980s reached the shores of Russia by the beginning of the 1990s. The term "privatization" became one of the most fashionable and indispensable attributes of proposed economic reform programs and discussions.

It is obvious that within the vast range of open or concealed interests, explicit political ambitions, and legal and spontaneous forms of privatization there can be no uniform interpretation of the process of privatization in Russia. This paper aims to describe, as much as possible, the state of privatization in Russia as of October 1993, with an emphasis on the main procedures and first results of mass privatization.

Alexander Radygin is the head of the Department of Privatization and Ownership Structure at the Institute for the Economy in Transition, Moscow, and has been an adviser to Yegor Gaidar, the former Acting Prime Minister of Russia.

One methodological note: in this paper, "privatization" is discussed in the narrowest sense of the word, i.e., as the process of complete or partial sale (transfer) of property (shares, assets) of state-owned enterprises to the private sector (both physical persons and legal entities). In the broader sense the notion of "privatization" also includes modification of management models for state-owned enterprises even without actual transfer of property rights, on the basis of leasing, franchising, contracting out, or other full or partial transformations of the legal status of state-owned enterprises.

The dominance of the public sector coupled with the long isolation of the Russian economy from the rest of the world make it inevitable that changes in property ownership will take place on an unprecedented scale. These two factors also mean that the privatization process will require intensive foreign investment. Foreign investment should not be used to achieve short-term objectives; it should help to establish effective economic units as an indispensable precondition for integrating the Russian economy into the world economy, thus making the economic reforms irreversible.

I. A General Overview, 1991–1993

In July 1991, well before the radical economic program of the Yeltsin-Gaidar government, the Russian parliament adopted two basic privatization laws, "On the privatization of state and municipal enterprises in the RSFSR" and "On personal privatization accounts and deposits in the RSFSR." These laws defined forms and methods of privatization in general terms: auctions, tenders, corporatization and sale of ownership interests (shares), sale of enterprises to their workers on preferential terms, free distribution of state property to all citizens, etc. Various political and economic factors, however, delayed the development of the necessary detailed regulations. Without these, actual privatization continued mainly in spontaneous forms.[1]

With the beginning of Gaidar's reforms in November 1991, privatization was declared a key element of the transition to the free market. According to the new economic program, price liberalization and other measures of financial stabilization preceded large-scale official privatization. This was in conflict with the prevailing theoretical paradigm for transition to a market economy and with the experience of a number of other countries.

The Main Provision of the 1992 Program of Privatization adopted by presidential decree in December 1991 became the first document that actually regulated the process of privatization. In January 1992, the official, non-spontaneous privatization program began.

The final version of the State Program of Privatization of Public and Municipal Enterprises for 1992 was adopted by the Russian Federation Supreme Soviet only in June 1992, after some delay. (See "Summary of Privatization Programs," p.223.) This program was in fact a compromise on two interrelated issues. The first issue was the debate between those who advocated "paid" privatization, through which only the active part of the population would become property owners, and those who called for "free" privatization, under which vouchers would be granted to all citizens with privileges to labor groups. The second controversy was between the "people's privatization for all" model, which was advocated by

4

the State Committee for the Management of State Property (GKI), and a model that would allocate property to enterprise employees, which was supported by Communists and trade unions.

The GKI's effort to make its program respond as much as possible to the interests of all Russian citizens made the document a hodgepodge of different privatization models. The program's inconsistencies may, in fact, be retarding the process of privatization significantly. Moreover, despite statements to the contrary by authors of the program, the interests of foreign investors appear to be last on the priority list.

Despite all the bitter political contention over privatization, the actual process moved fairly quickly in 1992 and 1993. By September 1, 1993, more than a third of all state and municipal enterprises had been privatized (77,810 enterprises, or 43.2 percent). About 1,500 applications for privatization were submitted in January, 1992; by September 1, 1993, more than 120,991 applications had been submitted, of which 64.3 percent had been processed (see Table 1). Even though the actual rate of privatization lagged behind the planned rate, the overall number and pace of Russia's privatization was higher in 1993 than in 1992 (see Table 2).

By September 1, 1993, more than 11,000 medium-sized firms not included in the list for compulsory corporatization set up working commissions to prepare for transformation into joint-stock companies. This is the best indicator of the actual response on a micro-level to the proposed "rules of the game." These data also suggest that if the current rate of privatization remains unchanged and no fundamental changes are made to the laws, the process of privatization is likely to become irreversible in 1994.

II. Mass Privatization

The widespread term "mass" privatization usually unites two independent but closely connected processes. The first is large-scale privatization, i.e. the transformation of large, state-owned enterprises (SOEs) into joint-stock companies (JSCs), with subsequent transfer of the companies' shares to citizens and other non-state legal entities. The second major process is the distribution more broadly through the population of vouchers or other similar certificates that give citizens the right to shares in these JSCs. In this framework, JSC shares represent supply, while the vouchers held by the population represent demand. The Russian privatization process joins the two processes together, mainly by selling shares both at open voucher auctions and by closed subscriptions for enterprise employees.

In fall and winter 1992 the implementation of Russia's model of "mass" privatization became one of the primary elements of the reform strategy. The development and launching of this model, notwithstanding all its drawbacks, can be regarded as the most favorable result of privatization in 1992 and 1993.

Corporatization

The Russian ideology of mass privatization values speed of privatization over quality of individual projects, and has therefore established one uniform, crude procedure.

5

There are at least two reasons for the GKI policy requiring compulsory transformation of a great number of large SOEs into open JSCs (about 5,000 in 1992 and 1993). First, the GKI sees vouchers as a means of maintaining "investment demand" on the part of the population. To provide a matching "supply" of potential investment it is essential that many enterprises turn into JSCs and issue shares. Second, property ownership in corporate form (even if the owner remains the same) is more successful at attracting and promoting the flow of capital among economic agents, given the crisis in financing whereby enterprises must rely primarily on their own profits, the state budget, and bank credits.

For large enterprises, the process of corporatization began without delay after Presidential Decree #721 of July 1992 was put into effect. On September 1, 1992 the list of large enterprises required to become JSCs comprised 4,452 firms, and only two companies were already registered as JSCs; by September 1, 1993 these numbers were respectively 5,056 and 2,118 (see Table 3). Including medium-sized enterprises and subdivisions of large enterprises that were incorporating separately from their parent firms, the figures for September 1, 1993 were 20,000 structures in the process of forming corporations, and 7,500 registered JSCs with a total chartered capital of 575 billion rubles according to official valuations set at the end of 1991.

Close to one-quarter of corporatized enterprises (24.2 percent) went through the process according to Option One of the privatization program. The second option was selected by 74.2 percent, while only 1.6 percent used the third option (see glossary for a full description of the government privatization program). These figures show that enterprise employees preferred in general to obtain the controlling block of shares. Such a large degree of insider ownership will probably negatively affect mobilization of internal investment resources, reduce opportunities for secondary share issues, and deter significant Russian and foreign investors or investment institutions, including voucher funds.

At the same time, the dispersion of ownership among the workers (combined with the broad distribution through vouchers to many small investors) may lead to a serious problem, as noted by Manuel Hinds [2]: without strong or controlling shareholder blocks, management would have a free hand.

The voucher program

The concept underlying the voucher program was adopted by the Russian government in June 1992. The privatization vouchers are federal securities with a limited period of validity and a face value of 10,000 rubles. By the end of January, 1993 almost all of the vouchers were distributed (98 percent of the 150.5 million total).

Two Presidential Decrees, adopted October 14, 1992, have been extremely important for keeping up the price of the privatization vouchers: "On promoting the system of privatization vouchers in the Russian Federation" (#1229) and "On the sale of houses, plots of land, and municipal property for privatization vouchers" (#1228). The first of these establishes that at least 80 percent of the shares of a privatizing enterprise must be sold for vouchers (previously, the requirement was 35 percent). The second decree not only expands the sphere in which vouchers can be used, but also enables medium-sized enterprises (those with an evaluated capital between one and 50 million rubles) to become joint-stock companies following the procedure set out in Decree #721. Both decrees thus broaden the use of vouchers.

Experts believe, however, that an increase in the number of shares sold for vouchers may lengthen the sale process. Secondary issues of additional stock and buyout by the enterprise of the land on which it is located are allowed only after the sale is completed of all B-shares (all preferred shares, including those retained by the state). Increasing the mandatory percentage of enterprises' shares to be distributed through voucher auction thus may diminish the likelihood of a second issue and, consequently, of real investment.

The market price of vouchers rose steadily until mid-December, 1992, although it was still short of the face value; it then fell sharply to one-third of the face value by early February 1993. From mid-February, the rate increased again, and was relatively stable by May (4100-4200 rubles). Large-scale clearing operations of 10,000-30,000 vouchers at a time helped to stabilize the market as opposed to short-term speculations with cash payments. By September-October, 1993, the price was between 10,000 and 12,000 rubles, varying according to the political situation and fluctuation both on exchanges and in private sales. It should be noted that due to rapid inflation throughout 1992 and 1993, 10,000 rubles at the end of 1993 was worth less in real terms than 4,000 rubles in the fall of 1992.

It is also worthy of note that in only 20 percent of the regions does the number of vouchers correspond to the fixed assets to be purchased. Therefore the voucher's market price varies from region to region. One tangible result of this could be localization of voucher markets in several centers and high profits (up to 200 percent) for speculators on the price differences between markets.

The government has only one tool left to support the vouchers: mass voucher auctions. At the same time, this tactic may be counterproductive, if the shares of privatized enterprises suddenly flood the market and result in a slump in share prices.

In many respects, the dynamics of the voucher price were influenced by the political situation as well as by turnover on the exchanges. This does not mean, however, that the price of vouchers should be treated as independent of the privatization process.

In the first place, it is the current market price that serves as the basis for tentative "market" evaluation of shares and enterprises, following the voucher auctions. For example, the voucher auction price at the Bolshevik cake factory in Moscow last January was 0.1 (i.e., one 1,000-ruble share for each 10,000-ruble face-value voucher invested), while the voucher's market price was 6,000 rubles. Thus, a share with a nominal value of 1,000 rubles could be assessed at 6,000 rubles in terms of "voucher worth." The total capital equity of the enterprise, accordingly, would also be raised by a factor of at least six. This calculation is, however, quite crude; it is clear that the true market evaluation of the shares put out for sale can only be made by a secondary market of privatized firms' securities, which, for the time being, is still in its embryonic state.

Second, the current market price of a voucher (the actual cost to buy one) is the basis for comparing the opportunities to acquire shares at particular voucher auctions. This interpretation, however, is also subject to a reservation: the prices of shares per voucher depend not so much on the financial performance of enterprises as on the total number of securities put out for sale.

For this reason, any attempt to assess the true value of vouchers is doomed to failure if the evaluation is based on just one procedure. A real understanding must take into account the multiple nature of the value price at present. Under current conditions, an attempt to evaluate vouchers on the basis of "profitability" of enterprises (even through acquired shares) is unlikely to be productive; only "quasi-market" or "proprietary" approaches are possible. The various approaches that would be useful include: a) the current market price in turnover both on exchanges and outside them (clearing and cash); b) market prices at the moment a given voucher was issued (e.g. fall of 1992, weighted appropriately for inflation); c) share-purchasing power of vouchers at auctions (number of nominal prices per voucher), also weighted appropriately (this is perhaps the most accurate indicator of the true situation); and d) prices at voucher auctions, weighted according to the revaluation of enterprise assets (given an average coefficient multiple of 20-22).

Average market prices can be expected to rise, provided political turmoil is not beyond reasonable expectations, due to a) the increasing number of shares sold through voucher auctions by giant, prestigious enterprises or fuel and energy facilities, and b) the gradual decline in the number of vouchers on the market as they are used.

Sales of stock

In November 1992 the chairman of the GKI issued an important order approving a procedure for the sale of shares of privatized enterprises and for special voucher auctions. These were the last procedures needed to complete the overall guidelines, when added to those specified by Decree #721 on transformation of enterprises into JSCs, management of closed internal subscriptions, registration for issues of stock, and a typical plan of privatization.

In line with the GKI's preference for privatization through vouchers, the documents stipulate a strict sequence for selling the shares of a specific enterprise: closed subscription for employees (see glossary), sale of individual shares (not in blocks) at the voucher auction, and only after that, sale of shares from the corporate fund of the employees and investment tenders for Russian and foreign investors. Hence, the participation of foreign investors is less likely, as they would thus have the opportunity to buy only 10-15 percent of an enterprise's chartered capital rather than a controlling block.

All corporatized enterprises were divided into five groups according to the date of their registration as JSCs; each group had its own deadline between March 1 and November 1, 1993 for holding the voucher auctions.

The first eight voucher auctions were held in Moscow, St. Petersburg, Vladimir, Nizhniy Novgorod and some other cities in December, 1992. By September, 1993, auctions had taken place in 79 regions of Russia, at which shares of 4,500 enterprises with a total evaluated capital of 187 billion rubles were sold.

The average weighted auction value for vouchers in January 1993 was four shares with a 1,000-ruble face value for one voucher, while in August this figure was 1.1 shares per voucher. It is significant that the voucher value has grown quickly in regions where voucher auctions are held.

At the same time, there is a striking range of prices. They can vary by region, from 0.175 in Moscow to 1.0 in Sakhalin, and by industrial sector, with lower prices (as low as half the nominal price) in machine-building, defense, and metallurgy enterprises. The highest prices— 30 to 50 times the nominal value—are expected in the fuel and energy complex.

The main participants in voucher auctions include representatives of employees, small investors, voucher investment funds, and larger institutional and private investors. While small investors seek, above all, to invest in enterprises that are reliable from the standpoint of a man in the street (sausage factories, breweries, etc.), the interests of investment funds and other large investors can include the land an enterprise stands on, its buildings, the profitability of its previous production, the possibility of reselling a large block of shares at a profit, potential for modernization or for improving production capacity, and export capability.

So far, foreigners (who may participate in voucher auctions only through representatives) have not been major investors in vouchers. Reasons include the generally unfavorable climate for foreign investments, the fact that fuel and energy enterprises have not yet gone to auction, the rules preventing purchase of controlling blocks at auctions, the unpredictability of auction outcomes, and a reluctance to disclose the amounts purchased.

When enterprise workers and managers buy up shares, they are motivated essentially by the desire to own at least a controlling block of shares, and as many shares as possible on top of that. They want to use majority control to ensure that profits go to employees, and to prevent the layoffs that might be imposed by outsider proprietors. These enterprises readily agree to take part in auctions for two reasons. First, once the government's share of ownership in an enterprise drops to 25 percent or less, that enterprise is legally allowed to purchase shares in other enterprises, or to control them by holding shares in trust. At the auctions in the Vladimir region, for example, workers' collectives acquired 50 to 90 percent of the shares sold. Second, an enterprise is only entitled to buy out the land it occupies following a voucher auction.

In practice, voucher auctions have revealed numerous problems. First, there have been difficulties financing the auctions. The funds allocated are insufficient, although a December 31, 1992 presidential decree stipulates that 5 percent of the shares sold at a voucher auction are to be sold for cash ruble payments, with the proceeds to go toward covering the costs of auctions.

Problems have also resulted from the practice of holding each auction only in the geographical area of the enterprise. This works to limit access for potential investors from other regions despite formal interregional tenders, as did the initial disproportionate regional distribution of vouchers (which led to regional differences in voucher price).

Third, voucher auctions have been hindered by opposition from some local and regional authorities and from sectoral ministries. The auctions have also suffered in some areas from the lack of clear procedural mechanisms and data, or from delays due to the slow rate of corporatization of SOEs, lawsuits in connection with closed subscription, and conflicts between committees and funds.

Technical problems have included dividing shares into fractions below the nominal price of ten rubles, returning vouchers to losing bidders, setting a minimum share price, and revising auction results when a large investor or investment fund acquires more than its respective limit of 35 percent or 10 percent of the shares.

Another problem is the fall in auction price in cases where most bidders are the enterprise's employees, or when the controlling block is known in advance to have already been purchased.

Most of these problems should be resolved by the creation of regional and interregional auction centers. The first permanent regional auction center for privatization was opened in Volgograd on February 8, 1993, with 20 enterprises on the block at the first auction. At the end of February, an interregional auction center was opened in Moscow: the first auction involved the shares of eleven Moscow enterprises and four enterprises of other regions. In May, such centers already operated in many regions, and this, along with a consistent policy of holding nationwide auctions for major enterprises, should be decisive in stabilizing privatization policy and practice.

It should be noted that for most privatizations (the initial public offering of these JSCs), and for all small ones, stock exchanges and most other mechanisms of capital markets are not yet realistic mechanisms for sale or sources of financing. Capital markets simply do not yet function to facilitate the flow of foreign capital into the Russian economy. In general, they will assume an important role only following the initial mass transfer of ownership, after voucher privatization and the first wave of employee stock purchases. In this context the role of investment funds within the model of mass privatization is exceptional.

Investment funds

By October 1993, rough estimates set the number of investment funds registered with the Russian government at more than 600. Russian legislation allows both for investment funds along the lines accepted worldwide, and for specialized privatization funds to accumulate citizens' vouchers. In both cases, any open joint-stock company is considered an investment fund if it is simultaneously involved in building up funds by means of issuing its own shares, investing its own resources in securities issued by other firms, and trading in securities. On the whole experts consider this legislation up to world standards. Theoretically, foreign citizens or legal entities could establish an investment fund in Russia, but so far there are no such examples. The lack of foreign-owned investment funds, however, may hinder the creation of a system of investment intermediaries for privatization.

Since investment funds are intended to reduce the risk for rank-and-file investors and to put together an extensive range of investments, all types of investment funds are subject to the following regulations: a fund is forbidden to hold among its assets more than 10 percent of the securities issued by one source, and it may not invest more than 5 percent of its net assets in securities of one source. Nevertheless, it is easy to get around these restrictions: if one fund cannot purchase more than 10 percent of a firm (i.e., a controlling block of shares), then a number of "friendly" funds can do it together without much trouble. It is also pointless to set limits on investment of net assets since there is no standard procedure for their evaluation.

All types of funds face major problems. At the moment, no safe investments exist in Russia. Furthermore, voucher auctions take place not all at once, but according to a schedule established by the government privatization program. This means that an investor does not have full information about all investment options at the time he must decide about a particular investment. It is thus impossible to create an extensive and diversified portfolio of securities and to maximize the likelihood of profitability for the fund's investors.

Unlike all other investment funds a voucher fund has the right to swap its own shares for vouchers. Such a voucher fund must be a closed JSC and can be licensed only by the GKI. These funds have been set up to spur long-term investment, which can be expected to increase shares' market value. They are also expected to reduce bank managers' chances to exercise majority financial control. Despite these aims, the non-liquidity of Russia's stock market sharply reduces a shareholder's right to vote by walking out. In practice, by exchanging his own voucher for shares of a specialized fund, a shareholder irrevocably becomes a hostage of the fund managers' operations.

Most of the established voucher investment funds engage primarily in speculation with blocks of vouchers and are tempted to raise the exchange rate of their shares for vouchers. This is already affecting the turnover of voucher privatization funds and is likely, at some stage, to impede the flow of vouchers to investment agents. Even more disturbing are cases of outright hoaxes by investment funds, e.g. in St. Petersburg. This calls for serious reconsideration of legislation in this sphere.

III. Foreign Investment in Privatization

Legal regime and restrictions

Formally, foreign investors may participate in privatization on an equal footing with Russian entities and citizens in auction, tender, or investment bidding. The legal regime for foreign investors "cannot be less favorable than the regime for the property, property rights and investment activity of the juridical persons and citizens of the Russian Federation" (article 6 of the Law on Foreign Investments). Foreign banks may finance privatization transactions on commercial terms without restrictions.

There are some regulations restricting foreign investors' participation in privatization to certain types of enterprises. Approval of the local authorities is required for foreigners to participate in the privatization of facilities of public catering, consumer services, small-scale industry, construction, and road transport. When the Russian government (or governments at republic level) sets up procedures for the privatization of enterprises and facilities of the fuel and energy complex; and enterprises that produce or process precious metal ores, precious and semiprecious stones, precious metals, and radioactive and rare-earth products, the authorities will also determine the degree to which foreigners may participate in the privatization of these enterprises.

If a foreign investor is the sole participant in an auction or tender, a special valuation of the assets of the enterprise shall be conducted. Direct bargaining has been rejected in favor of auctions and tenders, although this policy conflicts with world practices, according to which 50 percent of all privatization transactions worldwide in 1991 ($50 billion) were done by direct sale. Top officials of the GKI reason, first, that competition facilitates fair prices and simplifies the evaluation of enterprises; in the absence of competition, complex contradictory methods of evaluation generate delays, arguments, and corruption. Second, they favor competition because it guarantees the highest price for the seller.

As for land, there are a few regulations establishing the right of Russian and foreign individuals and legal entities to acquire a plot of land following the privatization of an
• enterprise, and the right to acquire more land to expand production. Nevertheless, failure to recognize the right of private land ownership, conflicts between executive and legislative authorities throughout Russia, and the fact that prices for land are set by administrators have led to legal instability in this sphere.

Technical problems and current opportunities

The following reviews the technical aspects of foreign investment only, putting aside such problems as political risks, general guarantees for property rights, etc.

11

Should privatization of a specific property be initiated, foreign investors, like Russians, must follow the procedures for processing and filing an application for the privatization of public and municipal enterprises. In general, the purchase of shares in a Russian enterprise by a foreign investor is treated by the legislation (Law on Foreign Investment, art. 13) as the establishment of a venture with foreign investment subject to general conditions. Some laws do suggest that there are legal "peculiarities" for foreign investors, but none specify what these are; in practice, such regulations do not exist.

A foreign investor is thus subject to the same simple procedures as a Russian participant. Beyond the barriers such as corruption that face all investors, however, a foreign investor will have to cope with the following problems: 1) obtaining copies of the relevant statutory documents, necessary information on privatization projects, and access to regional (local) publications and bulletins; 2) arranging deposits and final payments in rubles (despite a special note that payments in transactions with foreign investors are to be made in Russian currency through special bank accounts, the effective law virtually omits any provision for currency exchange; and 3) discrimination, compared with a Russian investor, regarding (a) direct contacts with the seller, (b) drafting of required papers, and (c) opportunities for preliminary visits to the enterprise, which are restricted by the need of obtaining a visa.

If an enterprise that interests a foreign investor is on one of the restricted lists of the State Privatization Program, the investor will also have to deal with a host of problems arising from interagency conflicts. No state body is capable of resolving alone the entire complex of issues associated with foreign investment. As a result, despite the formal equality and common regulations, a foreign investor will be at a disadvantage compared with Russian participants.

Without touching on ideology, it is clear that frequent changes of privatization and taxation mechanisms are a strong discouragement to any serious investor. The adverse effect will be especially strong on the organizational and technical side, in view of the heavy expenditures of foreign companies in time and money at the early stages of drawing up a major investment project study.

The goal of relatively fast privatization at a time of economic instability demands a comprehensive system of privileges as compensation by the state for investor risk. For the time being, this is not in the plans: moreover, any mention of privileges for foreign investors has been deleted from the State Privatization Program. On the other hand, the program provides for a "double investment" without any allowances for features of specific enterprises: a foreign investor must first redeem the shares of an enterprise from the state before embarking on investment programs. This leads many potential investors to prefer other options to privatization as such: setting up joint ventures; buying shares after the initial privatization, either in a secondary issue or on the secondary securities market; or using intermediaries to purchase shares.

Finally, one crucial contradiction of the privatization process remains unchanged: participation of the enterprise personnel in the selection and invitation of a foreign investor. Clearly, as employees in privatizing enterprises achieve more solid positions, foreign investors who aim to become majority shareholders will be discouraged.

In spite of the problems mentioned above, a few opportunities for foreign investors remain:

1) Participation in voucher auctions of shares in enterprises. The problems are the uncertainty of auction results and the fact that only non-controlling blocks of shares are for sale.

2) Participation in cash auctions of shares in enterprises. Foreign investors can pay for such transactions through special bank accounts or by using Russian partners as their representatives. The main difficulty is the extremely small number of shares available through these auctions.

3) Participation in investment tenders. Although foreign investors have not yet participated in many such competitions, nevertheless this is in practice the only way to get a controlling block of shares in an enterprise. If the winner of a tender has made an investment greater than 50 percent of the enterprise's net worth, he is entitled to request a secondary issue of new stock equivalent to his investment and will own these newly issued shares.

4) Direct negotiation with employee/manager groups. This option can include preliminary arrangements to buy their shares following the initial closed subscription.

5) Transactions in the secondary market after privatization.

Some of the most serious impediments to effective privatization and especially to the participation of foreign investors include the Soviet political and ideological legacy, old psychological stereotypes and collectivist traditions, ministerial or bureaucratic ambitions, and the extreme monopolization of the economy. On the other hand, it is natural that the initial legislation is not perfect and needs to be revised as experience accumulates.

Even if the basic infrastructure necessary for privatization is created in the foreseeable future, only then will the real work begin: the formation of a complex legal system of property rights and the economic and social structures that must accompany it, including an understanding of the market on the part of the masses. These are tasks that cannot be achieved by any privatization program.

For all its drawbacks, however, Russia's model of mass privatization (the creation of joint-stock companies combined with broad voucher distribution) has begun to work, although it neglects questions of efficiency, budget revenue, or future investment while overemphasizing a single, formal, and in many ways illusory task of creating a proprietor class. Yet the appearance of large joint-stock companies still does not mean that Russia's industry has adopted corporate property and management in the forms understood throughout the world. This is virtually impossible in the absence of efficient banking or financial market mechanisms to control the performance of corporations. The major task of privatization is the search for efficient owners and investment for future growth, and it still cannot be solved within the framework of the Russian model. So far, fears that stock ownership would be spread too thinly among small outsider owners have not been realized; in fact, voucher auction results suggest the reverse. A more serious problem lies in the "aggressive" behavior of workers' collectives (groups that include employees and managers) in the voucher auctions. This has led to significant ownership for these groups, resulting in dictatorial power for managers, even where their policies work to the detriment of outside owners. Thus, the so-called "fourth option" of privatization will effectively be in force even without a formal legal procedure.

It is unlikely that newly created joint-stock companies will be able to mobilize large-scale financial resources through additional issues of shares. This will be possible only for a rather small group of ventures with high profits and high liquidity.

One effective strategy could be rapid development of a secondary market for the stocks of privatized enterprises, a basis for which already exists in the form of regional auctions. This secondary market will involve stock exchanges in the sale of shares and the development of a telecommunications exchange system. Effective functioning of such a market will take time, since it requires efficient, knowledgeable owners—which it is to be hoped will be one of the results of privatization. Currently, however, voucher auctions represent only the first prerequisite for a true stock market.

It is insufficient to evaluate the privatization program's first results, even by formal quantitative criteria such as share or voucher price on the open market. The most significant positive result is quite different: the first step has been taken in what is necessarily a several-stage movement toward a new property rights system. It is only after these stages are a thing of the past, when a true capital market and a true system of property rights exist, that we will be able to speak of positive results of Russia's mass privatization model.

Notes

1. Alexander Radygin, "Spontaneous Privatization: Motives, Forms, and Main Stages," *Studies on Soviet Economic Development* 3, no. 5 (October 1992): 341-347.

2. Manuel Hinds, "Issues in the Introduction of Market Forces in Eastern European Socialist Economies, EDI/World Bank-IIASA. Seminar on Managing Inflation in Socialist Economies," Laxenburg, Austria, 6-8 March 1990, pp. 27-28.

Table 1

Main Indicators of the Privatization Process in the Russian Federation, January 1992–September 1993 (Cumulative totals)

Source: GKI Database. Not all Russian regions submitted complete information.

	As of April 1, 1992	As of January 1, 1993	As of April 1, 1993	As of September 1, 1993
Independent state enterprises*	139,904	204,998	194,190	180,837
Privatization applications submitted	18,366	102,330	114,725	120,991
Privatization applications rejected	656	5,390	6,879	9,011
Privatization plans accepted	12,677	46,628	42,788	35,234
Privatizations completed	5,023	46,815	61,810	77,810
Revenues obtained (in millions of rubles)	1,893	157,152	297,230	542,763
Total value of privatized enterprises (in millions of rubles)	1,171	193,189	405,177	531,219
Corporatized state enterprises offering shares for sale	59	2,376	4,805	10,159
Leased enterprises	9,451	22,216	19,435	17,735
Leased enterprises with a buyout agreement	7,581	13,868	10,850	14,504

*"Independent" state enterprises refers to the number of entities that can legally be counted as separate, with their own balance sheets, and thus are eligible for privatization as separate entities. This number rose between April, 1992, and January, 1993, because giant distribution networks for food and other consumer goods were divided into their subelements so that the smaller units could privatize separately.

Table 2

Analytical Summary of the Course of the Privatization Process in Russia (Average figures)

Source: GKI Database

	Avg. 1992	Jan. 1993	Feb. 1993	March 1993	April 1993	May 1993	June 1993	July 1993	Aug. 1993
Percentage of self-supporting state enterprises that submitted applications	43.0	44.6	45.9	46.8	47.9	48.1	48.6	48.2	52.7
Percentage of submitted applications that were processed	45.7	50.2	51.5	53.9	56.2	58.0	58.7	65.9	64.3
Actual rate of privatization (percentage of self-supporting state enterprises that had processed applications)	19.7	22.4	23.7	25.2	26.9	27.9	28.6	31.8	33.9
Planned rate of privatization (percentage of self-supporting state enterprises to be privatized, according to the government program)	53.2	53.2	53.2	53.2	53.2	53.2	53.2	53.2	52.4
Intensity of privatization (percentage of enterprises subject to privatization, according to the government program, that had processed applications)	36.9	42.1	44.5	47.4	50.6	52.5	53.7	59.8	64.7

17

Table 3

Main Indices of Corporatization in Russia According to Presidential Decree #721, as of September 1, 1993

Source: GKI Database

	Compulsory corporatization (large enterprises)	Voluntary corporatization (medium-sized enterprises)	Corporatization of separate subdivisions of enterprises
State-owned enterprises subject to corporatization	5,056	—	—
Enterprises selected by the GKI to corporatize	3,120	7,447*	1,261**
Enterprises where privatization plans were accepted and official evaluations were completed	2,629	6,269	775
Registered joint-stock companies	2,118	4,995	592
Total official value of registered joint-stock companies (in billions of rubles)	365.5	208.2	9.71
Total official value of assets transferred to employees and managers through privatization process	119.5	36.0	7.29

*11,229 medium-sized enterprises organized special working commissions for privatization.

**This figure does not include 2,275 structural units that local GKIs decided to commercialize.

2

The State of Public Finance, Fiscal Policy, and the Budget in Russia

Sergei Sinelnikov

The Soviet system of public finance had two stable, primary sources of budget revenue: deductions from corporate profits and a turnover tax. State spending steadily increased, however, and by 1990 the state's financial situation had worsened dramatically. The escalation of social welfare programs combined with increased government subsidies after a rise in agricultural prices in fall, 1990, and in wholesale prices of industrial goods in January, 1991 (while retail prices remained unchanged), produced a drastic financial situation. Both the federal and republic governments therefore sought to increase public revenues relative to GDP. Additional taxes were introduced, such as a sales tax and a payroll tax, to contribute to a stabilization fund. Social security payroll deductions were increased to 26 percent, while 20 percent of enterprises' depreciation allowances was withdrawn. Finally, exporters were required to sell part of their hard currency earnings to the state at an overstated ruble exchange rate. These measures were aimed at increasing the mandatory tax payment rate, which in previous years had ranged from 42 to 48 percent (around 55 percent of the GDP).

According to official estimates, under the new conditions taxes on corporate and personal incomes would go down sharply compared with taxes on enterprises' payroll and property (depreciation allowances), thus reducing the share of the items traditionally most important for a Soviet budget to increase revenues of extrabudgetary funds: the Pension Fund and the Economic Stabilization Fund.

These plans, however, remained unfulfilled. By the beginning of 1991, legal battles raged between the USSR and its constituent republics. In the course of these struggles, which threw the country's economic system into chaos, legislative bodies and governments at all levels

Sergei Sinelnikov is on the board of directors of the Institute for the Economy in Transition, Moscow, and has been an adviser to Yegor Gaidar, the former Acting Prime Minister of Russia.

made decisions that ran counter to the original budget projections in order to further their specific political agendas. Taxes on individuals and corporate profits were lowered, the sales tax was transformed from a cumulative *ad valorem* tax (as originally planned) into something like a value-added tax (VAT), and many goods were exempted from sales tax. Important macro-economic processes were also occurring, adversely affecting public finances by reducing the tax base.

As early as the end of the first quarter of 1991, it became clear that it would be impossible to implement the original budget plan: actual revenues to the Soviet federal budget were only 40 percent of planned revenues, and revenues to the Russian budget only 60 percent of those planned. The retail price reform of April 2, 1991 was an attempt to improve the budgetary situation. Retail prices were approximately doubled and partly liberalized. The aim of the reform was to reduce subsidies and increase income in the form of the turnover tax, the profit tax, and the sales tax. Unfortunately, this did not happen, primarily due to the almost complete disintegration of administrative control over prices and incomes. Price reform required corresponding wage increases, which increased the budget deficit. This resulted in the faster growth of wholesale prices compared with retail prices (295 percent and 240 percent, respectively, in 1991), which in turn meant increases in budgetary subsidies and reduction of the turnover tax receipts, and counteracted the positive influence price reform had on public finances.

In the first half of 1991, the Soviet federal budget deficit reached 60 billion rubles, approximately twice the planned target. In spite of substantial cuts in expenditures, the Russian republic's six-month budget deficit totaled 10 billion rubles, the figure originally planned for all of 1991. By the end of the year, the increasingly strained relations between the central government of the USSR and the republics' governments and the subsequent disintegration of the Soviet Union complicated the budgetary situation still further. The Soviet budget deficit for 1991 totaled 83.2 billion rubles, and together with the All-Union extrabudgetary economic stabilization fund amounted to 119.6 billion rubles. Taking into account use of state credits to keep farm produce prices from rising, the 1991 deficit of the Russian republic totaled 109.3 billion rubles. On the whole, the total budget deficit of the Soviet Union (including local budgets and extrabudgetary funds) increased from 8 percent of GDP in 1990 to about 15-16 percent in 1991, not including receipts from and expenditures on foreign economic activities.

The urgent financial situation, combined with the increasing slump in production and foreign trade, determined the need for immediate economic reform in Russia. The liberalization of many prices turned suppressed inflation into overt inflation, and the government's attempts to avoid hyperinflation while liquidating the "ruble overhang" demanded tough budgetary, credit, and monetary policies. To a great extent, this dictated the basic principles of the tax reform: stabilizing direct tax exactions at the levels of 1988-1990 (40-42 percent of GDP), increasing the share of indirect, *ad valorem* taxation, which would provide budgetary revenue from growing prices (by introducing VAT at a 28 percent rate), and creating equal taxation conditions for enterprises and firms under any forms of ownership.

In addition, the relation between revenues and implementation costs had changed radically. This is explained not only by the transitional nature of the Russian economy, but mainly by the fact that in 1992 the public finance system began for the first time to fulfill all the functions characteristic of the budget of an independent state.

The Russian State Budget in 1992

In 1992, Russia's financial policy went through three phases. The first phase, which lasted through the spring of 1992, was characterized by a relatively tough budgetary policy. In the summer, the government adopted a softer budgetary policy, leading to a sharp increase in the deficit. The third phase, from the fall until December, saw the implementation of emergency restrictive measures and a tougher budgetary policy.

The original budget estimates for the first quarter of 1992 provided for balanced revenues and expenditures through drastic spending cuts, primarily in the national economy and defense. As revised by the Supreme Soviet, by contrast, the first-quarter budget envisioned a budget deficit of 5.8 percent of the forecast Russian GDP. The first-quarter deficit in fact totaled around 3.8 percent of GDP, taking into account the expenditures envisioned by the Supreme Soviet's plan for the first quarter but financed in April. Not counting these expenditures, the budget deficit would be about 0.3 percent of GDP. This figure was achieved by implementing the budgetary expenditures, which were about 85 percent of the revised plan's target, as revenue came in. The emphasis on tough budgetary policies continued in April and May 1992. In April the budget deficit reached 1.1 percent of GDP, and in May 4.1 percent of GDP.

By spring, however, the president and the government faced mounting pressure to give financial support to enterprises and the population at large. As a result, the period from May to August saw the enactment of about two dozen laws, presidential decrees, and government resolutions that channeled about 400 billion rubles of extra funding to social needs. Industry, agriculture, and other economic sectors received government credits through the Central Bank.

Compared with the first quarter, budgetary expenditures in the national economy in the first half of the year grew from 7.9 percent to 9.7 percent of GDP, totaling 11.8 percent of GDP in the first seven months and 13.3 percent over the first eight months of 1992. Social spending increased from 6.8 percent of GDP in the first quarter to 9.3 percent of GDP in the first eight months of 1992, defense expenditures rose from 4.2 percent of GDP to 6.3 percent of GDP, and expenditures on the state administration bodies and law-enforcement agencies went from 2.9 percent of GDP to 2.5 percent of GDP.

Combined with the discrepancies between planned and actual revenue, these expenditures sharply aggravated the state of public finances. In the first half of 1992, Russia's budget deficit totaled 7.5 percent of GDP. By July, the deficit had reached 9.9 percent of GDP, climbing to around 13.5 percent by August.

The end of the summer saw the monetarization of the budget deficit through increasing loans to enterprises and trade surplus with the states in the ruble zone. This combined with the accelerating growth of the money supply resulted in rapid price increases and a plunge in the ruble exchange rate. Such structural factors as the introduction of new harvest prices for the use of agricultural raw materials and the September implementation of the next stage of fuel price liberalization played important roles in the rapid inflation. Resulting expectations of inflation boosted the demand for money, which in turn spurred on the inflation and caused the exchange rate to drop again in September.

The government consequently embraced tougher budgetary policies as a macro-economic priority in the fall of 1992. Government spending was slashed dramatically from September through November. By December, 1992, spending for the national economy shrank to 11.8 percent of GDP, social programs to 8.3 percent of GDP, and defense to 5.1

percent of GDP. Simultaneously, tax receipts from October-November 1992 grew considerably. The share of tax receipts in the budget revenue increased from 26 percent of GDP in September to 32 percent of GDP in November 1992.

As a result of these policies, in September the Russian budget deficit fell from 820 billion rubles to 716 billion rubles, or by 8.8 percent of GDP. At the same time, state payments for social sphere expenditures, for arms, and for the agricultural sector were delayed, and had to be covered by incoming revenue. In October, the actual federal budget deficit totaled 5.2 percent of GDP. In November, the budget deficit fell to approximately 4.0 percent of GDP (622.7 billion rubles).

The Russian federal budget deficit for 1992 totaled 985 billion rubles (4.9 percent of GDP), a figure only slightly above the limit set by the law "On the budgetary system of the Russian Federation for 1992." At the same time, the increase in the consolidated budget expenditures in December totaled more than 60 percent of the monthly GDP (the consolidated budget is the Russian federal budget, local budgets, and extrabudgetary funds added together), while the increase of the Russian Federation's budget deficit amounted to 13.4 percent of the monthly GDP. This data should be adjusted to take into account a number of the government's financial operations not included in the reports of the Ministry of Finance. Analysis of state revenues should include funds the government received in the first half of 1992 from the mandatory sale of hard currency from exports (at an overstated exchange rate of $0.018 per ruble). In the first six months of 1992, these budget revenues totaled about 110 billion rubles. An analysis of state expenditures should include import subsidies. Counting imports paid for by funds left by exporters abroad, imports paid for by Russia's Foreign Currency Reserve, and the imports paid for by external loans to be repaid by the state ($10.8 billion in 1992), import subsidies should total about 1,900 billion rubles (9.5 percent of the GDP), of which the lion's share was funded by external loans. State loans granted by the government should also be included in the budget, and in the consolidated public revenues and expenditures of the extrabudgetary funds.

As Tables 1 and 2 illustrate, in 1992 the balance of the Russian federal budget revenues and expenditures together with loans (minus the repayment deductions) totaled 21 percent of GDP. In regard to the impact of public finances on the moooney situation, the balance of the federal budget revenues, expenditures, and loans (minus the repayment deductions) shown above, but without subsidies to the importers, is a more informative indicator than the federal budget deficit calculated by the Ministry of Finance (5 percent of GDP). In 1992 this indicator was 11.4 percent of GDP. The Russian federal budget deficit was financed at the expense of foreign loans and loans granted by the Central Bank of Russia.

Out of all loans made by the Central Bank of Russia, the share granted to the government varied considerably during the year. Loans to the government made up 30 percent of the 70 percent first-quarter increase in the credit reserve, with loans to commercial banks accounting for 60 percent and loans to the states of the ruble zone for 10 percent. In the second quarter, loans to the government made up 38 percent of the bank's total loans, which increased overall by 192 percent (loans to commercial banks accounting for 32 percent, and loans to the states of the ruble zones for 30 percent). In the third quarter, loans from the Central Bank increased 131 percent, loans to the government this time accounting for 43 percent of the increase (with loans to commercial banks and states of the ruble zone at 40 percent and 17 percent respectively). In the fourth quarter, loans to the government made up 30 percent of the overall 75 percent increase in Central Bank credits (57 percent to commercial banks and 13 percent to states of the ruble zone).

Table 1. Public Revenues in 1992 (in billions of rubles)

	Republic Budget (% of GDP)	Local Budgets (% of GDP)	Extrabudgetary Funds (% of GDP)	Consolidated Budget (% of GDP)
Corporate Tax	646 (3.2%)	922 (4.6%)	–	1,568 (7.8%)
Income Tax on Individuals	–	431 (2.2%)	–	431 (2.2%)
Deductions for Social Insurance Fund	–	–	2,150 (10.8%)	2,150 (10.8%)
Internal Taxes on Goods and Services	1,701 (8.5%)	720 (3.6%)	–	2,421 (12.1%)
Taxes on Foreign Trade	689 (3.4%)	8 (0.08%)	–	697 (3.5%)
Other Taxes	112 (0.5%)	190 (0.9%)	–	301 (1.4%)
Extrabudgetary Funds	–	–	1,212 (6.1%)	1,212 (6.1%)
Other Revenues	53 (0.2%)	54 (0.2%)	not available	107 (0.5%)
Total Revenues	3,201 (16.0%)	2,344 (11.7%)	3,362 (16.8%)	8,907 44.5%)
Subsidies	–	299 (1.5%)	51 (0.3%)	–
Total Revenues and Subsidies	3,201 (16.0%)	2,643 (13.2%)	3,413 (17.1%)	9,257 (46.3%)

In 1992, federal budget revenues in Russia totaled 56 percent of consolidated budget revenues, with expenditures totaling 60 percent (without taking into account subventions to other levels of administration, loans and sums transferred under mutual settlements). Estimates made in 1992, however, had totaled revenues at 57.7 percent and expenditures at 69.9 percent, including December adjustments.

In many regions, local authorities tried to separate their finances from the Russian federal ones. In Bashkortostan, Tatarstan, Yakutia, and Chechnya, for instance, local authorities made declarations of sovereignty and adopted constitutions that gave regional laws priority over federal ones. As a result, all tax revenue in Bashkortostan and Tatarstan goes to the regional republics' budgets, and transfers of funds to the federal budget are carried out only with approval of the republic's Supreme Soviet. The amounts and procedures of these transfers are specified in annual or long-term agreements between the republics and the Federation. The agreement with the republic of Sakha-Yakutia, for example, stipulates an increase in the rate of deductions from Russian federal taxes towards Sakha's budget, along with the transfer to the republic of many expenditures previously funded out of the federal budget. In Chechnya, all taxes and payments collected go into the republic's budget. The Federation, however, does not fund any activities on the republic's territory.

Table 2. Public Expenditures in 1992 (in billions of rubles)

	Republic Budget (% of GDP)	Local Budgets (% of GDP)	Extra-Budgetary funds (% of GDP)	Consolidated Budget (% of GDP)
General State Services	42 (0.2%)	64 (0.3%)	–	106 (0.5%)
Defense	855 (4.3%)	–	–	855 (4.3%)
Law Enforcement Agencies	240 (1.2%)	5 (0.1%)	–	245 (1.2%)
Science	104 (0.5%)	3 (0%)	–	108 (0.5%)
Social Services	489 (2.4%)	971 (4.9%)	1,618 (8.1%)	3,078 (15.4%)
State Services to the National Economy	2,995 (15.0%)	964 (4.8%)	794 (4.0%)	4,753 (23.8%)
including: Investment in National Economy	315 (1.6%)	–	–	315 (1.6%)
Price Subsidies	313 (1.6%)	–	–	313 (1.6%)
Subsidies to Importers	1,900 (9.5%)	–	–	1,900 (9.5%)
Other Functions	1,184 (5.9%)	246 (1.2%)	–	1,430 (7.1%)
including: Foreign Economic Activity	417 (2.1%)	–	–	417 (2.1%)
Foreign Debt Servicing	120 (0.6%)	–	–	120 (0.6%)
Internal Debt Servicing	120 (0.6%)	–	–	120 (0.6%)
Subventions to Other Levels of State Administration	299 (2.5%)	–	–	
Other Expenditures	562 (2.8%)	–	–	562 (2.8%)
Total Loans Minus Repayments (Net Loans Outstanding)	907 (4.5%)	40 (0.2%)	–	947 (4.7%)
including: Loans **to Enterprises** Minus Repayments	876 (4.4%)	34 (0.2%)	–	910 (4.6%)
State Budget Loans to Enterprises Minus Repayments	72 (0.4%)	34 (0.2%)	–	106 (0.5%)
Central Bank Loans to Enterprises Minus Repayments	804 (4.0%)	–	–	804 (4.0%)
Total Expenditures Plus Net Loans Outstanding	7,378 (36.9%)	2,293 (11.5%)	2,412 (12.1%)	11,784 (58.9%)
Revenues and Subsidies Minus Expenditures and Net Loans Outstanding	-4,177 (-20.9%)	350 (1.7%)	1,001 (5.0%)	-2,879 (-14.4%)
Financing	4,177 (20.9%)	49 (0.2%)	–	4,226 (21.1%)
including: Domestic Central Bank Credit (Net)	1,912 (9.6%)	49 (0.2%)	–	1,961 (9.8%)
External (Net)	2,265 (11.3%)	–	–	2,265 (11.3%)

Taxation Policy in 1992

It is difficult to show the differences between the fiscal and budgetary structure of the Soviet Union and of the Russian Federation since the structure of public revenues and expenditures has undergone significant transformation. Meaningful comparisons must therefore be made by looking at the consolidated budget of the Soviet Union as well.

Between 1988-1990, the share of revenues in budgets at all levels totaled about 45 percent of the Soviet Union's GDP; in 1985-86, this figure was 47-48 percent of GDP. The accuracy of these figures is diminished due to the difficulty in assessing revenues from external economic activities at that time; nevertheless, these figures may be used for comparison. A reconstruction of the consolidated Soviet budget for 1991 shows a sharp decrease in budget revenues compared with preceding years and planned figures. According to our calculations, budget revenues for 1991 totaled 39 percent of GDP, which explains the catastrophic growth of the deficit.

In 1992, taxes increased to account for about 44 percent of GDP. The increase can be explained by both the successful tax reform and increased deductions in various social and production extrabudgetary funds.

If we consider the state budget alone, separately from the extrabudgetary fund, tax revenues increased during the year. In the first quarter they totaled about 20 percent of GDP, increased to 23 percent of GDP by July, and to 27 percent of GDP by the end of the year. The elasticity of tax revenues in terms of GDP in May, June, and September of 1992 was noticeably lower by one point.

Corporate income tax revenues for 1992 totaled 29.5 percent of the consolidated budget. The amount of real revenue from corporate profits was influenced by both tax remissions and the rate of wage growth as compared with changes in renumeration in prime cost regulated by the legislature. The interaction of these factors led to an increase in the corporate tax rate from 17 percent in the first quarter to almost 33 percent in the first half of 1992, and to 36 percent for the year as a whole. It should be noted that tax benefits for enterprises accounted for only one-third of those planned in the budget.

From January to December, the value-added tax accounted for 37.6 percent of all budget revenue, with excise taxes accounting for another 4 percent. In the first quarter, the elasticity of the VAT and excise tax revenue was fairly high with respect to GDP. This can be explained by small returns at the beginning of the year, and rapid growth in February and March after organizational difficulties in introducing *ad valorem* taxes, which replaced the turnover tax. The turnover tax had been calculated based on the difference between centrally fixed wholesale and retail prices. The steep decline in the growth rate of the excise and VAT revenues in the second quarter was caused by inter-enterprise debt and, to a certain extent, by the hoarding of finished products.

By July 1, 1992, inter-enterprise debt reached 3,004 billion rubles. Products marketed between January and May accounted for about 55 percent of the overall output. In the vast majority of enterprises, profits were assessed not when products were shipped, but when they had been paid. As a result, products already shipped to customers but not yet paid for are not considered when assessing taxable turnover of VAT payments, nor are they considered in the assessment of taxable profits.

The acceleration of the growth rate of VAT returns during 1992 can be largely explained by changes in exaction procedures for the tax. Until May, customers could make advance payments that were not based on actual turnover; they could therefore understate the advance and delay payment of the tax. Beginning in May, orders for more than 300,000 rubles required payments based on actual turnover. Furthermore, at the end of May it became illegal to subtract from enterprises' VAT liabilities the amounts of tax on inventories received (VAT credit) if the appropriate bills had not been settled. The substantial increase of VAT receipts in July versus June (2.6 times more) was due to the introduction of advance VAT payments. The amount of advance payments was worked out proceeding from the actual payments made in the first quarter, multiplied by 2.5.

The sharply increased VAT and corporate profit tax revenues in the fall can be attributed to precision in tax collection techniques. In October VAT accrued, due to a regulation restricting deductions from VAT to only material resources that can be written off as production costs, and also due to the inclusion in the taxable turnover of all the funds received by suppliers. (Before this change, one widely used method of avoiding taxes was understating prices and remitting to the supplier money designated for other purposes.) According to data supplied by the State Tax Collecting Service, the additional VAT and profit tax return based on actual turnover, as compared with advance payments, totaled about 200 billion rubles. Growth of tax revenues in October was aided by a new policy whereby funds received by enterprises were channeled primarily into the settlement of the debts to the state budget. According to the Russian Central Bank's data, the repayment of the outstanding VAT totaled some 220 billion rubles.

Starting in October, the procedures for advance VAT payments were toughened. Enterprises with a turnover of more than 100,000 rubles a month were to pay VAT every 10 days based on actual sales figures. The final tax figures for each enterprise were to take into account the VAT credit paid for material resources already used, as well as the results of the month as a whole.

In 1992 income tax on individuals accounted for 8 percent of Russian budget revenues and remained very stable. The elasticity of those receipts with respect to GDP is close to 1, which is explained by the similarity of the wage and GDP growth rates on the linear scale of tax levied at the source compared with 1991. Since the minimum taxable income was raised, receipts dropped from 12 percent to 8 percent of national personal income.

Budget Planning and Budget Implementation in 1993

By December the increasingly tough budgetary, credit, and monetary policies carried out in the fall of 1992 slowed the growth in prices and stabilized the ruble exchange rate. However, a substantial increase in the money supply in December owing to expanded crediting and the growing Russian budget deficit provoked a new spiral of price hikes as early as the middle of December and a nosedive of the ruble exchange rate in late January.

The replacement of Yegor Gaidar by Victor Chernomyrdin as the head of the government caused serious concern about the consistency of the measures designed to achieve financial stabilization. The retention of part of the old cabinet, however, as well as the appointment of Boris Fyodorov to the post of vice-premier and later simultaneously to that of minister of finance, made it possible to ensure continuity of the economic policy.

Two fairly distinct periods can be distinguished in the budgetary policy carried out in 1993. The first period lasted from January to September 1993, until the dissolution of the legislature on September 21, and was characterized by the fact that all the legislative and executive authorities made decisions escalating expenditures, which were not supported by increased revenues. Since in the same period the Russian Ministry of Finance pursued a relatively tough policy, from January to September the gap between the cash budget deficit and the planned one kept growing. Starting in October, however, the fundamental change in political forces made it possible to reduce this gap, giving hope that a more balanced budget could be achieved.

The First Part of 1993, January-September

In January, 1993, the Russian Supreme Soviet approved a resolution financing federal budget expenditures to one-third of the amount envisioned in the fourth quarter of 1992. Expenditures not planned in the fourth quarter could only be financed by a new decision of the Supreme Soviet.

As a result, revenues in January topped expenditures by 29 billion rubles (0.9 percent of GDP), with tax receipts totaling 37.4 percent of GDP (not counting extrabudgetary funds), and making up 23.4 percent of the Russian federal budget.

The Russian parliament did pass a resolution, however, under which the government was allowed during the first quarter to provide monthly funding for programs totaling one-twelfth of the combined appropriations outlined in the budget that had been submitted by the government. In February, this had not yet made any dramatic impact on the state of the budget. Tax receipts totaled 35.2 percent of GDP, and the republic's budget deficit stood at 34 billion rubles (.04 percent GDP).

In March, 1993, state expenditures rose steeply, from 21 percent of GDP in January-February to 26 percent in January-March. (The figure for expenditures rose 240 percent, but high inflation during the same period meant that in real terms the increase was not so dramatic.) As a result, the Russian federal budget deficit grew to 11.2 percent of the January-March 1993 GDP. The deficit was funded by increased Central Bank credits to the government, totaling 1.72 trillion rubles—11.5 percent of GDP.

At the end of March the Russian Supreme Soviet adopted the 1993 budget on its second reading with a deficit of about 18 percent of GDP, which was signed by the president in the middle of May in spite of the opposition of the Ministry of Finance. Almost immediately after it was signed, however, corrections began on the budget because of both the unrealistic precepts on which the 1993 budget had been based and the Ministry of Finance's objections to its extremely high planned expenditures. At the end of June, 1993, the Supreme Soviet considered the draft budget as revised by the Ministry of Finance, which envisioned reduction of the deficit from 18 percent of GDP to approximately 10 percent of GDP. After it had been debated by the parliament, however, the draft was corrected and on July 22, 1993, the Supreme Soviet adopted the law "On the specification of the indicators of the republican budget for 1993," envisioning a deficit of 22 percent of GDP. President Yeltsin refused to sign the law and sent it back to the Supreme Soviet. On August 27 the parliament passed this variant of the budget a second time and adopted the law "On the introduction of changes and additions to the law 'On the republican budget of the Russian Federation for 1993.'" In this version the deficit had been reduced by only 60 billion rubles—to 22.1 percent of GDP.

In spite of 1993's difficult and controversial process of financial planning, the implementation of the budget proceeded relatively smoothly. After a sharp rise in the deficit in the first quarter of 1993, beginning in May the Ministry of Finance succeeded in stabilizing the situation and, according to official data, in cutting the deficit to 4-5 percent of GDP.

In May, federal expenditures on the bodies of state authority, defense, the national economy, and the social sphere decreased slightly. As a result, the Russian federal deficit shrank to 4.5 percent of GDP or, taking account of the incomplete transfer of some federal budget revenues by the Central Bank, to 5.9 percent of GDP. In June, the slight decrease of the expenditure on the national economy and defense continued, while the other expenditures were stabilized. The total amount of loans granted to enterprises from the central budget minus repayments also became smaller (1.2 percent of GDP in April, 1.2 percent in May, and 0.8 percent in July). As a result, according to official data from the Ministry of Finance, the deficit totaled 3.4 percent of GDP for the first half of 1993 (in cash terms 5.5 percent of GDP), while revenues totaled about 15 percent of GDP.

Over six months, as in the first quarter of 1993, local revenues exceeded expenditures. Over six months this excess added up to 1.9 percent of GDP, the transfers from the Russian Federation budget in the form of subventions to other levels of state administration and budgetary loans also totaling about 2.1 percent. Tax revenues in local budgets fluctuated around 15.5 percent of GDP. Thus, in the first half of the year the revenues (including those not from taxes, which made up 0.2 percent of GDP) and subsidies of the local budgets reached 18-18.5 percent of GDP, with the expenditures totaling 16-16.5 percent of GDP.

In July and August negative trends in the budgetary situation increasingly made themselves felt. Changes in revenues were to a considerable extent independent of the policy of the Ministry of Finance and were connected mainly with growing inflation in the summer of 1993. The consolidated budget deficit increased from 4.2 percent of GDP in June to 6.6 percent of GDP in July and to 7.5 percent of GDP in August. The federal budget deficit increased from 6.1 percent of GDP in June to 8.8 percent of GDP in July and to 9.5 percent of GDP in August. In July and August the revenues coming in totaled about 29 percent of GDP (without the extrabudgetary funds).

No serious changes in the structure of the budget revenue and expenditure occurred in July and August. An important trend, however, was the decrease in taxes from 29.8 percent of GDP in June to 29.2 percent of GDP in July and 27.4 percent of GDP in August. This occurred mainly at the expense of tax revenues to the federal budget, which diminished from 13.9 percent of GDP in June to 13.3 percent of GDP in July and to 12.3 percent of GDP in August. The growing budget deficit was financed by selling hard currency and precious metals and stones (0.6 percent of GDP in June, 1.2 percent of GDP in July), and by selling the hard currency received as an IMF loan (1.2 percent of GDP in July). In July and August these sources brought in 2.3 trillion rubles (3.3 percent of GDP). In addition, in August part of the Central Bank revenues, totaling 260 billion rubles (0.4 percent of GDP), was counted as budget revenue. It should be noted that in the statistics of the Ministry of Finance, Central Bank revenues are counted under "financing," whereas in our tables they are counted as "non-tax revenues."

In September the situation continued to deteriorate. The consolidated budget deficit reached 8.3 percent of GDP, and the republican budget deficit reached 10 percent of GDP, while federal expenditures practically did not increase (from 19.4 percent of GDP in August to 19.5 percent of GDP in September) and expenditures plus subsidies minus repayments even decreased by 0.5 percent of GDP. Budget revenues, however, shrank to 11.8 percent of GDP. Central Bank profits, which totaled 0.5 percent of GDP, were added to budget revenues. Expenditures were financed by the government by selling hard currency (1.6 percent of GDP over nine months), precious metals (0.8 percent of GDP), and by using the IMF loan (1.6 percent of GDP).

The Second Part of 1993, October-December

The fundamental change in the balance of political power after President Yeltsin dissolved the Parliament in September 1993, and the resulting appointment of Gaidar as First Deputy of the Chairman of the Government, led to radical changes in budgetary policy.

The political change did not affect the cash implementation of the budget (in the fourth quarter the federal budget deficit remained at 9-10 percent of GDP), but it resulted in lower government expenditures. Without legislative interference, the executive branch had the opportunity to implement budget expenditures in accordance with incoming revenues and Central Bank credit limits. Excessive expenditures were reduced in several ways. Indexation of grain and other agricultural prices for state orders was cancelled, bread subsidies for the needy were abolished, import subsidies were liquidated, most preferential loans were cancelled (except for budgetary loans), and the Central Bank refunding rate was raised. State capital investment was sharply reduced, and federal budget expenditures for the fourth quarter of 1993 were sequestered at 20 percent.

The state also succeeded to a considerable degree in battling the centrifugal budgetary tendencies of a number of regions of the Russian Federation. Presidential Decree No. 1774 of October 27 enabled the government to fight violations of Russian law in transferring federal tax receipts to the republican budget. Regional indebtedness to the republican budget diminished considerably.

In spite of fairly tough measures taken in the fall of 1993, the lasting consequences of previous expenditure policies kept the deficit high. In addition, tax receipts as a percentage of GDP continued to shrink, although less precipitously (see Table 5). Cumulative tax receipts into the consolidated Russian budget dropped from 25.4 percent in September to 24.5 percent by December 1993, and receipts into the republican budget from 11.1 percent to 10.3 percent. The structure of republican budget expenditures remained approximately the same as in the first nine months of the year. Expenditures on the national economy decreased slightly from 3.1 percent to 2.8 percent of GDP. Subventions to local budgets increased from 2.5 percent to 2.7 percent of GDP, while loans minus repayments decreased from 2.4 percent to 1.7 percent of GDP.

As a result of this difficult process of going back on prior obligations (which turned out to be politically costly in the December elections), it was possible to keep the federal budget deficit to 9.4 percent of GDP. The government was able not only to avoid financial catastrophe, but to begin lowering inflation (from 16 percent in November to 13 percent in December 1993).

Under this policy, according to data of the Ministry of Finance, the overall sum of unfinanced expenditures, compared with the planned budget confirmed May 14, 1993, totaled 13.8 trillion rubles. Part of this sum made up the state's outstanding debt of about 8.5 trillion rubles. The most essential of these expenditures, totaling four trillion rubles, had to be financed in the first quarter of 1994; 2.9 trillion rubles were repayable at the expense of budget appropriations, while 1.1 trillion rubles were repayable through tax exemptions to enterprises (0.6 trillion rubles) and the issuing of medium-term treasury promissory notes (0.5 trillion rubles).

Tables 3 and 4 give a reconstruction of the consolidated budget of the Russian Federation in 1993. The analysis shows, first of all, a stabilization in Russia of the level of tax exactions at 43-44 percent of GDP. Tax receipts account for about 95 percent of state revenue. The rest is accounted for by the Central Bank's profits (1.3 percent of GDP), interest on loans to foreign countries, income from privatization, etc. Revenues of extrabudgetary funds remained at the level of 1992—about 17 percent of GDP.

Table 3. Public Revenues in 1993 (in billions of rubles)

	Republic Budget (%of GDP)	Local Budgets (%of GDP)	Extra-Budgetary Funds (% of GDP)	Consolidated Budget (%of GDP)
Corporate Tax	5,472 (3.4%)	11,302 (7.0%)	–	16,774 (10.3%)
Income Tax on Individuals	–	4,388 (2.7%)	–	4,388 (2.7%)
Deductions for Social Insurance Fund	–	66 (0%)	17,528 (10.8%)	17,594 (10.8%)
Internal Taxes on Goods and Services	8,908 (5.5%)	5,523 (3.4%)	–	14,431 (8.9%)
Taxes on Foreign Trade	8,360 (5.2%)	91 (0.1%)	–	8,451 (5.2%)
Other Taxes	37 (0%)	1,018 (0.6%)	–	1,055 (0.7%)
Extra-Budgetary Funds	–	–	9,902 (6.1%)	9,902 (6.1%)
Other Revenues	2,794 (1.7%)	2,345 (1.4%)	–	493 (0.3%)
Total Revenues	25,571 (15.8%)	24,733 (15.2%)	27,430 (16.9%)	77,734 (47.9%)
Subsidies	–	4,296 (2.7%)	–	–
Total Revenues and Subsidies	25,571 (15.8%)	29,029 (17.9%)	27,430 (16.9%)	77,734 (47.9%)

Table 4. Expenditures for 1993 (in billions of rubles)

	Republic Budget (%of GDP)	Local Budgets (%of GDP)	Extra-Budgetary Funds (%of GDP)	Consolidated Budget (%of GDP)
General State Services	658 (0.4%)	818 (0.5%)	–	1,476 (0.9%)
Defense	7,210 (4.4%)	–	–	7,210 (4.4%)
Law Enforcement Agencies	2,513 (1.5%)	111 (0.1%)	–	2,624 (1.6%)
Science	894 (0.6%)	49 (0%)	–	943 (0.6%)
Social Services	2,917 (1.8%)	12,413 (7.6%)	13,182 (8.1%)	28,512 (17.6%)
State Services to National Economy	6,473 (4.0%)	11,847 (7.3%)	5,024 (3.1%)	23,344 (14.4%)
including: Subsidies to Importers	1,930 (1.2%)	—	–	1,930 (1.2%)
Capital Investment	1,321 (0.8%)	–	–	1,321 (0.8%)
Total State Services to National Economy	2,849 (6.8%)	2,628 (6.3%)	1,003 (2.4%)	6,480 (15.5%)
Other Functions	15,784 (9.7%)	1,734 (1.1%)	–	13,190 (8.1%)
including: Foreign Economic Activity	6,111 (3.8%)	60 (0%)	–	6,171 (3.8%)
Foreign Debt Servicing	450 (0.3%)	–	–	450 (0.3%)
Internal Debt Servicing	989 (0.6%)	–	–	989 (0.6%)
Subventions to Other Levels of State Administration	9,328 (2.7%)	–	–	–
Other Expenditures	2,000 (1.2%)	–	1,136 (0.7%)	3,136 (1.9%)
Total Expenditures	38,449 (23.7%)	26,972 (16.6%)	19,342 (11.9%)	80,435 (49.6%)
Total Loans Minus Repayments (Net Loans Outstanding)	3,293 (2.0%)	586 (0.4%)	–	3,897 (2.4%)
including: Loans to Enterprises Minus Repayments	2,834 (1.7%)	586 (0.4%)	–	3,420 (2.1%)
Loans to CIS States Minus Repayments	511 (0.3%)	–	–	511 (0.3%)
Loans Minus Repayments Untransferred to Foreign States	-450 (-0.3%)	–	–	-450 (-0.3%)
Central Bank Arrears to the Government	322 (0.2%)	–	–	322 (0.2%)
Total Expenditures Plus Net Loans Outstanding	41,742 (25.7%)	27,588 (17.0%)	19,342 (11.9%)	84,314 (51.9%)
Revenues and Subsidies Minus Expenditures and Net Loans Outstanding	-16,171 (-10.0%)	1,471 (0.9%)	8,088 (5.0%)	-6580 (-4.1%)
Financing	16,171 (10.0%)	–	–	–
Domestic (Net)	13,021 (8.0%)	–	–	–
External (Net)	3,150 (1.9%)	–	–	–

31

The 2.4 points difference from the official Ministry of Finance GDP statistics can be explained by the different methods of assessing the government's external economic operations. We do not include the ruble cover for the centrally granted hard currency sums in the revenues from external economic activity. Under expenditures we do not take into account "purchase of goods for centralized export." Instead of these two items we take into account "revenues from the realization of the state monopoly on centralized export operation," which are assessed as earnings from the centralized export minus the expenditures on the purchase of goods for this operation. Moreover, according to our method the import subsidies item under expenditures takes into account the balance between hard currency sums centrally granted to the importers and the corresponding incomings of the ruble cover. As a consequence, in the annual report of the Ministry of Finance revenues from external economic activity account for about 1.4 percent of GDP, while in our estimates they account for 5.2 percent of GDP.

In 1993, the structure of state expenditure changed to some extent. Expenditure on the bodies of state authority and administration increased by 0.4 percent of GDP and social expenditures grew by 1.7 percent of GDP. Expenditures on the national economy diminished quite considerably, but this was due chiefly to the reduction of import subsidies. Capital investment also decreased to a certain extent (from 1.6 percent to 0.8 percent of GDP). On the whole, in 1993 expenditures totaled 51 percent of GDP, which was close to the 1992 figure. At the same time, subsidies minus repayments dropped from 4.7 percent of GDP in 1992 to 2.4 percent of GDP in 1993.

According to our estimate, federal budget revenues and subsidies with the deduction of expenditures and loans minus repayments totaled 9.9 percent of GDP. On the whole, state expenditures exceeded revenues by 4 percent of GDP. Internal financing supported 81 percent of this federal deficit, with loans from the Central Bank accounting for 64 percent of the total volume of financing. It should be noted that in 1993 loans to the government made up 65 percent of all Central Bank loans.

Taxation Policy in 1993

In 1993 the main changes in the tax system were based on taxation regulations adopted by the Supreme Soviet of the Russian Federation in July 1992, the law "On changes and additions to Russia's taxation system" passed in July, and the law "On changes and additions to the Russian tax laws for individuals" passed on December 22, 1992. In accordance with these laws and regulations, procedures for assessing and taxing corporate profits, VAT, and individual income substantially changed.

Provided that depreciation allowances are fully spent on renovation, from 1993 all production and non-production capital investment will be exempted from corporate profit tax.

The technique for regulating the spending of funds on consumption has been altered. The amount by which corporate expenditures exceed the maximum is subject to profit tax at the basic rate or, if it exceeds the maximum more than twofold, at a 50 percent rate. The maximum itself is four times the minimum monthly statutory wage, as it was in 1992. To prevent understatements of advance payments, the difference between the amount payable based on actual profits and the advance payments is indexed according to the Central Bank set interest rate of the preceding quarter.

From January 1, 1993, the VAT rates were reduced: to 10 percent on foodstuffs (except those subject to excise duty) and children's goods and to 20 percent on other goods. In addition to directly worsening the budgetary situation in 1993, the advance announcement of the measure led to a drop in sales in the fourth quarter of 1993. The reduction of the VAT rates did not produce the anti-inflationary effect desired by the legislators who made the decision, just as the lowering of VAT rates on dairy products, vegetable oil, flour, and other foodstuffs in February, 1992, failed to achieve it.

From February, 1993, existing procedures for VAT and excise payments were extended to cover imported goods. The only products exempted from VAT are imported foodstuffs, raw materials for food production, research equipment, and medical goods.

From January 1, 1993, value-added tax ceased to be gross VAT, the application of which makes it impossible to deduct tax on acquired capital resources from tax liabilities. It has not become a net VAT either, however, since the VAT credit, i.e., the part of the tax paid on fixed and intangible assets, is deducted from the tax due in equal installments over a two-year period, starting from the commissioning of the fixed assets and the recording of the intangible assets in the books. In agriculture such deductions can be done in a lump sum as the assets are entered in the books. Another measure that complicates corporate accounting and control over tax payments is the procedure that grants a VAT credit on acquired inventories (other than capital resources) only if their value is actually written off as production and distribution costs.

Aside from the numerous alterations of the method of assessing taxable income, the one fundamental change in the law on individual income tax is the indexing of the taxation scale. The new law raised the starting point for progressive tax from 42,000 rubles to 200,000 rubles; this is clearly not high enough, considering last year's high inflation, to achieve the Supreme Soviet's goal of saving most workers from income tax. In 1993, the taxation scale was indexed again and now taxes start from one million rubles a year. An important point is the exemption from taxation of money spent on new construction or the purchase of a house, apartment, dacha, etc., as well as any money spent repaying loans received for these purposes.

The rates at which national taxes are channeled into regional budgets have also been changed. Now regional budgets receive 20 percent of the value-added taxes, 19 percent of the corporate profit taxes, 50 percent of the excise duties on spirits and vodka, and 100 percent of the other national excise duties (except on automobiles). With a view to reducing the subsidies to local budgets, the Russian government has increased the percentage of VAT deductions to be channeled to many territories—up to 50 percent.

One worrisome tendency is the shrinking ratio of tax exactions to GDP from 31.1 percent of GDP in April to 27.5 percent of GDP in August. This occurred mainly because tax revenues coming into the national budget went down from 15.3 percent of GDP in April to 12.9 percent of GDP in August.

When analyzing the dynamics of the budget tax revenue in 1993, one should note that the high level of tax exactions at the beginning of the year is explained, first, by the fact that at the beginning of the year VAT was imposed in accordance with last year's rates (28 percent) and, second, by the reassessment of the actual corporate profit tax in accordance with the overall results of the fourth quarter and 1992. Therefore, the 1993 summer tax level should be compared either with the 1992 figures, when the tax exactions level (without the

Table 5. The Dynamics in 1993 of Tax Receipts, Gross Domestic Product, Debit Indebtedness, and Non-Payment of Arrears with Price Index Taxes

Source: State Statistics Committee of the Russian Federation, Ministry of Finance, State Tax Collection Service of the Russian Federation, author's calculations.

	Jan. 1993	Feb. 1993	Mar. 1993	April 1993	May 1993	June 1993	July 1993	Aug. 1993	Sept. 1993	Oct. 1993	Nov. 1993	Dec. 1993
Tax revenues to the consolidated budget (percent of GDP)	36.0	33.8	31.0	30.7	29.5	29.4	28.7	27.4	25.4	25.0	25.1	24.5
Tax revenues to the state budget (percent of GDP)	2.7	19.1	15.8	15.2	14.5	14.0	13.3	12.3	11.1	10.9	10.7	10.3
Growth rates of monthly GDP		2.38	1.68	1.22	0.94	1.09	1.1	1.19	1.31	0.98	1.13	1.37
Growth rates of nominal GDP		2.38	1.97	1.6	1.35	1.29	1.31	1.28	1.29	1.22	1.20	1.23
Growth rates of debit indebtedness (industry and construction)	1.12	1.29	1.21	1.20	1.18	1.27	1.24	1.18	1.18	1.18	1.19	1.20
Arrears in payments to the consolidated budget (percent of GDP)*	3.8	2.7	2.4	2.34	2.02	1.72	1.62	2.25	1.78	1.62	2.19	1.86
Arrears in payments to the state budget (percent of GDP)	2.4	1.82	1.52	1.29	1.14	1.14	1.09	1.48	1.13	0.99	1.22	1.08
Retail price index	1.27	1.26	1.21	1.23	1.19	1.20	1.22	1.26	1.23	1.20	1.16	1.13
Wholesale price index	1.32	1.32	1.23	1.24	1.19	1.17	1.29	1.27	1.21	1.19	1.15	1.11

*Arrears in payments to the consolidated budget include arrears in payments to the state budget.

extrabudgetary funds) totaled about 31 percent, or with the April figures.

The continual, month-by-month shrinking of tax revenues relative to GDP was mainly due to the decrease relative to GDP of such principal budget revenue items as corporate profit tax (from 13.0 percent of GDP in April to 11.6 percent of GDP in August) and VAT (from 9.1 percent of GDP in April to 7.9 percent of GDP in April), while the revenue from excise duties and individual income tax remained stable, relative to GDP.

The drop in corporate profit tax revenues in May 1993, compared with April, can be explained by the completion in April of the reassessment for the first quarter and 1992. In monthly calculations, the revenue decreased by more than 4 percent of GDP. In cumulative month-by-month calculations the decrease reached 1 percent of GDP. In cumulative month-by-month calculations VAT revenues dropped by 0.3 percent of GDP.

We believe that the main reason the tax revenue increase lagged behind GDP in 1993 was the method of imposing the corporate profit tax and VAT. The profit tax is paid twice a month in the form of advance payments, and the reassessment is done at the end of each quarter; the actual sales are assessed not by the shipment of the goods, but when payment is made. In current conditions, when payment transactions between enterprises take from a few days to several months, enterprises' tax obligations at the time of each assessment are calculated not on the basis of the last quarter, but of a considerably earlier period. The higher inflation gets, the greater the loss in actual tax receipts due to the lag between the manufacture or shipment of goods and the receipt of payment by the manufacturer.

A similar situation is observed with VAT. Major payers pay it three times a month (less important ones only once a month) in accordance with goods actually sold. The reassessment, taking into account VAT on materials purchased, is made by monthly results. So at the moment of payment enterprises pay tax on goods, which were sold considerably earlier and, consequently, at considerably lower prices than those existing at the time of the assessment of tax obligations and the payment of the tax.

Thus, the elasticity of Russia's taxation system depends greatly on the rate of inflation, the length of the delay in settlements between enterprises, and the frequency of reassessment by actual results (the period for calculating the profit tax has been lengthened to 30 additional days after the end of the quarter). The inflation factor was especially strong in July and August, when there was a sharp price increase: wholesale prices increased from 17 percent a month in June to 29 percent in July and retail prices from 20 percent a month in July to 26 percent in August (see data above).

The absence of a strong surge of corporate profit tax receipts in July can be attributed to enterprises' adaptation to the introduction of criminal sanctions for understating advance payments. It should be noted that in 1992 this tendency of tax receipts to drop was not apparent because of the extremely low tax base at the beginning of the year, the worsening non-payments crisis (which lasted until fall), mutual non-payments cancellation, and the continual modifications of the taxation methods (which resulted in increased revenues).

The data given in Table 5 show no serious impact of the dynamics of indebtedness on the decrease of tax revenues, with the possible exception of July; the rate of buyers' indebtedness to their suppliers increased from 17 percent in June to 24 percent in July, which was nevertheless smaller than the growth of the nominal GDP in July (31 percent) and the growth of wholesale prices (29 percent).

According to the Russian Federation State Tax Collecting Service's statistics, the arrears in payments to the budget had no impact on the drop in the tax revenues either, with the exception of August, when tax receipts rose from 1.62 percent of GDP in July to 2.25 percent of GDP in August.

The increase of tax arrears in August and September was to a large extent due to the tax deferral granted to enterprises. Permission to defer tax payments to the Russian federal budget was granted by the Russian Ministry of Finance under the amendment to Article 24 of the law "On the foundations of the taxations system" passed on July 16, 1992. Similar rights with respect to the territorial budgets were granted to the local bodies of state authority. Growth in arrears was also encouraged by Resolution #672 of the Council of Ministers of the Russian Federation of July 13, 1993, "On measures to stabilize the financial situation of the enterprises and production associations of the fuel and energy complex." This resolution undermined the priority of payments to the budget, since it allowed enterprises to keep at their own disposal 40 percent of the money due to them and paid into their accounts, rather than paying it into the republican budget to reduce their debt .

The shrinking of the tax revenues of the Russian federal budget is partly due to the indebtedness of Tatarstan, Bashkortostan, and Yakutia. All taxes on the territory of these republics are collected in accord with a "one-way system," under which the republics transfer sums fixed by bilateral agreements to the federal government budget. However, these sums are transferred with a long delay (as of January 1, 1994 their debt totaled 465 billion rubles, i.e., 0.3 percent of GDP).

In the fourth quarter of 1993, with the slight drop in inflation and slowing growth of the nominal GDP, the decrease in tax receipts as a percentage of GDP also slowed. In comparison with September 1993, revenues in December dropped by less than 1 percent of GDP.

1994

With the departure from government of Gaidar and Fyodorov, short-term budget policy will be determined primarily by the pace of repayment of the government's outstanding unfunded expenditures and by its commitment to following through on promises made in the spring and summer of 1993.

As of mid-February 1994, the draft federal budget envisioned revenues totaling 16.7 percent of GDP, expenditures totaling 23.6 percent of GDP, and a deficit totaling 7.1 percent of GDP. The structure of the budget is roughly similar to that of 1993. This year, however, it envisions an increase in expenditures on the national economy (by 1.9 percent of GDP), on law enforcement bodies (0.25 percent of GDP), on external economic activity (1 percent of GDP, which incidentally is balanced by planned growth in revenue), on the state administration, the judicial system, and public prosecutors' offices (0.3 percent of GDP), and on financial support for the territories (1.3 percent of GDP).

Obviously, a final judgment on the budget cannot be made until it has been approved by Parliament. So far the Ministry of Finance and the government have in general been continuing the policies carried out last year.

Part II

Management, Corporate Governance, and Enterprise Directors

3

Agency Problems in the Privatization of Large Enterprises in Russia

Michael McFaul

I. Introduction

The Russian privatization program has been heralded as the crown jewel of Russia's economic reform. While other aspects of Russia's economic reform have been less successful, privatization has continued unimpeded throughout the first two years of economic reform. On paper, Russian privatization appears to be more successful than any other government privatization program in history. By January 1994, 90,000 state enterprises were privatized.[1]

The size and speed of Russia's privatization program are truly impressive. The kind of privatization occurring at large enterprises, however, is less encouraging. Directors are acquiring control of their enterprises. By the summer of 1993, insiders held majority shares in two-thirds of Russia's privatized firms. Estimates for 1994 suggest that insiders will acquire majority shares in 75 percent of all privatized enterprises.

Managerial control, in and of itself, is not necessarily an impediment to the development of effective private enterprises. If their individual well-being can be maintained during the transition, former Soviet directors may adapt to the market. Many directors, in fact, seem already to have made this transition. Nonetheless, the privatization program adopted in Russia—a strategy that gave incumbent enterprise directors extensive ownership and control over their enterprises—has created barriers to the emergence of effective ownership. Russia's privatization program has not separated ownership from management, and has thereby

Michael McFaul is a research associate at the Center for International Security and Arms Control, and an assistant professor in the department of political science at Stanford University.

reinforced key problems inherent in the Soviet enterprise model.

The rest of this introduction describes what the Yeltsin government wanted to achieve through privatization, and how these goals were embodied in the government's original privatization program. Section Two then describes what this program was up against: the actual preexisting property rights as allocated during the Soviet era. Section Three demonstrates how the original program was altered to reinforce rather than transform the existing system of property rights. Section Four discusses the consequences for manager behavior of the privatization program that resulted.

Privatization has been one of the Russian government's most effective tools for implementing radical economic reform. While Russian government officials and Western advisors alike believed that a comprehensive program must undertake several economic reform measures in parallel,[2] they also viewed privatization as the cornerstone of a successful transition.[3]

Privatization aims to "rationalize" the use of resources and thereby maximize the overall productive capacity of the economy.[4] Privatization accomplishes more efficient use of resources by internalizing costs and benefits of production for the individual enterprise,[5] while also providing incentives to both managers and employees. By escaping the government budget, privatized enterprises also are less subject to politically motivated state interference. In postcommunist economies, privatization also should rationalize the size of enterprises, meaning that large conglomerates will be broken into several entities while each newly privatized enterprise will likely be scaled down dramatically.[6] Privatization will also involve liquidation of non-viable enterprises—an essential mechanism for reorganizing property and capital.[7]

To achieve these benefits, the process of privatization was designed to separate management from ownership. As two chief Western advisors to the Russian government, David Lipton and Jeffrey Sachs, argued:

> The shift to a West European ownership structure will require that enterprise governance be removed from the workers' councils and managers and be placed squarely with a supervisory board (or board of directors) controlled by the owners of the enterprise. In essence, privatization requires first that certain ownership rights, now vested in the enterprises, and particularly in the workers' councils, be eliminated so that property rights to an enterprise can be transferred to the real owners.[8]

Separation of ownership from management of large enterprises exposes managers to the disciplines of the market.

In the initial privatization program of the Yeltsin government, this separation was to be achieved by the mandatory transformation of all large state enterprises into open joint-stock companies. Closed joint-stock companies were prohibited.[9] Yeltsin's team wanted to force enterprises to accept outside ownership. Second, ownership was to be dispersed. Although 25 percent of each enterprise's shares was to be distributed to the workers' collective free of charge, these shares were to be non-voting. Another five percent of voting shares was offered to the management at full price, but all the rest of the shares were to be distributed through a mass voucher program. This distribution aimed to disperse ownership of large enterprises so that millions of Russian citizens would have a stake in privatization.[10] By outlawing closed joint-stock companies, and creating a voucher market to serve as a transitional substitute for capital markets, the privatization program planned to expose entrenched directors to the discipline of financial markets as well as product markets.[11] Toward this end, boards of directors were decreed into existence and given, on paper, the same fiduciary responsibilities as in American and European corporate law.[12]

The privatization program thus originally intended to create Western-style corporations out of state-owned enterprises. By doing so, this original draft of the privatization program challenged the previously existing organization of property rights at Soviet state enterprises.

II. Property Rights and Directors' Power Under the Soviet State

The state, the de jure owner of Soviet enterprises, over time conceded many property rights to the directors of these enterprises. How these directors—formally employees of the Soviet state—assumed rights linked to property ownership can best be explained with the aid of agency theory. Complex organizations, whether in capitalist or socialist economies, require a division of labor and a hierarchy of authority. Agency theory explores these relationships. In the simplest terms, "An agency relationship is said to exist between two (or more) parties when one, designated as the agent, acts on behalf of another, designated the principal."[13] In reference to property rights, an agency relationship is formed

> when a principal delegates some rights—for example user rights over a re-
> source—to an agent who is bound by a (formal or informal) contract to represent
> the principal's interest in return for a payment of some kind.[14]

In capitalist economies, the classic agency relationship exists between owners of assets (principals) and managers of these assets (agents). As first underscored by Berle and Means sixty years ago, the rise of the modern corporation in capitalist economies has served to disassociate ownership from control.[15]

As defined in capitalist economies, ownership of property consists of three basic rights: the right of use, the right to profits from that use, and the right of transfer.[16] Agency theory's analysis of firms in capitalist economies has highlighted two basic problems inherent to large organizations such as corporations in which agency relationships are present: uncertainty and goal conflict among members within the organization.

Because principals cannot observe the behavior of their agents all the time, agents have the opportunity to withhold information from their principals about the utilization of the principal's assets. Without the ability to monitor agent behavior constantly, principals cannot know what opportunities they are missing. Incomplete knowledge about an agent's ability and behavior makes optimization of assets impossible.

Closely related to uncertainty is the second problem, conflicting goals. Principals and agents can have different utility curves. Because information gained through the use of the principal's resource(s) cannot be totally controlled by the principal, agents can limit their own effort—i.e., shirk—or use the information they have to maximize individual gain at the expense of the principal.[17] This conflict of goals coupled with uncertainty about agent behavior creates real impediments to efficiency and/or profit maximization for principals.[18]

These dilemmas of agency were especially acute in the relationship established between the Party-state as principal and enterprise directors as agents during the Soviet era.[19] The fact that the Soviet economy was a command economy may seem to complicate the notion of a contractual relationship between principal and agent, but interactions between the Soviet state and its agents actually did approximate a contractual relationship (specified in five-year plans, yearly quotas, etc.). The principal's ability to monitor the agent's performance grew increasingly weaker as the number of transactions to be monitored grew, while the organizations mandated to monitor these agents (KGB, CPSU, Soviet ministries) weakened. The principals in the Soviet system were huge centralized bureaucracies of the Party-state, so individual *apparatchiks* within these massive, complex organizations had no personal incentive to monitor agents closely at the enterprise level. Profits of individual enterprises were determined by bureaucrats rather than markets. Moreover, production measurements in the Soviet economy were quantitative, not qualitative, creating easy opportunities for shirking. The loss of profits to agents had no direct adverse effect on any individual; rather, the Soviet state as a whole was the loser.[20]

The problem of principal control over agents already had begun to undermine the Soviet command economy well before the appearance of Gorbachev.[21] Under a "depersonalized" owner, the state, no principal authority has either the knowledge, incentive, or technical ability to intervene at the enterprise level concerning control issues.[22] The Party-state established production targets as well as a whole package of social benefits for employees that defined and constrained the powers of the directors. Through the Brezhnev period, however, actual decisions regarding five-year plans, industrial output targets, and even output goals for individual enterprises were made increasingly at lower and lower levels in the agency chain. Agents, the directors, began to acquire de facto property rights through their control of information about their enterprises. Most importantly, directors increasingly assumed control over the operation and use of their enterprises. Over time, the plan—the main control mechanism for the principal in the socialist economy—was written "from the bottom up" rather than from the top down.[23] The principal (the Party-state) increasingly lost the ability to enforce its priorities in agency relationships.

Empowered with increasing control over their enterprises, directors could also supplement their individual wealth by hiding profits or skimming extra production.[24] An extensive gray economy provided tremendous incentives for opportunistic behavior.[24] Moreover, the forces inhibiting shirking and corruption in market economies, such as labor markets or the threat of outside takeover, did not exist.[25] Of the three classic property rights—use, profits from use, and transfer—the only one not acquired by enterprise directors was the power to alienate property. Yet, within a socialist economy, the principal—the state—did not recognize anyone else as a legitimate owner, and thus would not exercise this right either.

With Gorbachev's reforms in the late 1980s, it might have been expected that the state would try to challenge the pervasive corruption and reclaim some control over its directors. These reforms, however, did not challenge the relationship between the director and the state. On the contrary, they strengthened existing institutional arrangements regarding property rights and enterprise organization. In a search for prospective allies against the entrenched CPSU apparat, Gorbachev offered directors incentives to support his reform course.

A series of new laws and regulations in 1987 and 1988 concerning small enterprises, cooperatives, and enterprise organizations essentially codified the spontaneous transfer of property rights that had begun several years before. Moreover, this new set of laws stimulated even greater transfer of property rights from the principal to the agent.[26] Because cooperatives, "small businesses," and leased assets were allowed to undertake economic activities forbidden to state enterprises, entrepreneurial directors set up parasitic cooperatives, collectively owned entities, lease agreements, and joint ventures, which became profit centers feeding off the assets of large state enterprises.[27] By October 1990, it was estimated that 215,000 cooperatives were operating while another 12,500 lease arrangements had been set up.[28] Profitable transactions with outside contractors, especially foreign contractors, were channeled through these small enterprises, leaving profits "off-shore" outside the budgets of state enterprises.[29] Overhead and many externalities of these small firms were paid, directly and indirectly, by the state. Monies allocated to state enterprises were siphoned off by directors and laundered through these cooperatives and joint ventures.

In other cases, entrepreneurial managers used the ambiguously defined entity of the collectively owned enterprise to privatize state properties spontaneously.[30] Most of these privatizations were carried out in the name of the workers' collective, but control was firmly in the hands of management.

The Party-state—the principal—took few punitive actions against these directors—their agents—for two reasons. First, many within the state believed that these activities promoted the development of market reforms, while those who opposed these activities had little knowledge about the mysterious ways of the market. Second, even if state leaders had wanted to intervene to curtail these activities, the state was too weak to do so.[31]

What might have provided another check on directors' power, the potentially opposing interests of industrial workers, was not a realistic possibility. During the same period that directors' control over state enterprises increased, relationships between directors and employees developed along very paternalistic lines. Under Stalin, Soviet enterprises assumed responsibility for several social services typically not associated with the workplace in capitalist economies. Especially in small, one-company towns reconstructed after World War II, enterprises provided housing, schools, and medical facilities to their employees, while large conglomerates often ran their own farms and stores. Some enterprises even provided local electricity and transportation services. Because all enterprises were owned by the state anyway, distinctions between private and public facilities were not important.

This institutionalized arrangement at the enterprise meant that directors were looked upon as providers to workers for everything.[32] At the same time, workers had few opportunities to organize so as to represent their interests in opposition to the directors. Communist Party trade unions provided several services to workers, but union representatives colluded with the director rather than defend worker interests against management. With no other representative body to turn to, workers relied on their directors to represent their interests vis-a-vis the state planners, the local bureaucratic authorities, and the central Party bosses.[33]

Under *perestroika*, this paternalistic relationship between managers and workers was further reinforced. The uncertainty of living in a collapsing economy made workers even more dependent on and loyal to their directors at the plant level. The 1988 law on enterprises did create a workers' council (*sovet trudovogo kollektiva*, or STK) at each enterprise, a new organizational unit vested with powers over the operations of the enterprise. Most importantly, these workers' councils were given the right to vote on the general director of their enterprise. The workers' councils actually had little leverage over their managers, however, as they had poor information about the activities and responsibilities of directors and they still depended on their directors for their housing, social services, and employment. Directors were removed by workers' councils in only a few instances, a testament to the institutionalized paternalism already established between director and worker. The specter of unemployment, combined with the ascendancy of the workers' council and the weakening of the official communist trade unions, served to isolate and localize worker demands to the enterprise level.[34] Likewise, the more general collapse of first all-Soviet and then all-Russian state structures reaffirmed in the short run the role of the enterprise as the provider of social services and welfare.

Thus, when privatization began in earnest in 1992, workers were not psychologically in a position to hinder management control that took the guise of "employee ownership."

III. Amending the Privatization Program

By seeking to replace the Soviet state with outside private owners, the Russian privatization program threatened to "take back" these property rights from the factory directors. Not surprisingly, these directors mobilized to protect their claims to ownership and control. The first postcommunist Russian government hoped to avoid political struggles over its program by ambushing directors and workers' collectives with a simple yet comprehensive program for privatization. As described above, this original program included significant benefits for managers and employees in an effort to co-opt their support.

Privatization in Russia, however, could not escape politics. Understanding the implications of the Gaidar/Chubais plan, Russian directors fought to protect the de facto property rights they acquired during the Soviet era. Given the weakness of the new Russian government, directors' lobbies presented a formidable political challenge to Yeltsin's original privatization formula. Their power to hinder the government program was particularly important given that if privatization were not rapid, it might never be fully effective.[35] Under pressure from industrialists, whose support they felt they needed, the architects of privatization amended their original program.[36] The allocation of ownership as initially envisioned remained in the program, but only as one of three options. It became Option One—25 percent of shares, non-voting, to be given free of charge to the workers' collective, five percent voting shares to the management at full price, and ten percent more voting shares for the workers' collective at full price—while the two new options introduced more favorable conditions for directors. Option Two allowed directors and workers of an enterprise to purchase 51 percent of all shares, while Option Three allowed for manager buyouts when effective management assumed responsible control of an ailing enterprise. Each workers' collective was granted the right to select between the options, a tacit recognition by the state of the control that insiders—directors and workers—already had at the enterprise level.

Option Three ended up having very little impact, as less than two percent of privatizing enterprises selected it in 1992. The inclusion of Option Two in the privatization program, however, radically altered the Russian path of privatization. Of the 46,815 enterprises that had been privatized by the end of 1992,[37] 63.7 percent had chosen Option Two, while only 34.5 percent had chosen Option One, the original privatization design.[38] In 1993, more than 75 percent of all enterprises were privatized according to Option Two.[39]

The provisions of Option Two are extremely effective in serving the interests of directors. They prevent outside investors from gaining majority ownership in enterprises, while putting shares the managers themselves don't buy into the hands of workers who are highly susceptible to their influence. Although it may seem that 51 percent ownership for the

44

workers' collective would give control to ordinary workers, in fact they will not assume a major controlling position in most privatized companies.

This hypothesis may seem counterintuitive. Several analysts in both Russia and the West, in fact, have pointed to the popularity of Option Two as a positive indicator of the development of employee ownership ideas in postcommunist Russia.[40] In April of 1993, vice premier and head of the state property committee (GKI) Anatoliy Chubais proclaimed, "tens of millions of workers have already become shareholders."[41] These positive assessments, however, have failed to take into account the institutionalized relations between worker and director left over from the Soviet era. The relationship between workers and managers created during the Soviet era and sustained through the present suggests that what looks like employee ownership will in fact be a formula for managers to retain and expand their de facto property rights accrued before privatization.

Threatened by rapid and dramatic economic changes, and confused by the maze of new regulations and procedures governing this new economy, workers have become not less but more dependent on their managers to represent their interests. Alternative forms of worker representation have only just begun to form, while old worker associations and trade unions such as the Federation of Independent Trade Unions serve the interests of the directors first, and workers second.[42] In this setting, directors have made all major decisions about the method of privatization chosen; workers then ratified these decisions.[43] After privatization, directors will continue to maintain control of their enterprises. Though the process is only beginning, most former directors, in fact, have been elected chairmen of the newly created boards of directors at the first stockholder meetings.[44]

In many cases, directors will be content to have ownership dispersed among workers as long as a controlling share is still held by employees of the company. This situation allows old directors to wield their institutionalized leverage over the workers' collective regarding crucial decisions. Other directors, however, have attempted to acquire a controlling block of shares through a variety of manipulative schemes against their own workers. The most direct method is simply to buy workers' shares before they have any market value. At one plant, for instance, "a manager put up signs on the doors of the employee bathrooms, offering to buy their shares for 5,000 rubles each. Within a few days, he controlled 20 percent of the company."[45] Another opportunity for accruing a majority interest arises during the closed subscription for shares that takes place under Option Two. In the subscription process, each worker must bid how many shares she or he wishes to purchase. The number of shares available and the cost of each share is determined by the privatization committee at the enterprise (usually dominated by the management) with the approval of the GKI. If the number of shares bid for exceeds the total number of shares available, shares are then distributed in proportion to the size of each bid. The price of each share, however, remains constant for this first offering. Directors are acquiring controlling blocks of shares by making astronomical bids, realizing that the maximum they will actually have to pay can be no more than the nominal price of all shares. Because workers make their bids based on the real amount of money they are willing to pay, they actually receive significantly fewer shares than the amount hoped for if directors submit these very large bids that dwarf all others. In this manner, the directors can obtain the bulk of the 51 percent total offered to workers. As with any other option, they are then free to use vouchers to purchase as many shares as possible of the 49 percent offered publicly.[46] Directors frequently collaborate with either a commercial bank or investment fund in purchasing these additional shares.

45

IV. Implications for the Progress of Economic Reform

Even if the revised privatization program does allow managers to acquire the lion's share of enterprise ownership, it might be argued that this is not a problem. It may be unjust to rank-and-file workers if what passes as employee ownership is actually manager control, but does it necessarily hinder the goals of efficiency and market reform?

The concentration of enterprise ownership in the hands of directors does run counter to the goals of privatization for several reasons. Not separating ownership and management will have real consequences for the Russian economy.

Manager-Owner Behavior

Directors as owners in the Former Soviet Union have a different set of incentives than owners of securities in Western market economies. If the motivations of Western owners are framed in accordance with the ultimate objective of profit maximization, Soviet directors/owners often have a different overriding priority: maintaining the status quo at the enterprise. In developed capitalist economies, these two objectives can be compatible, as competition eliminates those enterprises that cannot make a profit. In the Russian context they are not compatible, as directors can maintain the status quo without seeking a profit. Directors' control of their enterprises, therefore, threatens to undermine the original rationale for privatization. As Kevin McDonald has observed of Eastern Europe,

> Without the support and prodding of shareholders, Eastern companies tend to operate very much along the lines learned in the days of central planning, insider control, and relentless focus on production.... [C]ompanies without strong, capable shareholders are apt to perform no better after a public offering than they did as state-owned enterprises.[47]

Without outside ownership, enterprises are not compelled to make a profit. Rather, they seek only to avoid bankruptcy and survive. As originally conceived, shock therapy was designed to bankrupt inefficient state enterprises. Enterprises, however, have found a variety of ways to avoid bankruptcy without having to become profit maximizers. Given that many overhead costs are minimal and investment is nil, a positive cash flow can be maintained without seeking profits. Payroll costs are often the only significant expenditure. In the context of high inflation, three-month delays in paying workers' wages—a common practice in Russia—can drastically reduce the burden of this expenditure. When wages are finally paid, they often can be covered by accruing state subsidies.[48] By the spring of 1993, these subsidies were estimated to be 22 percent of gross domestic product.[49] Because Russia's fragile state cannot survive massive, simultaneous bankruptcies and worker layoffs, enterprises have tremendous leverage in seeking continued state support.

In addition to state subsidies, enterprises continue to borrow from each other to maintain "positive" cash flows. From January to July of 1992, interenterprise debt jumped from 37 billion to 3.2 trillion rubles, an eighty-fold increase.[50] This method became even more attractive and accessible after Victor Gerashchenko became head of the Russian State Bank in the spring of 1992. In one of his first actions, he allowed enterprises to swap debts, an act which cleared the books, encouraged accumulation of further debts, and stimulated new production without regard to market demands.[51]

In sum, the enormous flow of state credits to support ailing companies coupled with giant interenterprise arrears has prevented the introduction of hard budget constraints at these enterprises, even if privatized. This continued level of state subsidy seriously undermines the very notion of "private" property. For conservative politicians opposed to privatization, this is the exact intention of issuing credits.

This situation does not mean that directors will not maximize their personal profits. In fact, through the creation or in most cases the further development of parasitic, subsidiary companies attached to the parent enterprises, these directors have the opportunity to make profits for themselves at the expense of the enterprise as a whole. If profit-seeking, outside shareholders could exercise their property rights, these kinds of activities would not be allowed. Without such outside forces, however, directors can continue to channel revenues into these small, closed joint-stock companies in which profits are divided among a handful of directors rather than thousands of shareholders. By obtaining state credits and subsidies for the parent company, the manager/owner pays for many of the externalities and much of the overhead of his smaller firm. In extreme instances, directors simply resell a line of credit obtained from the state to a commercial lending institution.[52] More generally, in the absence of defined property rights and in the context of high inflation, directors and workers will seek short-term exploitation of state properties and forsake long-term investments. If directors currently control their enterprises, but know that government subsidies may soon end, they have huge incentives to strip the state-owned enterprises of all sellable fixed assets.

Another negative consequence of tight director control combined with significant stock ownership is that necessary structural reorganization will not occur. A report of the Russian government and the World Bank explains that the privatization program was designed "to leave any necessary *restructuring* to new private owners, on the assumption that they will know better than the Government what changes are needed."[53] If incumbent managers remain in charge and acquire legal ownership, however, while budget constraints are not put in place, they will have little incentive to restructure, downsize, or close down unprofitable parts of the operation.[54] Rather, directors of large enterprises are searching for organizational models to enhance and expand their control over economic activities related to the firm.[55] Several have adopted the holding company as the organizational model for preserving control and reducing transaction costs between economic entities. In interviews at more than twenty large industrial enterprises, every director complained that the greatest threat to the continued viability of his operation was spin-offs and the breaking up of the enterprise.[56]

In fact, there is growing evidence that centralization and amalgamation is increasing, not decreasing. Most significantly, former Soviet ministries and their Russian counterparts have begun to reassert their control over enterprises by establishing large concerns, holding companies, and parastatals.[57] These supra-enterprise conglomerates seek to assume equity positions in a whole range of enterprises affiliated with a particular industry as a way to insure stable suppliers, maintain horizontal and vertical integration, and thereby preserve monopolies. Before being closed down, the Russian parliament encouraged this recentralization process by passing regulations conducive to the formation of giant holding companies and concerns.[58] The growth of this complex maze of holding companies, cross-ownership between related enterprises, and ministerial retention of golden shares (i.e., shares with veto power) could jeopardize restructuring or, at best, lead to a distinctly non-Western structure of ownership.[59] In the best-case scenario, Russia's economy will more closely resemble

Japan's "keiritsu" system than the United States or even Germany. A more likely analogue, however, is India—an autarchic system dotted with large parastatals and inefficient but protected private firms.

Potential Mechanisms to Control Manager-Owners

The post-Soviet environment in Russia is thus rife with opportunities for shirking and corruption on the part of enterprise managers. Personal profit incentives are not tied to incentives for corporate profit, resulting in widespread corruption. The situation is even less conducive to market reform because the lack of separation between owners and managers makes managers almost invulnerable to any sort of discipline or incentive for different behavior.

Theories of the firm in developed capitalist economies have described several different mechanisms for disciplining managers. Fama has argued that "the primary disciplining of managers comes through managerial labor markets, both within and outside of the firm,"[60] while Moe writes:

> The corporate form allows for decisional specialization and unrestricted risk-
> · sharing, both conducive to efficiency in large-scale enterprises, while, at the same
> time, important mechanisms are available for mitigating shirking problems
> inherent in stockholder-manager relation [*sic*]. (1) The unrestricted sale and
> ownership of stock means that stockholders can pull their investment out
> whenever management decisions fail to yield profits that compare favorably with
> of those of other corporations. (2) Corporations whose potential for profit goes
> unrealized due to managerial shirking are prime targets for takeovers by other
> organizational management teams. (3) Stockholders generally delegate most
> control and monitoring functions to small boards of directors, which have far
> better information and resources for mitigating shirking problems. Under a
> variety of economic conditions, therefore, the modern corporation emerges as an
> optimal organizational form.[61]

None of these mechanisms, however, are present in the Russian economy. First, real securities markets do not exist yet in Russia.[62] Any check on directors' control that might be exerted by the relatively few outside shareholders that remain under the revised program is considerably weakened by the lack of investment infrastructure. Nascent stock markets and ill-defined regulations on disclosure mean that outsiders have little if any information about enterprises. Individual investors will lack the capital or information to diversify and thus will assume greater risk than investors in Western capital markets, who can diversify their investments to protect against single company failures. With weak institutions of corporate governance, stockholders will also have little access to information about the profits and losses of even the enterprises in which they invested. If directors were able to operate with virtual autonomy from the state during the Soviet era, they will have even greater opportunities for withholding information from these new principals—uneducated and uninformed stockholders. For the immediate future, individual investors will be tied to the fate of one enterprise alone, and thus shareholder dissatisfaction cannot function to discipline managers.

The Russian government has encouraged the creation of investment funds and allowed commercial banks to participate in equity markets. Investment funds, numbering in the thousands by the end of 1993, allow individual voucher holders to invest without direct knowledge about particular enterprises. Such funds may be better placed than individuals to divest from one company and reinvest in another, if their motivation is to maximize profits for stockholders. It remains to be seen, however, whose interests these funds represent—individual investors, enterprise directors, or third-party speculators. Some investment companies were established by directors as a way to acquire further shares in their own enterprises, and others have been exposed as fronts for laundering Mafia money. Even if these funds were serving the interests of investors, however, they would still have great difficulty in acquiring sufficient information to know where to invest more profitably. Moreover, both investment funds and commercial banks are restricted by law from acquiring majority positions in privatized enterprises.

The threat of outside takeovers—a second mechanism for disciplining managers—is also absent at enterprises where the workers' collective owns 51 percent of the stock. If the primary goal of these employee-owners were profit maximization, then outside tender offers would operate in a similar manner as they do in developed capitalist economies. Given that initial stock issues are generally considered very undervalued, such tender offers could be very profitable for outside investors. The owners who make up the workers' collective (including the directors), however, are not disinterested investors seeking to maximize returns on their shares. On the contrary, the first priority of the managers is control, and the first priority of the workers is job security. Neither, then, has an interest in selling out, especially considering the small stake that each worker owns.[63] Loyalties to the firm, the directors, and fellow workers will also obstruct potential buyout attempts.

Third, disciplinary action by the board of directors against management is also highly unlikely in the near future. Though board formation is still nascent in Russia, it appears that most places on boards are being assumed by the managers themselves. Yet, even if these boards did try to exercise their fiduciary responsibilities, laws governing the rights and responsibilities of boards of directors either do not exist or are very underspecified. If, for instance, a board did try to fire a director and the director resisted, would the courts intervene on the board's behalf? At the same time, the stakes are very low for those now assuming ownership positions through the voucher program. Because vouchers were issued for free, stockholders assumed no risk in becoming owners. The lack of risk combined with the small size of each individual's investment minimizes shareholders' incentives for demanding fiduciary responsibility from the board of directors.

A fourth disciplinary institution for managers—the labor market for managers—is as yet very weak in Russia.[64] Few managers have been fired because few qualified managers are available for hire. Most current directors were trained as production engineers, making their skills not easily transferable. Moreover, those directors who are qualified can assume greater ownership of their current firm (through Option Two), and thus will have little incentive to move to another.

An important corollary to the labor market problem is the manner in which these relationships between owners and directors are being created. Most principal-agent relationships are constructed when the principal chooses an agent, offers a contract to the agent, and then the agent decides to accept the terms of the relationship. In the case of Russian privatization of large enterprises, owners (principals) do not select directors with whom they want to enter into incentivized, contractual relationships. Instead, directors are already in

49

place; the newly created owners simply inherit them. This sequence magnifies all the problems of control between principals and agents outlined above.

In sum, none of the mechanisms that might be expected to control a powerful managerial class under market conditions will operate in Russia today. Having won the struggle to amend the privatization program, the directors' corps is reaping the benefits of Option Two in the form of near-complete autonomy from outside shareholders and their demands for enterprise profits.

Conclusion

The Yeltsin government did not succeed in implementing a tough privatization program that could reduce the power enterprise directors have achieved under the Soviet system. Even with the transfer of some assets to private hands, the necessary incentives to change managers' behavior are not present.

Actual restructuring and pressures toward increased efficiency will begin only when hard budget constraints are introduced. If the Russian state has the capacity to enforce hard budget constraints, then even inside owners will be forced both to make the difficult changes of enterprise reorganization and to accept the risks of allowing greater outsider ownership.

In the long run, capitalization will be more crucial to the success of individual enterprises than privatization.[65] Irrespective of the initial balance of insider/outsider ownership, only enterprises that succeed in attracting new investment—a process that will inevitably tilt the equity balance toward outside owners—will survive. Thus, directors may be the first owners of privatized properties, but will probably not be the last.

Notes

[1] Alexander Ivanenko, "Privatization in Russia," *Business World Weekly*, No. 9/102 (March 7, 1994): 5.

[2] David Lipton and Jeffrey Sachs, "Creating a Market Economy in Eastern Europe: The Case of Poland," *Brookings Papers on Economic Activity*, no. 1 (1990): 99. Privatization was not pursued in isolation, and in fact was preceded by price liberalization and attempts at macroeconomic stabilization. On the synergistic benefits of carrying out a set of economic reforms simultaneously, see Anders Aslund, *Post-Communist Economic Revolutions: How Big a Bang?* (Washington: Center for Strategic and International Studies, 1992); Susan Gates, Paul Milgrom, and John Roberts, "Complementarities in the Transition from Socialism: A Firm-Level Analysis" (unpublished ms., 1993).

[3] See, for instance, Andrzej Brzeski, "Post-Communism From a Neo-Institutionalist Perspective," *Journal of Institutional and Theoretical Economics* 148 (1992): 195; Eirik Furubotn, "Eastern European Reconstruction Problems: Some General Observations," *Journal of Institutional and Theoretical Economics* 148 (1992): 202; Leonid Grigoriev, "Ulterior Property Rights and Privatization: Even God Cannot Change the Past," in Anders Aslund, ed., *The Post-Soviet Economy: Soviet and Western Perspectives* (London: Pinter Publishers, 1992), 196-197.

[4] See Jozef von Brabant, *Privatizing Eastern Europe: The Role of Markets and Ownership in the Transition* (Drodrect: Kluwer Academic Publishers, 1992), especially 148-174; and John Nellis, "Privatization in Reforming Socialist Economies," in Andreja Bohm and Vladmir Kreacic, eds., *Privatization in Eastern Europe: Current Implementation Issues* (Ljublana, Yugoslavia: International Center for Public Enterprises in Developing Countries, 1991), 16.

[5] See Robert Cooter, "Organization as Property: Economic Analysis of Property Law Applied to Privatization," in Christopher Clague and Gordon Rausser, eds., *The Emergence of Market Economies in Eastern Europe* (Oxford: Blackwell, 1992), 77-98; and Stanley Fischer and Alan Gelb, "The Process of Socialist Economic Transformation," *Journal of Economic Perspectives* 5, no. 4 (Fall 1991): 98.

[6] Aslund, *Post-Communist Economic Revolutions*, 80-81; Philippe Aghion, Kenneth Arrow, Robin Burgess, and Jean-Paul Fitoussi, "Industrial Restructuring in Eastern Europe" (unpublished ms., 1993).

[7] See the remarks of Deputy Prime Minister Boris Fyodorov in Oleg Polukeyev, "Finansovie Maneri Pravitel'stva," *Nezavisimaya Gazeta*, January 20, 1993: 1.

[8] Lipton and Sachs, 35.

[9] Presidential Decree No. 721 "On Organizational Measures To Transform State Enterprises and Voluntary Associations of State Enterprises into Joint-Stock Companies" (July 1, 1992) required that all enterprises subject to privatization be converted to open joint-stock companies by November 1, 1992.

[10] See *Ekonomika i Zhizn'*, No. 31 (August 1992): 18.

[11] See Nellis, "Privatization in Reforming Socialist Economies," 16.

[12] Jeffrey Sachs, "Privatization in Russia: Some Lessons from Eastern Europe," *American Economic Review* 82, no. 2 (May 1992): 47.

[13] Daniel Levinthal, "A Survey of Agency Models of Organizations," *Journal of Economic Behavior and Organizations* 9, no. 2 (March 1988): 155.

[14] Thrainin Eggertsson, *Economic Behavior and Institutions* (Cambridge, England: Cambridge University Press, 1990), 40-45.

[15] The classic work on this subject remains a book first published in 1932 by Adolf Berle and Gardiner Means, *The Modern Corporation and Private Property* (New York: Transaction Publishers, 1991).

[16] Yoram Barzel, *Economic Analysis of Property Rights* (Cambridge, England: Cambridge University Press, 1989).

[17] Terry Moe, "The New Economics of Organization," *American Journal of Political Science* 28, no. 4 (November 1984): 756.

[18] See Michael Jensen and William Meckling, "Theory of the Firm: Managerial Behavior, Agency Costs, and Ownership Structure," *Journal of Financial Economics* 3 (1976): 305-360.

[19] See Eirik Furubotn and Svetozar Pejovich, "Property Rights and Economic Theory: A Survey of Recent Literature" *Journal of Economic Literature* 10, no. 4 (December 1972): 1137-1162; and Steven Solnick, "Understanding the Soviet Collapse: Institutional Transformation in Periods of Political Chaos," paper presented at the annual meeting of the American Political Science Association, September 3, 1992.

[20] Janos Kornai, *The Socialist System: The Political Economy of Communism* (Princeton, NJ: Princeton University Press, 1992), 73.

[21] See Vitali Naishul, "Institutional Development in the USSR," *Cato Journal* 11, no. 3 (Winter 1992): 495.

[22] Kornai, 75.

[23] Naishul, 490; and Alexander Bin, "Role of the States in Transitional Postcommunist Economies," in Anders Aslund, ed., *The Post-Soviet Economy: Soviet and Western Perspectives* (London: Pinter Publishers, 1992), 189.

[24] Ratchet effects on production goals and worker performance standards provided agents with margins of opportunity. John Litwack, "Ratcheting and Economic Reform in the USSR," *Journal of Comparative Economics* 14 (1990): 254-268. See also Gregory Grossman, "The Second Economy in the USSR and Eastern Europe: A Bibliography," *Berkeley-Duke Occasional Papers on the Second Economy in the USSR*, no. 1 (1985).

[25] On these inhibitors, see Louis De Alessi, "Property Rights, Transaction Costs, and X-Efficiency: An Essay in Economic Theory," *American Economic Review* 73, no. 1 (March 1983): 67; and Eugene Fama, "Agency Problems and the Theory of the Firm," *Journal of Political Economy* 88 (April 1980): 288-307.

[26] See John Nellis, *Improving the Performance of Soviet Enterprises*, World Bank Discussion Papers, no. 118 (Washington: World Bank, 1991); Naishul, 494.

[27] Leonid Grigoriev, 200.

[28] Nellis, *Improving the Performance of Soviet Enterprises*, 4. In an interview with the author, Academician Vladimir Tikhonov, President of the Union of Cooperatives and Entrepreneurs of Russia, said that these private enterprises accounted for 7 percent of Soviet GNP in 1990 (Moscow, April 1993). Leased properties then became some of the first to privatize. See, for instance, Mikhail Glukovsky, "Conversion Voronezh Style," *Delovie Lyudi*, May 1993: 20-21.

[29] Grigoriev, "Ulterior Property Rights and Privatization," 201.

[30] Heidi Kroll, "Managerial Strategies for Spontaneous Privatization," *Soviet Economy* 7, no. 4 (October-December 1991): 281-316. For instance, the Saratov Aviation Plant (SAP) and the Saratov Electrounit Production Organization (SEPO) were privatized by managers using collective ownership as a interim step towards full property rights. Author's interviews with managers at SAP and SEPO (Saratov, August 1992).

[31] See Michael McFaul, "State Power, Institutional Change, and the Politics of Privatization" (unpublished ms., 1994).

[32] Ken Jowitt, *New World Disorder: The Leninist Extinction* (Berkeley, CA: University of California Press, 1992), 289-290. See also "The Western Executive and the Soviet Executive: A Talk with Nikolai Kaniskin," in Sheila Puffer, ed., *The Russian Management Revolution* (Armonk, NY: M.E. Sharpe, 1992), 41-51.

[33] Joseph Berliner, *Factory and Manager in the USSR* (Cambridge, MA: Harvard University Press, 1957), 230; John Willerton, *Patronage and Politics in the USSR* (New York: Cambridge University Press, 1992).

[34] Of course, there were notable exceptions such as the coal miners' activism in 1989 and 1991. See Stephen Crowley, "Barriers to Collective Action: Steelworkers and Mutual Dependence in the Former Soviet Union," *World Politics* (forthcoming, July 1994).

[35] Lipton and Sachs wrote, "[U]nless hundreds of large firms in each country [of Eastern Europe] are brought quickly into the privatization process, the political battle over privatization will soon lead to stalemate in the entire process, with the devastating long-term result that little privatization takes place at all." "Privatization in Eastern Europe: The Case of Poland," in Bohm and Kreacic, eds., *Privatization in Eastern Europe*, 27. The importance of timing for privatization has also been observed in other countries. See Joan Nelson, "The Politics of Stabilization," in R.E. Feinberg and V. Kallab, eds., *Adjustment Crisis in the Third World* (New Brunswick, NJ: Transaction Books, 1984); Joan Nelson, *Fragile Coalitions: The Politics of Economic Adjustment*, Overseas Development Council (New Brunswick, NJ: Transaction Books, 1989); Stephan Haggard and Robert Kaufman, eds., *The Politics of Economic Adjustment* (Princeton, NJ: Princeton University Press, 1992); and Adam Przeworski, *Democracy and the Market: Political and Economic Reforms in Eastern Europe and Latin America* (Cambridge: Cambridge University Press, 1991).

[36] On the politics of these negotiations, see McFaul, "State Power, Institutional Change, and the Politics of Privatization"; and Michael McFaul, "Russian Centrism and Revolutionary Transitions," *Post-Soviet Affairs* 9, no. 2 (July-September, 1993): 196-222; and Maxim Boycko and Andrei Schleifer, "The Politics of Russian Privatization," in Olivier Blanchard, et al., *Post-Communist Reform: Pain and Progress* (Boston, MA: MIT Press, 1994), 37-80.

[37] "Chubais Schitaet Shto Glavnaya Zadacha 1993 Goda—Perekhod k Kachestvennoi Privatitizatsii," *Izvestiya-FP*, March 12, 1993: 1.

[38] "Obzor Investii i Privatizatsii," *Kommersant'*, no. 7, February 15-21, 1993: 16.

[39] Industrial groups such as Civic Union and the Industrial Union faction even pushed for a fourth option whereby the workers' collective would receive 90 percent of all equity. The distraction of the referendum in the spring of 1993 derailed this version of the plan. "Privatizatsiya: Etap Vtoroi," *Rossiyskiye Vesti*, February 4, 1993: 1; Vitaliy Klyuchnikov, "Chetvertyi Variant Privatizatsii v Tsentre Politicheskoi Bor'by," *Rossiyskaya Gazeta*, February 23, 1993: 3.

[40] See, for instance, Cory Rosen, "Employee Ownership May Be Next Russian Revolution," *We/My*, April 19-May 2, 1993: 7.

[41] Interview with Chubais, in "Snova 'Fabriki-Rabochim'?" *Argumenty i Fakty*, April 16, 1993: 4.

[42] See Michael Buroway and Kathryn Hendley, "Between *Perestroika* and Privatization: Divided Strategies and Political Crisis in a Soviet Enterprise," *Soviet Studies* 44, no. 3 (1992): 371-402.

[43] Author's observation on visits to more than twenty large state enterprises in Moscow, St.

Petersburg, Saratov, and Ekaterinburg in 1992 and 1993. The enterprise privatization committees that were tasked with drafting the privatization plan were dominated by management. A trade union or workers' collective official often held a seat in the committee, but in almost all situations observed by the author, these officials only loosely "represented" workers and their interests.

[44] The author attended the first stockholders' meeting at the Saratov Aviation Plant (February 1993) at which the plant director, Alexander Yermishin, was elected chairman by an overwhelming majority. All other board members elected were managers, except the old trade union representative.

[45] David Brooks, "You're Privatized. Now What?" *Wall Street Journal* , April 23, 1993: A14.

[46] Unlike the preset price of shares offered through closed subscription to the workers' collective, the price of these shares is determined by the auction, and thus could be significantly higher than the subscription price.

[47] Kevin McDonald, "Why Privatization Is Not Enough," *Harvard Business Review*, May-June 1993: 5 and 11.

[48] Subsidies have many forms. They can be loans with interest rates that are effectively negative, given inflation; debt forgiveness; money allocated according to special programs (e.g., conversion funds); payments on state orders; or direct transfers of funds.

[49] World Bank, "Subsidies and Directed Credits to Enterprises in Russia," Report No. 11782-RU, April 8, 1993: v.

[50] Barry Ickes and Randi Ryterman, "The Interenterprise Arrears Crisis in Russia," *Post-Soviet Affairs* 8, no. 4 (1992): 331.

[51] Gerashchenko also allowed a 40 percent increase in credit from the Central Bank during his first month in office. See Steven Erlanger, "Russian Aide Says Central Bank Is Trying To Undermine Reforms," *New York Times*, September 15, 1992: A6.

[52] See Pyotr Filippov, "End Policy Leading to a Thievish Economy," *New Times*, no. 16, April 1993: 10; Filippov, "Kak Ostanovit' Kriminalizattsiyu Ekonomiki," *Daidzhest-Kuranty*, no. 24 (91), June 1993: 6.

[53] The World Bank and the Government of the Russian Federation, "Structural Reform in the Russian Federation: Progress, Prospects, and Priorities for External Support" (April 20, 1993): 19.

[54] See Aghion, et al.

[55] At Svetlana Corporation in St. Petersburg, management transfers money from profitable production lines to subsidize others. At the Saratov Aviation Plant, directors managed to reincorporate two small business through strong-arm tactics rather than subcontract with them at higher prices. Author's interviews with Svetlana managers, August 1992, and John Battilega in this volume, "A Case Study of Russian Defense Conversion and Employee Ownership: The Saratov Aviation Plant." See also Oliver Williamson, *Markets and Hierarchies* (New York: Free Press, 1981).

[56] Disputes over control of spin-offs have become one of the largest legal issues in the privatization process. See the interview with the Chairman of the Russian Arbitrage Court, "Privatizatsiya—Anatomiya Konfliktov," *Ekonomika i Zhizn*, no. 31, July 1993: 1.

[57] Aviaprom and the Russian Space Agency have been most active in this regard in reconsolidating the aerospace industry. Investment consortiums in other defense-related industries, such as the Military-Industrial Investment Corporation (VPIK), also have begun to organize aggressively. See Vyacheslav Limonov, "Aviabank Nabiraet Vysotu," *Federatsiya*,

no. 47, 1993: 7; Natal'ya Kalinichenko and Pavel Krizhevskii, "Chif-Chif-Chif! Ptitchka po Zernyshku Klyuet, Chif VPK—po Vaucheru," *Kommersant'*, no. 17, April 26-May 2, 1993: 20; Leyla Boulton, "Co-operation Lifts Russian Aero Industry," *Financial Times* (London), March 30, 1993: 10; and Dennis Holeman, *The Structure of the Civil Aviation Industry in the Former Soviet Bloc Countries*, document no. d91-1599 (Menlo Park, CA: SRI International, December 1991).

[58] See the resolution issued by the Chairman of the Supreme Soviet and commentary in "Privatizatsiya i Kholdingi," *Kommersant'*, no. 26, June 28-July 4, 1993: 24.

[59] See "Izmenenie" (to Presidential Decree No. 721), Prilozhenie No. 2, *Ekonomicheskaya Gazeta*, no. 48 (November 1992): 19.

[60] Fama, 295.

[61] Moe, 753.

[62] On the implications of this absence of capital markets for other, more developed post-communist economies, see Christian Kirchner, "Privatization Plans of Central and Eastern European States," *Journal of Institutional and Theoretical Economics* 148 (1992): 4-19.

[63] For instance, a worker who owns shares worth 20,000 rubles can easily make twenty times his original investment, or 400,000 rubles. Given the rate of inflation in Russia, however, this is a small amount to sell out for if the risk of sale is future unemployment.

[64] Kirchner, 14. On the labor market for defense enterprise directors, see Peter Almquist, *Red Forge: Soviet Military Industry Since 1965* (New York: Columbia University Press, 1990), 46-47.

[65] I am indebted to David Bernstein for our numerous conversations on this point. Insider privatization, of course, brings in little new capital. See Richard Bauxbaum, "Privatization Plans of Central and Eastern European States: Comment," *Journal of Institutional and Theoretical Economics* 148 (1992): 26.

4

Attitudes of Enterprise Managers Toward Market Transition

Irina Starodubrovskaya

Economic transformation in Russia is determined not only by government policies such as liberalization, rigid monetary policy, and privatization, but also by the reaction of enterprises to these serious changes. Surveys taken in the first half of 1992 indicated that Russian enterprises were not behaving like classic market firms. Enterprises that faced a sharp decrease in demand and hard budget constraints did not try to enter new markets, devote energy to attracting new clients, change products, or increase their efficiency. Despite the fact that many no longer had funds for production, enterprises tried to keep their traditional partners, began charging higher prices from any new clients that did appear, and preserved their existing technology. Furthermore, most enterprises expected the state to continue its support.

Has enterprise behavior changed after a year and a half of economic reforms? In the spring of 1993, I distributed a survey to enterprise managers to assess attitudes toward economic reform, and to trace possible changes in management behavior since the previous year. Alvira Nabiulina of the Expert Institute and the Russian Institute of Management Consulting helped me with this survey. The Expert Institute conducted its own social survey at the same time.

I selected 105 enterprises in different sectors of the economy, of different sizes and with different ownership status. The bulk of the enterprises are in Moscow and the Moscow region, and the remaining are in Central Russia and the Volga and Ural regions. The survey was conducted by way of personal interviews, and was given to top managers, primarily directors and deputy directors. The same survey was given to 107 directors at a meeting of the Association of Private and Privatized Enterprises in April 1993. Since this second survey

Irina Starodubrovskaya is an economist at the World Bank. The views expressed in this paper are those of the author, and not of the World Bank.

was conducted in written form rather than by personal interview and is therefore less reliable, I have used the results of the second survey for comparison only. (A note regarding methodology: sometimes a number of managers did not answer some questions, or chose the option "difficult to answer"; in this case, the total of responses may be less than 100 percent. For some questions it was possible to choose more than one answer; here the total may be more than 100 percent.)

Table 1   Distribution of Enterprises by Industry

	First Survey	Second Survey
Machine-Building	21.9%	23%
Food Processing and Agriculture	36.2%	4%
Light Industry	11.4%	7%
Chemical and Petrochemical	8.6%	6%
Others	9.5%	38%
No answer	12.4%	22%

Table 2   Number of Employees

	First Survey	Second Survey
Fewer than 200	18.1%	22%
200-1000	42.9%	18%
1001-5000	28.6%	41%
More than 5000	9.5%	13%
No answer	0.9%	6%

Table 3   Ownership Status

	First Survey	Second Survey
State Owned	19%	11%
Privatized	49.5%	38%
In Process of Privatizing	25.7%	28%
Initially Private	–	16%
No answer	5.8%	7%

Table 4   Age of General Director

	First Survey
Under 40 years	10.5%
41-50	29.5%
Over 50	55.2%
No answer	4.8%

The main goal of the survey was not to determine what problems enterprises in Russia face, but rather how enterprise directors felt about the economic transition. We cannot conclude, for instance, whether or not an enterprise faces competition, but can gauge a manager's appraisal of this issue. The survey's outcomes therefore only indirectly reflect the development of the economic situation.

The survey indicated that the main shock of the rapid economic transition was past, and that the majority of managers were finding ways to survive the transition. A very small number of managers (2.9 percent) viewed the economic position of their enterprise in 1992 as catastrophic. Only 17.1 percent viewed the situation as very difficult and 43.8 percent as complicated (but manageable), while 33.3 percent were more or less satisfied by their position. A good portion of the directors (52.4 percent) did not consider their difficulties serious, believing their enterprise to have good prospects for the future. Yet only 41.9 percent of the directors understood the necessity of restructuring their enterprises. The results of the survey handed out at the meeting of the Association of Private and Privatized Enterprises paint a similar picture. Once again, only 1 percent of managers viewed their enterprise's economic position as catastrophic. While 24 percent of managers were more or less satisfied by their current economic position, 42 percent considered it complicated and 28 percent perceived it as very difficult. A smaller number of managers (38 percent) than in the first survey did not believe their difficulties were serious, but a more encouraging 55 percent understood the necessity of restructuring to overcome their difficulties.

The Expert Institute's survey supported the conclusion that the majority of managers were finding ways to survive the economic transition. Only 5 percent of the directors believed their enterprise might have to file for bankruptcy.

Overall, managers were moderately optimistic about their enterprise's present and future economic position. It is hard to find an interdependency between the size of an enterprise and its economic position since our sample was not large enough for such an analysis. It is interesting to note, however, that in the second survey, which included more large enterprises, managers' assessments of both the current situation and future prospects were more cautious.

Constraints and Competition

The survey tried next to understand whether the constraints enterprises felt in 1992 were market or non-market by comparing difficulties in supplies and sales. Results showed that supply constraints were much stronger than sales constraints. While 79 percent of managers from the first survey stressed supply difficulties in maintaining normal production, only 39 percent emphasized difficulties in sales. (Some directors chose two answers.) The figures from the second survey were 41 percent and 22 percent respectively, but one should note that 37 percent of the directors did not answer the question. Responses also show that monetary constraints were more important than non-monetary ones. The majority of managers (54.3 percent) mentioned lack of money as one of their main difficulties in obtaining supplies, and 38.1 percent viewed lack of customers with money as their main sales problem. Other important factors behind supply difficulties were the disintegration of the Soviet Union and the Council for Mutual Economic Assistance, and the subsequent disruption of economic links between enterprises. These factors were mentioned by 41.9 percent of the directors. Only 2.9 percent of the directors cited lack of resources with which to barter, which previously could have been a more important obstacle. The Expert Institute's survey produced similar results: the bulk of directors saw lack of money as their main difficulty in supply and sales, while a smaller number blamed instead the instability of economic links between enterprises.

A very limited number of managers (2.9 percent) faced difficulties due to lack of demand for their products. Indirectly, this result may be considered an indicator of the lack of structural changes in the economy. Considering that 41.9 percent of managers related their difficulties to the structural changes in the economy, and that the most popular strategy for the future appeared to be changing output mix, entering new markets, and reacting to sales demand, it is evident that directors considered structural changes an important factor in their future development.

It is interesting to compare issues of constraints with competition. Surprisingly, only 21.9 percent of the directors said they faced no competition at all. A larger 37.1 percent believed they generally faced competition, while 40 percent thought they faced competition in only part of the market. Even among those managers who believed competition was a real threat, however, less than half mentioned problems with sales as one of their main difficulties. These answers must therefore reflect potential rather than real competition, i.e. the directors' knowledge that other enterprises produce similar goods, rather than actual market struggles. Furthermore, most directors said they were not afraid of competition. Nevertheless, answers to this question indicated that directors were beginning to view competition as something they would not be able to ignore in the future.

Future Strategies

Next, I tried to determine what strategies enterprises would choose in the next few years: would strategies reflect the old administrative system or new market conditions, would they be more open or closed, and so on. The first strategy described in the responses, a supply-oriented strategy, maintained existing networks. In the first half of 1992, most enterprises maintained existing economic links with suppliers and buyers, even those with temporary financial difficulties. By the summer of 1992, this strategy had created a serious crisis in interenterprise arrears. However, 30.5 percent of directors from the first survey and only 18 percent from the second chose this strategy. The fact that a minority of the managers opted for this old-fashioned model was a positive sign, even though it does not completely eliminate the possibility of another such crisis occurring.

A greater number of directors (37.1 percent from the first survey and 37 percent from the second) focused instead on ensuring reliable payment, stressing the necessity of selling products to clients with money, and demanding prepayment or payment guarantees.

A strategy based on economizing on all types of expenditures and reducing costs, thus attracting customers by limiting price increases, was not very popular (chosen by 13.3 percent of directors in the first survey and 20 percent in the second). While any of several factors (uncertain ownership status; high inflation; a feeling that this strategy is typical of the old system of management) may explain this situation, it is clear that managers saw more ways to improve conditions outside the enterprises than inside, and they preferred not closed, but open types of strategies.

The most popular strategy, however, was demand-oriented, focusing on shifts in output mix, production of new commodities, and entrance into new markets. A large number of directors (41 percent of managers from the first survey and 53 percent from the second) thought this the best strategy for maintaining and expanding sales.

Since this demand-oriented strategy is the one that should lead to greater market success, about half of the directors, therefore, seemed psychologically ready for structural changes and prepared to work in a competitive environment. (The Expert Institute's data also supports this conclusion: 80 percent of surveyed enterprises had begun changing their suppliers and buyers.) In the future, managers who have based their decisions on the likelihood of payment (about 37 percent) will have to choose between supply-oriented and demand-oriented strategy. Depending on their choice, therefore, the economy as a whole could retreat to being supply-driven or could progress to appropriate demand-driven market relations.

Links with Other Enterprises/Interest Representation

Links with other enterprises were the next subject for analysis. After the old Soviet administrative system collapsed, many of the branch ministries and their departments did not disappear, but were transformed into various kinds of organizations and associations linking enterprises within a given industrial sector. These associations no longer have official government authority, but still exercise a good deal of authority to organize production and promote their members' interests through lobbying.

The general impression that the bulk of enterprises are members of such associations is not quite right. Only 58.1 percent of enterprises from the first survey and 52 percent from the second belonged to associations, while 34.3 percent and 41 percent of enterprises respectively did not. Enterprises' best means for lobbying, however, is through associations of various types, and directors (40 percent from the first survey and 51 percent from the second) recognized this. Further, 33.3 percent of directors from the first survey and 21 percent from the second believed that these organizations provide high-level consulting and information services, and perform functions that enterprises are not yet ready to undertake.

Yet managers seemed to want more from associations with other enterprises. Only 25.7 percent of directors from the first survey and 30 percent from the second felt that associations are successful in defending the interests of their enterprise in relation to their partners and state bodies. Some directors, albeit a minority (26.7 percent from the first survey and 36 percent from the second), believed that associations impede the initiative of enterprises and their overall adjustment to the market economy. A smaller number of directors (10.5 percent) responded that these enterprise associations do not work at all, and/or that the directors preferred to work independently. Two directors said that associations were no better than the former state institutions.

Table 5 compares the attitudes of managers who were members of associations to those who were not. The table contains the results of both the first and the second survey.

The number of directors who expressed negative feelings about associations is about the same as the number with positive feelings, but the distribution of answers among those who were and who were not members is quite different. This difference is significant, because it provides some evidence as to whether, in general, enterprises join associations voluntarily or are pressured or coerced by their former ties into doing so. Approximately two-thirds of directors who belong to associations spoke positively of the activities of associations, while about three-fourths of directors who do not belong expressed a neutral or negative attitude toward them. (This tendency is clearer in the first survey than in the second one.) This suggests that most managers are free to join or not to join.

This cannot be true for all managers, however, since there were some directors who expressed negative feelings toward associations, yet continue to belong to them. At the same time, there are also managers who assessed the role of associations positively, but are not members. One can assume, therefore, that some restrictions and obstacles still exist, both to entering and exiting these associations.

Enterprises do have means of safeguarding their interests other than these associations. Lobbying government officials directly, for instance, is often effective. Meetings with top officials were considered more successful means of lobbying than contacts with state bureaucracy (according to 21 percent and 15.2 percent of directors from the first survey; 31 percent and 14 percent from the second, respectively). These results indicate that directors of enterprises continued to have access to the highest levels of state hierarchy, and that not

Table 5 Managers' Attitudes Toward Associations

	First Survey	Second Survey	Average
Respondents that belong to associations —"members" (as percentage of all respondents)	59.0%	52.3%	55.7%
Respondents that do not belong to associations—"non-members" (as percentage of all respondents)	34.3%	41.2%	37.7%
Respondents that expressed a **positive** attitude toward associations (as percentage of all respondents)	49.5%	42.1%	45.8%
(as percentage of members)	74.2%	58.9%	66.9%
(as percentage of non-members)	16.7%	27.3%	22.5%
Respondents that both a) are members and b) expressed a **positive** attitude toward associations (as percentage of all respondents)	43.8%	30.8%	37.3%
Respondents that both a) are **not** members and b) expressed a **positive** attitude toward associations (as percentage of all respondents)	5.7%	11.3%	8.5%
Respondents that expressed a **neutral or negative** attitude toward associations (as percentage of all respondents)	43.8%	41.1%	42.4%
(as percentage of members)	25.8%	28.5%	27.1%
(as percentage of non-members)	83.3%	63.6%	72.5%
Respondents that both a) are members and b) expressed a **neutral or negative** attitude toward associations (as percentage of all respondents)	15.2%	14.9%	15.1%
Respondents that both a) are **not** members and b) expressed a **neutral or negative** attitude toward associations (as percentage of all respondents)	28.6%	26.2%	27.4%
Respondents that did not respond to question concerning associations' activities (as percentage of all respondents)	—	10.3%	5.2%
(as percentage of members)	—	12.6%	6.0%
(as percentage of non-members)	—	9.1%	5.0%

everything depends on bureaucracy. Some directors also saw the mass media as playing an important role in representing the interests of enterprises (20 from the first survey and 17 percent from the second). A similar number of directors relied upon the relatively new political/networking organizations of industrialists (e.g. Arkady Volsky's Union of Industrialists and Entrepreneurs, or Yegor Gaidar's Association of Private and Privatized Enterprises) to fulfill this task. Peoples' deputies, on the other hand, were not seen as very effective. No directors from the first survey and only 6 percent from the second believed that the deputies of the Supreme Soviet could represent their interests. The relevant figures for local soviets are 9.5 and 3 percent. At the same time, however, some directors thought highly of local government officials in this capacity.

Attitudes Toward Economic Policies

Due to the complexity of the overall economic situation, assessing the attitude of directors toward economic policies in 1992 can be complicated. In general, however, directors strongly supported privatization (about 70 percent from both surveys), and as a whole reacted positively to the free exchange of rubles to hard currency (about 70 percent of the directors had positive or neutral attitudes, but the share of neutral answers fluctuates from 10 to 30 percent). A good portion of the managers had neutral (about 45 percent) or positive (40 to 50 percent from the second survey) attitudes toward the licensing of export activity and state regulation of enterprise monopolies.

There was a negative attitude toward price liberalization, which had the support of only about one-third of the directors. Rigid monetary policy was also unpopular, opposed by approximately one-half to two-thirds of the directors. During 1992, however, the number of directors who were against rigid monetary policy declined somewhat, from 73.3 percent to 64.8 percent. From 50 to 70 percent of directors were against the liberalization of prices for fuel and energy (the number of negative responses rose during 1992, when the liberalization took effect). Surprisingly, more than half the managers were against import restrictions. These last results may be indicative of the lack of real competition: import restrictions for managers are now additional expenditures for import inputs, not additional barriers to entry for newcomers.

These results are ambiguous, however, because they can be understood as reactions to policy or to its implementation.

The attitude of the managers to the different directions of economic policy was perhaps the key issue of the survey. To analyze the results on this point, I compared the answers of two questions. The first question contained four options concerning the particular enterprise's strategy, asking if in the process of creating such strategy the manager 1) relied only upon his own abilities and the resources of the enterprise, 2) tried to find domestic or foreign investors, 3) thought that authorities would understand the necessity of supporting domestic production, which would make survival easier, or 4) relied on the help of local powers or other state bodies. In reality, these choices can be divided into two camps: relying upon one's own forces (options 1 and 2) versus relying upon the state (options 3 and 4). I put directors who mentioned 1 and 2, but chose either 3 or 4 into the second camp. In a second question, directors were asked to choose among three options for a future economic policy: rigid monetary policy, strong government support of producers, or freezing of prices and wages.

The best way to analyze the responses is to take into account the interdependence of the questions. If a manager opts for a rigid monetary policy while relying upon the state for financial support, it is clear that he either does not fully support a rigid policy or does not fully understand its meaning. At the same time directors who prefer to rely upon their own forces but would support an economic policy of continued financial support from the state

64

would not seem to be psychologically prepared to become independent market agents. I will proceed with a combined analysis of these two questions together, and then address the most interesting aspects of each.

The number of defenders of a rigid monetary policy in both the first and second survey was little more than 40 percent, a figure which could be an objective reflection of support for real market reforms among directors. In general, managers of enterprises with fewer than

Table 6 Managers' Attitudes Toward State Economic Policy

	First Survey	Second Survey
Respondents that rely primarily on their own abilities (as percentage of all respondents)	64.7%	67.3%
Respondents that rely primarily on the state (as percentage of all respondents)	35.3%	32.7%
Respondents that favor rigid monetary policy (as percentage of all respondents)	54.3%	60.7%
(as percentage of those who rely primarily on their own abilities)	64.7%	61.1%
(as percentage of those who rely primarily on the state)	35.1%	60.0%
Respondents that favor financial support from the state (as percentage of all respondents)	16.2%	13.1%
(as percentage of those who rely primarily on their own abilities)	14.7%	12.5%
(as percentage of those who rely primarily on the state)	18.9%	14.3%
Respondents that favor price/wage controls (as percentage of all respondents)	11.5%	16.8%
(as percentage of those who rely primarily on their own abilities)	4.4%	16.7%
(as percentage of those who rely primarily on the state)	24.3%	17.1%
Respondents that mentioned other economic policy ideas (as percentage of all respondents)	18.0%	9.4%
(as percentage of those who rely primarily on their own abilities)	16.2%	9.7%
(as percentage of those who rely primarily on the state)	21.7%	8.6%
Respondents that both a) rely primarily on their own abilities and b) favor rigid monetary policy (as percentage of all respondents)	41.9%	41.1%
Respondents that both a) rely primarily on their own abilities and b) favor financial support from the state (as percentage of all respondents)	9.5%	8.4%
Respondents that both a) rely primarily on their own abilities and b) favor price/wage controls (as percentage of all respondents)	2.9%	11.2%
Respondents that both a) rely primarily on their own abilities and b) mentioned other economic policy ideas (as percentage of all respondents)	10.4%	6.6%
Respondents that both a) rely primarily on the state and b) favor rigid monetary policy (as percentage of all respondents)	12.4%	19.6%
Respondents that both a) rely primarily on the state and b) favor financial support from the state (as percentage of all respondents)	6.7%	4.7%
Respondents that both a) rely primarily on the state and b) favor price/wage controls (as percentage of all respondents)	8.6%	5.6%
Respondents that both a) rely primarily on the state and b) mentioned other economic policy ideas (as percentage of all respondents)	7.6%	2.8%

1000 employees were slightly more market-oriented than those of larger enterprises (more than 45 percent in the first group, and less than 40 percent in the second). I failed to find any connection between the attitude of the manager and the enterprise's ownership status, except for the understandably high number of market-oriented managers in companies that were private from the beginning. It is much more difficult to understand how many directors were against market reform. Only one response considered necessary the state-regulated distribution of consumer goods (through rationing, for example) and a guaranteed order from the state for 30 percent of an enterprise's output. I do not believe that more than 5 to 7 percent of directors would support such policies (taking into account their attitude toward privatization and their strategies).

Thus, although managers might be expected to exert united political influence as a powerful interest group, in fact their proxy preferences are ambiguous and diverse; different political forces can gain support from different parts of this group.

The difference between the results of the first and second surveys is straightforward. The results of the first survey showed that among managers who relied upon the state, the number of defenders of freezing prices and wages was much higher than among those who relied upon their own forces. To some extent, therefore, managers viewed a rigid monetary policy as synonymous with a free market economy, and the freezing of prices and wages as synonymous with state regulation. In the second survey, by contrast, managers who relied on their own forces expressed similar preferences in economic policy to those who relied on the state. This suggests that managers see no inherent contradiction between free market competition and state support.

Two different explanations can be found for the outcome of the second survey. The high number of defenders of rigid monetary policy among directors who also relied upon the state could be the result of these directors' participation in the Association of Private and Privatized Enterprises, where rigid monetary policy was directly connected with Yegor Gaidar. The high number of directors who opted for freezing prices and wages while relying upon their own forces indicated that for some managers this combination was attractive not because of its similarity to the old administrative system, but because it could be seen as the first step in stopping inflation.

If the two questions are analyzed separately, two results in particular stand out. In the first place, few directors (about 17 percent in the first survey and about 20 percent in the second) will try to find outside private investors in the near future; they prefer to rely upon the state. A good portion of managers who lacked investment saw no opportunities or had no desire to deal with outside investors.

The other interesting issue to note is the managers' own proposals for economic policy. A portion of directors who gave their own economic recommendations proposed support of selected sectors of the economy, but none of the directors supported the idea of state help for enterprises that are losing money. Other proposals called for determining the goals of economic reform and establishing stable and long-term economic rules, establishing profit-margin ceilings for all the enterprises, and strengthening the struggle against corruption and organized crime.

One final note: two main observations stand out when examining the difference in answers between the first and second survey. First, the number of directors who based their strategy on preserving existing networks was much smaller in the second survey than in the first (18 percent in the second survey and 30 percent in the first). Second, the managers who participated in the meeting of the Association of Private and Privatized Enterprises were much more involved in creating various market structures such as banks, exchanges, and joint ventures. One may assume, therefore, that the same directors were more politically involved and had more dynamic strategies in the economic sphere.

References

1. V. Kashin and A. Nabiulina, "Definite 'Rules of the Game' are Necessary," *Economic Bulletin of the Russian Union of Industrialists and Entrepreneurs*, #2: May 1993.
2. A. Nabiulina, *Enterprises in Conditions of Reform: New Models of Behavior* (Moscow: Expert Institute, April 1993).
3. *Russian Enterprises: Life in Crisis Conditions* (Moscow: Expert Institute, 1992).
4. *Russian Enterprises: The Process of Adjustment* (Moscow: Expert Institute, October 1993).

5

Privatization and Corporate Governance in Russia: An Empirical Study

Katharina Pistor

This paper presents the results of an empirical survey of privatized enterprises conducted in Russia during the summer of 1993.[1] It should serve as a first appraisal of mass privatization in Russia with regard to the emergence of a system of corporate governance. The questions addressed concern the development of a secondary market of shares, as well as the legal framework currently in place for Russian corporations.

The results obtained in this study suggest that the privatization program, adopted in combination with an insufficient framework for corporate law, has facilitated entrenchment by management of the former state enterprises. The Russian privatization program gives insiders a large stake in companies, and the lack of a strong legal framework has enabled management to reinforce its position in corporations. Influential outside investors with a substantial amount of shares relative to insider ownership are absent in Russia, leaving management largely uncontrolled. Furthermore, there is no efficient capital market as a substitute for monitoring management through "voice."[2]

This paper is divided into four parts. Part I gives a brief overview of the framework for Russian corporate law. Part II describes the sample, and Part III presents the main results of the survey. The implications of these results for the emergence of a system of corporate governance in Russia are discussed in Part IV.

I. The Legal Framework for Privatization

The Russian privatization program gives employees (both workers and management personnel) of state enterprises considerable control over the privatization process. A privatization

Katharina Pistor is studying for a master's degree in public administration at Harvard University.

commission set up at the enterprise adopts a privatization plan, which includes the selection of one out of three privatization options.[3]

Prior to privatization of an enterprise through the sale of shares, an enterprise is required to corporatize as an open joint-stock company. To this end, President Yeltsin's Decree No. 721 of July, 1992 drafted a model charter that all enterprises are mandated to adopt as their charter of corporatization. Changes to the charter require a three-fourths majority of common stock and may be vetoed by the Property Fund, as long as it holds 50 percent or more of the total stock. The model charter is based on Decree No. 601 of the RSFSR Council of Ministers, which dates back to December 1990. Decree No. 601 confirms the statute on joint-stock companies, and provides a two-tier management structure consisting of the Council of Directors and the Management Board. Both of these bodies are headed by the general director, who simultaneously is chairman of the Council of Directors. The members of the Council of Directors as well as the general director are elected at the first shareholder meeting, while other members of the Management Board are nominated by the general director and then appointed by the Council of Directors. While Decree 601 does not provide a clear demarcation of powers and responsibilities between the two management organs, the model charter allocates most strategic decisions to the Council of Directors, leaving the Board of Management with more routine management decisions. The Council's potential to exercise control over the general director and the Board, however, is weakened by the fact that the general director is appointed and dismissed by the shareholder meeting rather than the Council itself. This structure differs clearly from Western corporate law systems, in which either the board (in the Anglo-American system) or the supervisory board (in the German system) have the key responsibility of appointing and dismissing the chief executive officer(s). Without this power, the Council of Directors could become a mere shadow organ. In view of the initial distribution of shares according to the privatization options, this also implies that outside shareholders might not be able to exert substantial influence on an enterprise's performance even if they gained a seat on the Council of Directors.

The implementation of an internal system of corporate governance is further complicated by the fact that enterprises are corporatized under the guidance of the old management. The management remains in place at least until the first shareholder meeting, which has to be convened only within twelve months after registration of the company as a joint-stock company. According to the model charter, the first general director is appointed or confirmed by the Committee for the Management of State Property (GKI), or its regional representative. The Council of Directors should consist of the general director and one representative each from the labor collective, the local soviet, and either the Property Fund or the GKI. While the general director has two votes, the remaining representatives only have one vote each. Thus, until the first shareholder meeting, insiders have the majority of votes on the Council.

II. The Sample

My data is based on interviews conducted with the general directors and high-level managers of 36 enterprises in six regions throughout Russia: Moscow, Novgorod, Yaroslavl, Ivanovo, Perm, and Sverdlovsk. Regions were selected based upon the progress of privatization in the area, while enterprises were selected from the GKI database according to the completion of voucher auctions and the size of the enterprise. All enterprises except one had completed voucher auctions at least two months prior to the interview, and in most cases by the end of April 1993. The sample includes both medium-sized enterprises with a charter capital of 25 million to 50 million rubles and an average of 630 employees, and large enterprises with a charter capital of more than 150 million rubles and more than 2500 employees.

III. Results of Interviews

Privatization Option

Reflecting a trend throughout Russia, the majority of enterprises in my sample (26 out of 36) chose Option 2, which gives both employees and former employees an opportunity to acquire up to 51 percent of an enterprise's common voting stock in a closed subscription. No enterprise in the sample adopted Option 3, while all six enterprises I interviewed in the Ivanovo region chose privatization Option 1. In order to buy up the 51 percent of voting stock under Option 2 in the closed subscription, enterprises usually set up a privatization fund from profits, and allocate a certain share to employees and former employees. Enterprises with relatively large charter capitals[4] and without sufficient profits to guarantee the buyout of the total 51 percent see Option 1 as a way to gain control over the enterprise by reducing the total number of voting shares, and they hope to buy an additional block of shares on the market.

Current Distribution of Shares

The distribution of shares of each enterprise at the time of the interview is presented in Table 2. As the table shows, in most cases insiders managed to gain an additional block of shares at voucher auctions, on average acquiring 57 percent of the voting stock.[5] Only in four cases did insiders not buy more shares at the voucher auctions.

Outsiders, including investment funds, commercial structures,[6] foreign investors, and persons other than employees or former employees of the enterprise, acquired shares during privatization in 25 of the enterprises. Outsiders acquired a mean of 19 percent of the total stock, with the largest stake acquired by a single outside investor 31 percent. On average, the largest amount held by a single outside shareholder amounts to 10.4 percent. Since voucher investment funds are restricted by law from acquiring more than 10 percent of a single enterprise,[7] the largest outside investors are commercial structures, in some cases joint ventures with foreign partners. While some investment funds succeeded in acquiring up to 10 percent of the total stock, in most cases investment funds hold around 3 percent or less each in a given enterprise.

The total amount of shares acquired by outsiders depended less on the size of the charter capital than on the location of the enterprise and its production line. Lowest outside shareholdings were in the regions of Yaroslavl and Ivanovo,[8] in which only very small blocks of shares were offered in voucher auctions (1 percent in most cases in Ivanovo, and around

71

11 percent in Yaroslavl). The regional Property Funds apparently supported this strategy, making it less attractive for outside investors to participate. On the whole, this practice highlights the drawbacks of a decentralized auction system.[9]

Another factor contributing to regional disparities is the concentration of industries in different regions. Perm and Sverdlovsk, for instance, are centers for oil, gas, and timber, all of which are industries with potentially lucrative export markets. Ivanovo, on the other hand, is home to the textile industry, which is in serious difficulty due to the collapse of the supply network from the former republics of the Soviet Union.

Foreign investors bought shares at voucher auctions in only two enterprises. Local investment funds hinted, however, that more foreign investors are actually participating in voucher auctions by commissioning Russian intermediaries, e.g. voucher investment funds, to buy on their behalf.

There is not much hard data on the distribution of shares among insiders, i.e. ownership by managers as opposed to workers. In one case, the general director acknowledged holding 38 percent of the stock in his enterprise.[10] Several large enterprises claimed that the largest inside shareholder—usually a member of top management—held only 1 to 2 percent of the total stock. Even where management does not hold a controlling block vis-a-vis other insiders, however, it may still control decisions made by insider shareholders. Management typically initiates privatization and "educates" workers on what decisions to adopt and how to use their voting rights. In addition, on the secondary market there seems to be a tendency toward concentration of insider shares among managers. In large enterprises, management often sets up a separate trading company that acquires a license to deal in securities and buys shares of the joint-stock company on the secondary market. The new company raises funds partly by trading in vouchers, and partly from resources it receives from the parent company.

Trading of Shares

Post-privatization trading of shares took place in most companies. In general, trading volumes were low, and usually occurred among employees and former employees. "Trading among employees" often is a synonym for increasing share ownership by managers, who advise employees not to sell their shares, at least not to outsiders. Trading takes place mostly regionally, since the absence of a nationwide depository system makes national trade rather cumbersome. Under Decree 601, shares can be legally transferred only by registering the new shareholder in the company's registry. In most cases the new shareholder has to travel to the company and present the sales contract and the share or share certificate in person. Currently, the major channel for trade among different regions is the few large investment funds with a countrywide network. A few newly emerging financial institutions[11] also provide shareholder registry services, however, and have started to organize a depository system.

None of the enterprises interviewed had stock trading on the market yet, and information about prices of shares on the secondary market in general was scarce. According to a few regional investment funds, prices for shares bought from individuals on the secondary market are considerably lower than share prices at voucher auctions.[12] Apparently, employees and former employees who received their shares in the closed subscription with means provided by the enterprises are the first ones to sell. According to GKI data, shares are being sold at voucher auctions at a weighted average auction rate of 1.78.[13] Given the heavily undervalued charter capital of enterprises, especially in light of rapid inflation, these prices are already very low.

Shareholder Meetings

Of the enterprises in the sample, thirteen had already held their first shareholder meeting, and the remaining had scheduled one before the end of the year.[14] Most enterprises notified shareholders about the meeting in writing, yet one company only announced it at work.

Given the number of shareholders, especially in large companies, most companies are not able to invite all shareholders to attend the shareholder meeting, or are reluctant to do so.[15] In general, enterprises tend to use a system of delegation to reduce the number of shareholders attending a meeting. Some larger enterprises use workers' conferences, an old Soviet institution, to elect delegates to shareholder meetings. A quota is established for the election representatives, such as one representative for a certain number of shares. Candidates for the Council of Directors occasionally present their platform at workers' conferences, and some enterprise representatives commented that the shareholder meeting only confirmed the decisions that had already been adopted by the workers' conference. Enterprises that do not use workers' conferences usually encourage shareholders to authorize a representative. In two enterprises, management prepared authorizations for either the Council of Directors or other delegates it proposed, while in other cases blank forms were issued to workers.

Decree 601, unamended by the model charter, requires that the power of attorney (*doverennost'*) issued by shareholders to their representatives at the shareholder meeting be certified by a notary, which is both difficult and costly.[16] In order to reduce the technical and financial problems involved, management sometimes hires a notary to validate the certifications first issued by management, giving management considerable control over who will be authorized. Thus, current legal regulations heavily restrict shareholders' freedom to issue authorizations either in the form of blank authorizations or with precise instructions for how to vote on their behalf.

Amendments to the Model Charter

Most of the enterprises interviewed had either already amended the model charter or were preparing to do so at the shareholder meeting. Most of the amendments concern the structure and powers of the Council of Directors and the Board of Management, but there is little data available so far on the actual content of these changes. However, the fact that the model amendments concern the allocation of powers between the two management organs suggests that powers are being shifted from the Council of Directors to the Management Board. This was confirmed by representatives of a few enterprises who suggested that the Board of Management be in charge of strategic decisions, rather than the Council of Directors.

Russian corporate law has erected some defenses against amendments to the charter, namely the super majority (three-fourths) requirement, and the right of the Property Fund to veto changes as long as it holds 50 percent or more of the total stock. The Property Fund relinquishes its veto right upon completion of the voucher auction, however. Furthermore, in light of the large block of shares allocated to insiders or acquired by them at voucher auctions and/or additional share sales, the three-fourths majority requirement does not pose a serious obstacle for charter changes. The attempt to improve the weak corporate structure of Decree 601 by a more elaborate model charter has thus proved to be short-lived. Unless a more sophisticated corporate law is adopted, management, with the backing of other insiders, has considerable leeway to design the charter in a way that solidifies its position and further mitigates the influence of outsiders.

The Council of Directors

The model charter prescribes the staff of the first Council of Directors of the corporatized enterprise. The overall activity and effectiveness of a corporatized enterprise's first Council of Directors is hard to assess. In most cases, those interviewed only confirmed that this organ existed, and that it was required to meet once a month. In two corporations, however, the Council of Directors had met only twice since corporatization of the enterprise roughly a year earlier, and in three cases not even once. Thus, the Council of Directors is a rather passive or even superfluous organ in many enterprises. Generally, its role was not apparent given the fact that the former management single-handedly administered the affairs of companies. Even in enterprises in which the Council was more active, outsiders could easily be outvoted by the general director and the representative of the workers' collective, who together have three of the five votes. Three companies in the sample did not change the original composition of the Council of Directors, despite the fact that in the meantime shares had been privatized. Such a solution appears to give insiders a comfortable cushion against outside interference.

Outside investors are represented on two Councils of Directors in the sample, and are expected to gain a seat in the forthcoming shareholder meeting in a number of enterprises where they have gained a fairly large stake at the auction (around 8 percent and more). However, there was no company in which outsiders gained a majority of seats on the Council.

In the absence of legally or otherwise established voting standards, many enterprises still hold hand votes. To provide some secrecy, some companies use voting cards indicating the number of shares a representative may vote on. Candidates for the Council of Directors must get a majority of all shares present to be elected. Cumulative voting rules have not been established, which makes it even harder for outsiders to obtain a seat. Representatives of investment funds reported that they gained a seat on the Council of Directors only with the support of the workers' collective over the objections of management.

General Director and Management Board

Without exception, the general directors appointed by the GKI upon founding of a joint-stock company were the former directors of the state-owned enterprise. The same directors were then elected at the first shareholder meeting as the new general directors of the company, with only two notable exceptions. In the first case, the director was replaced after attempting to sell the enterprise to an outside investor during the process of privatization. In the second case, the director was replaced by the chief engineer of the company at the first shareholder meeting of the privatized company after supposedly helping an outsider to gain a large stake in the enterprise.[17] In other words, anti-outsider takeovers by insiders were responsible for the two cases where the former general director was replaced.

74

Dividend Payments

Most enterprises in the sample are currently not paying dividends even if they report profits (which only four have so far) and are not planning to pay dividends on common stock in the near future. Many of these enterprises have adopted, or plan to adopt, a moratorium on dividends for one to four years. One enterprise representative stated explicitly that the company preferred to pay higher wages to workers rather than share profits with outside shareholders. In general, enterprises appear to be reluctant to pay dividends to shareholders who have not made any capital contribution to the enterprise during privatization.

Social Assets

State enterprises provided many social services for their workers and thus owned many social assets and local infrastructure, including cultural and sporting facilities, as well as schools, roads, and housing. Privatization regulations on social assets divide these facilities and services into those that may be privatized as part of the enterprise's assets and those that shall be transferred to state ownership exercised by the municipality. In general, social assets that are important for the local infrastructure, such as schools, housing funds, and roads, are to be transferred to ownership of the municipalities, while cultural and sporting facilities may be privatized as part of the assets of the enterprise.

Currently, however, even social assets that are being transferred to the municipalities are still fully financed by the enterprise. In the majority of cases they are transferred back to the enterprises on the basis of full economic jurisdiction, a property concept developed during *perestroika*.[18] Full economic jurisdiction leaves enterprises responsible for the management and direct financing of these assets, but without the right to transfer them freely. Enterprises interviewed declared that they are spending between 25 percent and 50 percent of their net profits to cover the costs of social assets, including those legally owned by the municipality.[19] In some cases, enterprises are slowly reducing payments for assets owned by municipalities, while other enterprises are planning to create closed joint-stock companies or partnerships with the municipality and the local GKI to whom these assets will be transferred, again reducing their financial responsibility over time.

The large financing burden for social assets calls into question the ability to enforce hard budget constraints once an enterprise has been privatized, since it is not only responsible for profit maximization, but also for a large part of the social infrastructure in a given community.

Changes in Economic Behavior

The implicit goal of privatization is not only a formal reallocation of property rights, but the establishment of a new property regime that provides incentives for changes in enterprises' economic behavior toward greater efficiency and responsiveness to the demands of the market.

In most cases, changes in economic behavior reported by the directors and managers interviewed were changes that had already taken place prior to privatization.[20] A few enterprises converted from military production in the late 1980s. In other cases, changes in the supply system occurred either because of the disintegration of the Former Soviet Union, because suppliers collapsed, or because of increases in imports due to trade liberalization. While trade liberalization also provided a number of companies with new export markets,[21] the Russian internal market seemingly provided more obstacles than opportunities and was regarded as unstable and unpredictable.

Although most companies were faced with considerable decreases in their production volumes over the last two years, none of them had laid off employees. Two companies stopped just short of laying off workers, instead sending up to 40 percent of their workforce on extended vacation. An additional four enterprises had "not yet" dismissed workers, but expected to be forced to do so in the near future. Ten companies had considerably reduced the number of their employees over the last year or two by not replacing pensioners who had left the enterprise. While unemployment was regarded as a real possibility by most company representatives, two of the companies in the sample had become virtually self-sufficient over the last couple of years. They claimed to be able to "feed their workers" for up to two years.[22]

Most companies only address the question of a new economic strategy or a new "business plan" immediately before the first shareholder meeting, in preparation for it. Management had little incentive to restructure prior to the first shareholder meeting, because far-reaching restructuring programs, which might jeopardize job security, are likely to endanger management's chances in elections at shareholder meetings where employees are majority shareholders. Since in the majority of enterprises in this sample the shareholder meeting had not been held at the time of the interview, it appears to be still too early to assess changes in economic behavior induced by privatization.

Changes in Financial Behavior

The managers and directors interviewed were usually most reluctant to answer questions regarding their financial situation and the possibility of obtaining credits. Most companies appear to have high debts (though the amount in real terms is not possible to assess) and have a great demand for credits. Fifteen enterprises cited "the state," the Ministry of Finance, or the Central Bank as one of their credit sources, but only in three cases were these institutions said to be the only creditors. Eleven enterprises claimed to obtain credits only from commercial banks. The fact that most privatized companies still have easy access to state credits is not surprising given the November 1992 decree by President Yeltsin prohibiting discrimination between privatized and state-owned enterprises in obtaining credits from the state.

Without exception, companies expressed great need for additional capital. Some actively lobbied the Property Fund to hold an investment tender for the shares that had not yet been privatized in order to produce a "real" investor.[23] A secondary emission of shares as an alternative financing strategy was considered by four companies, two of which regarded the organizational problems involved in a secondary emission as a major obstacle. Another four companies explicitly rejected the possibility of a secondary emission, mostly because of the lack of sufficient capital on the internal market. In many companies, management had a clear preference for setting up joint ventures with outside investors over participation of investors as shareholders in the parent company. One company had actually adopted a business plan at the shareholder meeting according to which 18 joint ventures with various, mostly foreign, partners were to be established. This indicates that the expropriation of enterprise assets by management and the transfer of them to newly created entities, a typical feature of "spontaneous privatization" prior to the implementation of the state privatization program, has not been brought to a halt by privatization. Curiously, sanctioning by shareholders has now legalized this procedure.[24]

76

Privatized companies are only starting to establish a new network with other entities. A number of companies expressed their wish to sell shares of the company to suppliers or customers and/or are planning to buy shares from them. Since enterprises are prevented under current legislation from buying shares in privatized entities as long as the state still holds 25 percent or more of their stock, the development of strong cross-shareholder relations was not possible during the early stages of privatization when most enterprises were still state-owned. Based on the comments made by interviewees and their distrust of outside investors who are not "related" or "friendly" enterprises, the development of strong post-privatization vertical integration with suppliers and customers appears to be very likely. The intention seems to be partly to protect the company against hostile outside shareholders who are not controlled through trade relations and/or cross shareholdership, and partly to preserve the security of the old supply system.

IV. Discussion and Conclusions

While in terms of sheer numbers, privatization has made considerable progress in Russia since the beginning of 1993,[25] judging by the results of this survey there is some reason to be cautious about actual changes in company behavior induced by privatization. A number of different factors need to be evaluated in assessing the survey results: the economic and political uncertainties paralyzing the country, among others. However, one of the factors that has been neglected is the absence of a sufficient legal framework for corporations. Corporatization in Russia has occurred without a corporate law in place that assigns specific functions to the different management organs of the corporation,[26] and, most of all, that limits the extent to which powers can be shifted from one organ to another. Amendments to the model charter provide a perfectly legal avenue for transferring powers from the Council of Directors, where outsiders might be represented, to the insider-controlled Management Board.[27] The lack of a legally established governance structure has given management of the former state-owned enterprises a chance to solidify their position and shield themselves against substantial influence by outside shareholders, and the majority of enterprises in the sample have in fact realized this opportunity. The power of management is further enhanced by its control over the organization of shareholder meetings, including the authorization of delegates. Thus, mass privatization in Russia has not only paid a political premium to management of state enterprises, but the weak legal framework has offered the opportunity to legalize management entrenchment.

In the absence of a governance system through "voice" with accompanying legal provisions for enforcement, an alternative corporate governance would allow exit by shareholders, who could signal their discontent with an enterprise's performance by selling its shares on the market. Such a system, however, requires the development first of a functioning capital market, and second, the responsiveness of management to developments on the market. The results of this survey suggest that a capital market, i.e. a secondary market of shares after privatization, is only slowly evolving. Most of the few shares exchanged are being traded regionally in the absence of a nationwide depository system.

While it seems likely that trading volumes will increase as shareholders who received their shares at steep discounts in the closed subscription begin to sell their shares, such an increase does not necessarily indicate a response to an enterprise's performance, since cash-strapped shareholders may be tempted to sell shares at any price. Increased trading volumes might lead to the desirable consolidation of shares, giving new shareholders a greater impact. However, consolidation of share ownership does not necessarily imply that shareholders who actively monitor the enterprise will emerge. It seems that a large proportion of those currently competing for shares on the secondary market are management personnel and entities controlled by them, or client or supplier enterprises who are free to buy shares in other entities after they have been privatized themselves. Investment funds may play the role of vigilant shareholders in the future, but it seems difficult to assess the role they currently play in the market.

Table 1   Enterprises in the Sample

ID #	Region	Industry	Charter Capital (in rubles)	Number of Employees
1	Moscow (city)	bread & products	20,200,000	1,161
2	Moscow (city)	equipment	18,489,000	479
3	Moscow (city)	construction	15,036,000	479
4	Moscow (oblast)	system construction	30,033,000	915
5	Moscow (city)	timber	26,151,000	850
6	Moscow (city)	concrete	35,884,000	568
7	Moscow (city)	concrete	40,000,000	812
8	Novgorod	furniture	35,536,000	
9	Novgorod	chemicals	539,690,000	5,000
10	Novgorod	beer, soft drinks	16,490,000	300
11	Novgorod	milk products	80,000,000	450
12	Novgorod	energy	248,000,000	3,500
13	Yaroslavl	synthetic rubber	230,570,000	2869
14	Yaroslavl	motors for aircrafts	757,369,000	27,351
15	Yaroslavl	chemicals	34,002,000	1,800
16	Yaroslavl	motors, parts	614,489,000	7,401
17	Yaroslavl	textiles	46,012,000	800
18	Yaroslavl	trade	42,753,000	
19	Ivanovo	textiles	241,887,000	2,766
20	Ivanovo	textiles	230,201,000	3,358
21	Ivanovo	textiles	177,188,000	3,993
22	Ivanovo	metals/quartz	164,262,000	5,026
23	Ivanovo	textiles	279,105,000	3,787
24	Ivanovo	textiles	175,968,000	4,600
25	Perm	engines/rockets	817,617,000	35,000
26	Perm	paper	229,816,000	5,456
27	Perm	machinery	568,824,000	22,500
28	Perm	construction	21,744,000	430
29	Perm	chemicals	210,847,000	3814
30	Sverdlovsk	electro-mechanics	16,152,000	1,091
31	Sverdlovsk	machinery	1,803,191,000	34,041
32	Sverdlovsk	electro-technicals	441,287,000	7,392
33	Sverdlovsk	aluminum products	700,000,000	10,000
34	Sverdlovsk	chemicals	215,659,000	3,839
35	Sverdlovsk	metal products	1,352,227,000	24,198
36	Sverdlovsk	construction materials	22,715,000	1,788

Table 2   Equity Distribution

ID #	Priv. Option	% Insiders	Voting Stock Held by Insiders	% Property Fund	% Outsiders	% Largest Outsider	Type/Largest Outsider
1	2	83	83	0	17	2	VIF
2	2	0		0	100	100	Holding Company
3	2	56	56	20	24		VIFs, Individual
4	2	70	70	0	30		VIFs, Individual (jur)
5	2	53	53	20	27	3	Individual
6	2	62	62	20	17		Supplier, CS
7	2	72	72	0	28	13	Foreign CS
8	2	62	62	20	18		Individual, VIFs
9	2	51	51	0	49	31	JV (US/Russia)
10	2	56	56	0	44	12	CS
11	2	56	56	20	24		Kolkhozy, Sovkhozy
12	1	31	19	56	0	0	
13	2	51	51	18	31	20	Foreign CS
14	2	48	48	37	15		Individual
15	2	80	80	11	9	9	Individual
16	2	70	70	25	5	5	Individual
17	2	80	80	20	0	0	
18	2	78	78	20	2		Individual
19	1	59	39	20	21	20	JV (AO cofounder)
20	1	80	55	20	0	0	
21	1	80	55	20	0	0	
22	1	75	50	25	0	0	
23	1	75	50	25	0	0	
24	1	75	50	25	0	0	
25	2	51	51	20	29	4	CS
26	2	63	63	20	17	10	VIF (national)
27	2	68	68	20	12	8	VIF (national)
28	2	60	60	20	20	20	VIF
29	2	54	54	20	26	0	*
30	2	80	80	20	0	0	
31	1	40	15	31	29	18	CS
32	1	74	49	26	0	0	
33	1	50	25	32	18		*
34	2	61	61	20	19	4	VIF
35	2	56	56	20	24	4	VIF
36	2	54	54	20	26	8	VIF
Mean		61.8	57	19.3	19	10.4	

VIF - Voucher Investment Fund (local unless otherwise specified)   CS - Commercial Structure
JV - Joint Venture   AO - Joint Stock Company
* Not provided.

80

Notes

[1] I would like to thank Jeffrey D. Sachs, Maxim Boycko, Andrei Shleifer, and Robert Vishny for cosponsoring the survey; and the GKI (the Russian privatization agency) and the Property Funds in the regions in which I conducted interviews, for their support.

[2] Albert O. Hirschman, "Exit, Voice, and Loyalty," (Cambridge, MA: Harvard University Press, 1970).

[3] See "Summary of Privatization Programs," page 223.

[4] The companies in Ivanovo all had charter capitals of between 165 and 280 million rubles.

[5] It should also be noted that three of the enterprises (16, 17, and 32) had previously been leased enterprises, in which insiders were already regarded as owners of part of the stock prior to privatization. The collective's ownership share depends on the amount of profits generated by the company during the lease. When these companies began privatizing, employees already owned 58 percent (#16), 63.3 percent (#17), and 24 percent (#32) respectively.

[6] "Commercial structure" is a general term in Russia referring to any private, profit-making entity.

[7] This limit was increased to 25 percent in late 1993.

[8] Compare #13 to #24 with the remaining cases in Table 2.

[9] For a discussion of different auction systems and the reasons to adopt a decentralized system for Russia, see Maxim Boycko, Andrei Shleifer, and Robert W. Vishny, "Voucher Privatization," forthcoming in *Journal of Financial Economics*.

[10] It is not quite clear whether the general director acquired these shares from employees after privatization, or whether this was a result of the distribution of the shares that were allocated among insiders as a result of the lease (see note 10).

[11] These financial institutions are often subsidiaries of investment funds, both regional and national.

[12] A rate of three to four times below the auction rate was mentioned by one investment fund in Perm.

[13] Calculated for all enterprises for which vouchers had been accepted. The rate is calculated as the sum of charter capital offered (e.g. 29 percent of the total stock) divided by the sum of vouchers accepted (GKI database, 2 July 1993).

[14] The only exception is an enterprise that scheduled its meeting for April 1994. The state will retain 49 percent of the enterprise for the next three years, and will thus have considerable influence in the enterprise's affairs.

[15] See, however, a newspaper account of the shareholder meeting of Vladimir Traktornii Zavod, which was so large it took place in a sports stadium. Mikhail Berger, "First-Ever 'Auction Match' at the Vladimir Stadium 'Torpedo': Shareholders of Tractor Factory Decided Their Fate," *Izvestiya*, June 26, 1993: 1.

[16] According to a representative from a local investment fund in Ekaterinburg, the fee for each single authorization was 25,000 rubles, at a time when the average wage was 35,000 rubles per month. In Soviet and post-Soviet Russia, notary certification has been required for far more transactions than it is in general in the West. With respect to issuing proxies, this formal requirement apparently acts as an impediment to free transactions rather than as a guarantor against fraud.

[17] See company #9 in Table 2, where a single outsider acquired 31 percent of stock at the voucher auction where 49 percent of the total stock had been offered at once.

81

[18] This property concept is almost identical to the legal definition of ownership, giving the enterprise the right "to possess, use, and dispose of" the asset, though within certain constraints established by law.

[19] These are usually large enterprises where the city had virtually grown around the enterprise. These enterprises had always provided the most important local infrastructure, and therefore assumed a great financial burden for the social sphere.

[20] This is obviously the subjective view of those interviewed and would have to be verified by a closer analysis of company behavior both before and after privatization.

[21] Nine out of 36 companies reported that they were exporting to new markets they had previously not supplied in Western Europe, North America, or Asia.

[22] Apart from the social assets mentioned above, a number of companies own farms (*kolkhozy*) that provide employees with meat, fruits and vegetables at lower prices.

[23] Those participating in voucher auctions were mostly regarded as speculators, not "real" investors, which explains the contradiction of managers' attempting to buy out the company on the one hand, and lobbying for an investment tender on the other hand.

[24] An investment fund representative who attended the shareholder meeting of the company that is planning to set up 18 joint ventures reported that the business plan was ratified in five minutes. A discussion of one and a half hours followed about whether dividends will be paid once or twice a year.

[25] At the end of August 1993, roughly 3000 enterprises had completed voucher auctions according to GKI data.

[26] Even in countries where corporate law does provide a clear legal framework, the actual power structure within a given company may not correspond to what is provided by law. Nevertheless, at least with regard to changes in management, such a legal framework does exert some control.

[27] Some companies referred explicitly to the vague formulations of Decree 601 in their proposals for amendments.

References

R. Joseph Blasi and James Gasaway, "Corporate Governance and Employee Ownership: Comparing The United States and Russia," unpublished paper prepared for a presentation at the Fifth Annual Conference of the Society for the Advancement of Socio-Economics, New School for Social Research, New York, New York, 28 March 1993.

Maxim Boycko, Andrei Shleifer, and Robert W. Vishny, "Voucher Privatization," forthcoming in *Journal of Financial Economics*.

Maxim Boycko, Andrei Shleifer, and Robert W. Vishny, "Privatizing Russia," forthcoming in *Brookings Papers on Economic Activity*.

Jenny Corbett and Colin Mayer, "Financial Reform in Eastern Europe: Progress with the Wrong Model," *Oxford Review of Economic Policy* 7, no. 4 (1991).

John S. Earle, Roman Frydman, and Andrzej Rapaczynski, et.al., *The Privatization Process in Russia, Ukraine, and the Baltic States* (London: Central European University Press, 1993).

Roman Frydman and Andrzej Rapaczynski, "Markets and Institutions in Large-Scale Privatization: An Approach to Economic and Social Transformation in Eastern Europe," in Vittorio Corbo et al., *Reforming Central and Eastern European Economies: Initial Results and Challenges* (Washington, D.C.: The World Bank, 1991): 253-274.

Roman Frydman and Andrzej Rapaczynski, "Privatization and Corporate Governance in Eastern Europe: Can a Market Economy Be Designed?" in G. Winkler, ed., *Central and Eastern Europe: Roads to Growth* (Washington, D.C.: IMF, 1991).

Kathryn Hendley, "Legal Development and Privatization in Russia: A Case Study," *Soviet Economy* 8, no. 2 (1992): 130-157.

Manuel Hinds, "A Note on the Privatization of Socialized Enterprises in Poland," in Vittorio Corbo et al., *Reforming Central and Eastern European Economies: Initial Results and Challenges* (Washington, D.C.: The World Bank, 1991): 275-287.

Albert O. Hirschman, "Exit, Voice, and Loyalty " (Cambridge, MA: Harvard University Press, 1970).

David Lipton and Jeffrey Sachs, "Privatization in Eastern Europe: The Case of Poland," in Vittorio Corbo et al., *Reforming Central and Eastern European Economies: Initial Results and Challenges* (Washington, D.C.: The World Bank, 1991): 231-251.

Peter B. Maggs, "Taking the 'Poison Pill': A Commentary on a Case Study," *Soviet Economy* 8, no. 2 (1992): 158-163.

Kevin R. McDonald, "Why Privatization is Not Enough," Harvard Business Review (May–June 1993): 49.

Edmund S. Phelps, Roman Frydman, Andrzej Rapaczynski, and Andrei Shleifer, "Needed Mechanisms for Corporate Governance and Finance in Eastern Europe," *Economics of Transition* (1993).

Brian Pinto, Marek Belka, and Stefan Krajewski, "Transforming State Enterprises in Poland: Evidence on Adjustment by Manufacturing Firms," *Brookings Papers on Economic Activity* 1(1993): 213-270.

6

Political Origins of Corporatist Order:
The Politics of Enterprise Reform

Mari Kuraishi Horne

Introduction

The politics of enterprise reform in Russia, more than any other political process taking place there today, will determine the nature and limits of state intervention in the economy for the foreseeable future. Enterprise reform may lack the drama of the conflicts between the president and the legislature, or even of tensions between the central government and regional authorities. No one has had to call up the tanks to force an enterprise to submit a privatization proposal, though such eventualities have been joked about in Russia. Nevertheless, the political path of enterprise reform in Russia will determine whether Russian capitalism as it emerges will be "atomistic, competitive, organized, or statist."[1]

Enterprise reform will define the nature of the future Russian state. In no other process are the limits and distribution of state power and authority so much at stake, as the process of privatization simultaneously releases spheres of activity formerly held by state organs to the private sector, and opens avenues of political access and leverage to agents hitherto excluded from the policymaking process. The state, by legitimizing certain groups' control

Mari Kuraishi Horne is an operations analyst in the Europe and Central Asia Division for the World Bank. The views expressed in this paper are those of the author, and not of the World Bank. The author is grateful to Lev Freinkman, Geoffrey Lamb, Irina Starodubrovskaya, and Paulo Vieira da Cunha for very helpful comments at various stages of the paper.

over productive assets, is effectively empowering these actors to an unprecedented extent. In other words, in Russia today, a key group of people—enterprise insiders—is acquiring real political influence over the state, without significant opposition. These people are moving rapidly to a position of unequaled political power almost before they realize their collective interests as an economic or social class.

In the short to medium term, the political consequences of enterprise reform pose the greatest possible challenge to bureaucratic rationalization and state autonomy.[2] This is the heart of the institutional and political dilemma faced by the state in post-communist transition. State autonomy and capacity are essential to achieve not only the transition to, but the preservation of modern liberal capitalism.[3] At the same time, democratic development presupposes the growth of an independent civil society—of which the most fundamental basis is private property. Moreover, if the transition to a market system is to be completed, the sphere of state action will necessarily diminish. This process must be managed in a context of diminishing consensus at the center, and the trend of decentralization. While efforts to shore up state capacity and authority will be necessary, ultimately the state must aim at creating a private enterprise sector that will perceive its interests not in continued applications for state support, but in countervailing pressures against state intervention in its sphere of activity.

Russia is trying to develop what I will call "corporatist" arrangements.[4] Corporatism seeks to economize on the use of state authority through the institutionalization of regular negotiation between state and non-state actors. Such arrangements can place the conflicts associated with economic policymaking within known bounds. Corporatism refers to a special relationship between state and civil society, which is often associated with authoritarian regimes or with advanced welfare state economies. In authoritarian states, the gains to intermediary associations at the apex of civil society tend to be economic, while the price they pay is largely political (they restrain themselves from overthrowing the order). In advanced welfare states, on the other hand, the gains to intermediary associations of both employers and workers are political (formal inclusion in the policymaking process), while the price paid is economic (worker restraint from wage strikes and employer retention of agreed-upon levels of employment). In both of these instances, the state is relatively strong, and corporatism is often understood to be an orchestration of civil society by the state. Indeed, the absence of corporatist arrangements is sometimes understood to be an indication of the weakness of the state.

The impulse to corporatism, however, does not necessarily arise from the strength of the state. In fact, *weakness* may cause both the state and the enterprise sector to seek accommodation from each other—the state attempts to borrow the power and authority of market actors, in return for the enterprise sector's use of public resources. This tendency is encouraged when, as in the Russian context, the transition to a market begins from a background of extensive state involvement in the economy, as well as from an oligarchic political culture. Representatives of both the state and civil society in Russia (to the extent that industrial interests tend to form the core of civil society) would probably be satisfied if their system ended by resembling this description of Japan:

> Business enjoys privilege, systematic inclusion in the policy process, access to public goods, and rights of self-regulation. It reciprocates by agreeing to state jurisdiction in the definition of market structures and by participating in the distribution of benefits.[5]

Enterprises and their associations have exploited the lack of agreement among central state leaders on the pace, and at times even the direction, of reform in Russia to extract privileges and subsidies, and to exercise power over ministerial appointments; and regional authorities have kept the center incessantly occupied in bargaining over fiscal and political aspects of decentralization. In the context of high macroeconomic instability and declining output, both the state and newly formed "private" interests have been inclined to arrive at corporatist-type compromises (these arrangements tend to be ad hoc at first, and thus might be described as quasi-corporatist). Through such agreements, the state seeks to augment its authority by cooperating with emerging "private" interests,[6] and these interests try to leverage the political, as much as the economic, potential of their newly acquired assets.

This has had two consequences for enterprise reform. First, the state, in order to induce these newly empowered agents to cooperate, has had to resort to a variety of stratagems, including but not limited to subsidies, privileges, and delegation of power. Second, representatives of enterprises (including privatized or privatizing enterprises) who lobby for continued state intervention have tended to strengthen the hand of those in government who are reluctant to see the state's (and thus their own) power diminished.

A corporatist state is by no means a certain outcome for Russia. Moreover there are many forms of corporatism, and the term itself is perhaps too loosely defined to have much explanatory power. Nonetheless it might be argued that when corporatist arrangements are accompanied by a weak state—as the Russian state is likely to be for some time to come—they will prove particularly inimical to robust economic development. Given the Russian economy's current condition such dampening effects could prove to be far more damaging than in other countries.

The State Context for the Development of Corporatist Institutions

The Central Government

The political costs of pursuing a reform program in a country with an uncertain constitutional base have been high. Throughout 1992, conflict over the division of powers between the legislature and the executive exacerbated substantive disagreements on reform. While these tensions lessened with the president's victory in the referendum of April 1993, they grew again until by the fall of 1993, Yeltsin shut down the Parliament and used force to restrain his opponents. In part in response to these violent events, the December elections recreated a divided government by putting politicians from a wide array of views in the Duma. Thus, despite his decisive action, in the spring of 1994 Yeltsin once again faces significant opposition both within and outside the legislature. He has responded by making personnel changes in the executive branch, so that once again consensus cannot be reached even within a single part of the government.

In general, two opposing views dominate debate on the future course of enterprise reform. One approach to the issue emphasizes the primacy of privatization, stressing the need to avoid supporting former state structures, and above all to avoid trying to "pick the winners" in the Russian economy. The argument is that the state cannot articulate and implement coherent policies, especially with respect to enterprises; the state cannot exercise diligent supervision over public resources; and state decisions are heavily influenced by interest groups and possibly by corruption. Many believe that the industrial and technological might of Soviet industry was vastly exaggerated—and thus the emphasis should be on restructuring to introduce new managerial and organizational skills, as much as new technologies. In allowing the market to guide new developments, this strategy leans toward the development of smaller and leaner firms emerging from the collapsing structure of excessive integration and the belief in unlimited economies of scale. The underdeveloped domestic consumer and services market would offer potential for immediate expansion, with full price and trade liberalization and strong growth in exports from resource-intensive industries. Privatization, this school argues, is critical to clarify conflicting and uncertain incentives resulting from fuzzy ownership rights (which characterize the bulk of non-corporatized SOEs).

The other perspective would encourage large financial-industrial groups to form, most likely under state auspices in major sectors or sub-sectors of industry. These, it is hoped, would become the engines of Russia's future economic growth, increasing the country's competitiveness in the international market in particular. Among the rationales cited for such groups are that they will allow for the concentration of resources, with a resulting increase in investment potential, both for external investors and the Russian population. Ultimately the entire concept is driven by the perception that international competitiveness cannot be achieved without such structures. Most proponents of this view would not believe it to be opposed to the privatization process; rather they would suggest that the processes are complementary.

These antagonistic views would hinder consensus within the government on reform policy even if the conflict took place only on an ideological plane. The problem becomes more difficult, however, when some of the more interventionist views are reinforced by enterprise organizations that could benefit quite directly from such approaches. Moreover, this basic conflict is overlaid by the dynamics of the relationship between the center and the regions.

Regional Governments

In a context where sources of political power and influence are inchoate and uncertain, regions offer players at the center one possible organizing principle. At the same time, regional authorities are even more closely tied to the fate of enterprises located in their territory and seek to lobby the central authorities on their behalf. In addition, because local authorities have primary responsibility for social expenditures, the divestment of social assets from enterprises involves local authorities directly in the negotiations between the state and the enterprise sector. Political decentralization also affects the power and coherence of the state in general, and may lead to situations where policies decided at the center are not always implemented by the local authorities delegated to do so. Another impact the center-regional dimension can have on enterprise reform stems from the fact that local conditions can vary widely, which means that enterprises face very different external environments. These differences can be particularly telling for certain issues in enterprise reform.

Last, but possibly most important, an interesting dynamic is beginning to develop between the corporatist tendencies of the enterprise sector and the incipient corporatism of local authorities. The enterprise sector is not alone in exhibiting corporatist tendencies—local authorities are developing their own regional associations, and pursuing very similar strategies vis-a-vis the central government. Currently there are eight regional associations that have been officially recognized by the central government, and though most began their existence as bottom-up, grassroots organizations they are beginning to face pressures and incentives to play politicized roles that inevitably put these associations in a position to exert top-down influence. One of the first signs of the interaction between the corporatism of the enterprise sector and that of regional authorities can be seen in some of the proposals concerning financial-industrial groups; while some advocates of financial-industrial groups attempt to exploit economic potential wherever it may be found, others attempt to use these groups as a means for regional equalization and cross-subsidization.

The Privatization Program and Other Government-Initiated Corporatist Arrangements

The designers of the privatization program (as represented by Maxim Boycko, Andrei Schleifer, and Robert W. Vishny) have asserted that it was created in an institutional and political context in which the primary cause of inefficiency was the state—and its ownership and control of enterprises.[7] Between 1987 and the beginning of the privatization program in 1992, according to this argument, enterprise managers steadily gained so much control over enterprises that the state increasingly had to pay them subsidies or "bribes" to pursue the social goals of maintaining employment and output. In other words, the government did not allow enterprises to pursue economic efficiency. The Russian privatization program, therefore, was designed to give managers the greatest possible incentive to break free from the state and its insistence on social/political, noneconomic goals.

In early 1992 Russian reformers chose to emphasize rapid transformation of the economy, despite the accompanying pain of transition and the potential political instability. They adopted an approach emphasizing speed and irreversibility over a gradual, potentially less destabilizing approach, and this decision led to a privatization program that was unprecedented in scope and scale.

The ambitiousness of the program dictated a highly decentralized and bottom-up approach, which relied very much on inducing enterprises themselves to undertake privatization. As a result, Russian privatization is remarkable in the extent to which it does *not* initially alter the existing structure of control over the enterprise. Since passage of the Soviet State Enterprise Law in 1987, and the weakening grip of most branch ministries, the bulk of control rights over enterprises has rested with insiders—managers and workers.[8] The privatization program of the Russian government, initiated in 1992, did little to change the constellation of forces controlling the enterprise; both the small-scale privatization program and the mass privatization program were notable for the generous benefits offered to enterprise insiders.[9] These incentives have enabled privatization to proceed at a pace all the more remarkable given the limited institutional resources at the reformers' disposal. Not only have most of the ambitious targets initially set for privatization been met, but many enterprises initially exempted from mandatory privatization have been seeking ways to avoid these strictures.

From the conventional view of privatization, of course, this approach has one fundamental drawback—by allowing insiders to gain control of enterprises, it has failed to control the agency problems in the enterprise (see Chapter 3 of this volume, "Agency Problems in the

Privatization of Large Enterprises in Russia" by Michael McFaul). The Russian privatization program has failed to resolve thorny issues related to the corporate governance of privatized enterprises.

This model does describe well, however, the political incentives opening up to the enterprise insider. It clearly points to the process by which enterprise managers move from a position under the command economy of almost complete political subservience despite relative economic autonomy to one in the emerging market economy in which they can begin to exploit that economic power to command political concessions from the state. That is, the process by which it becomes increasingly more expensive for the state to subsidize enterprises is the same process by which enterprise insiders begin to exercise greater political control over the state.

The privatization program was designed to sharpen that process, to make it ultimately too expensive for the state to continue subsidizing enterprises to pursue these objectives—when manager ownership is high enough, the argument runs, "the government gives up trying to subsidize the firm to maintain high output and employment, the budget constraint hardens, and restructuring occurs."[10]

A number of questionable assumptions underlie this model of privatization. These include an assumption of high state autonomy (problematic in the best of times, but particularly so in the Russian context), a simplistic understanding of labor-management relations, and a disregard for the incrementalism of the process. Also, the government in this model is understood to be an "existing bureaucracy," a government ideologically committed to pursuing social objectives. While it is possible to argue that Russian government policy is indeed hampered by an existing bureaucracy intent on maximizing employment and output, this existing bureaucracy is plausibly as insulated as managers from the political problems caused by unemployment and low output.[11]

This paper diverges from the Boycko/Schleifer/Vishny model described above, however, primarily because of a different assumption about how managers will use their increased political leverage. Given the background and perception of most enterprise managers in Russia today, they are unlikely to keep raising the cost of influencing their behavior to levels prohibitive for the state. That is to say, most Russian managers, perceiving themselves to be ill-equipped to compete in a market context, will have incentives to keep the stakes of the game from escalating; they will try to find an equilibrium state where it is just cheap enough for the state to continue bribing the enterprise, which translates into the highest rents the managers can hope to extract from the state. After all, given the training and experience of most Russian managers, their comparative advantage lies in using their assets to extract political, not economic, advantages.

No durable corporatist arrangements have yet developed in Russia. Since late 1991, however, the state has repeatedly offered policy influence to organizations representing "private" interests. If such organizations can determine public policy in areas that are of central concern to them, the state can thereby hold them responsible for the effective implementation of these policies.

In the course of 1992 and 1993 the state initiated at least four discrete attempts to form corporatist frameworks for policy implementation. These included:

- The creation of a tripartite commission in early 1992 between the Federation of Independent Trade Unions of Russia (FNPR)[12] the government, and associations of enterprises, the most influential of which was the Union of Industrialists and Entrepre-

90

neurs (RSPP). The ostensible function of the commission was to mediate labor disputes. In Russia generally, however, enterprise managers and their employees do not see themselves as having antithetical interests; this function, therefore, was seldom needed.

- The government began more significant bargaining with the enterprise sector in the spring and summer of 1992 when a campaign against the government's policies in the combined names of industry and labor culminated in a stream of credits to industry, and a number of appointments of industrialists to the government.[13] The futility of this approach (from the government's point of view) became evident in November and December 1992, when an intensively negotiated agreement between the government and Civic Union[14] to keep Yegor Gaidar in place as acting Prime Minister could not be translated into a majority in the Parliament. No institution in Russia is strong enough at this point to hold legislators to certain positions in such a volatile environment.

- Another attempt to institutionalize interaction between the state and the private sector was a proposal drawn up by a "forum of social and political forces." This Roundtable was convened in January 1993 by the Parliament and the government from representatives of business circles, work collectives and trade unions, political parties and movements, science, and the civil service. The proposal suggested preparing a series of National Economic Agreements, which would form the basis for specific economic policies. As the main proponent of this arrangement—that is, the Parliament—was discredited, this initiative has faltered; it remains to be seen whether the new Duma will recreate it.

More recently, the executive has taken the lead, by proposing a so-called civic accord in January 1994. Although accounts of its details have varied, at different points it was said to have included a reintroduction of price controls, indexation of wages, and employment guarantees. Suggested signatories included enterprise associations, political parties, government representatives, and social organizations.

The Organization of the Enterprise Sector: Industry-Initiated Corporatist Arrangements

The enterprise sector in Russia today is saturated with associations, a term used loosely here to cover an immense variety of enterprise organizations.[15] Many enterprise organizations grew out of former state bodies, the successors not only of the former Russian republic's bureaucracy, but of the Soviet Union as well. However, the number and variety of enterprise organizations also point to the difficulty in arriving at a clear definition of enterprise interests. In addition to fundamental changes in their ownership and administration, enterprises have been subject to an accelerating series of changes in their external environment. It is therefore hardly surprising that enterprise associations vary widely, and that few among them can claim to represent enterprise interests definitively.

Enterprise associations in the Soviet Union were originally defined as production associations, "integral industrial (or scientific-industrial) complexes consisting of enterprises and subunits which are engaged in certain types of production activity," as stated in the USSR Law on Producing Associations of 1965. These associations often performed supervisory and administrative functions vis-a-vis their subunits, but also had the status of independent legal entities, and economic relationships with other enterprises were regulated by the civil code and economic legislation. By the late 1980s, the first voluntary associations of enterprises emerged in the then-Soviet Union, and in 1991 the Russian Law on Enterprises and Entrepreneurial Activity gave enterprises the right to create unions and associations of all types, on a voluntary and contractual basis, provided that all enterprises retained their status of independent legal entities and that associations did not have any supervisory powers over enterprises.

The disintegration of Soviet authority, and the interenterprise links supported by that authority, not only induced enterprises to seek membership in overarching organizations but provided employment for former bureaucrats. Reform-oriented associations centered around enterprises in the military-industrial complex, particularly those with significant scientific and technological capacity, whose managers believed that the preferential treatment they had received during the Soviet era would make them competitive in a market environment. Other enterprise associations, particularly in construction, transport, or traditional weaponry, were less reformist (some were instrumental in persuading the Soviet leadership to move away from the "500-Day" reform program in the fall of 1990). These associations were, however, still closely associated with one another, and operated in a context where ministries had significant vestigial control over enterprises.

The final disintegration of the Soviet Union threw many of these associations into disarray, as they were organized on a Union-wide basis. Ministries, of course, were similarly affected: the Soviet ministries were all abolished, and some reorganization also took place in the Russian bureaucracy. While the older associations regrouped, many of the erstwhile ministries and *glavks*[16] also sought to perpetuate their existence by transforming themselves into organizations in various forms—associations, concerns, trusts, and the like. In addition, with the shock of price liberalization in January 1992 and a sharp decline in state orders for the military-industrial complex, enterprises themselves were no longer certain about their own future prospects, nor which government institutions would, if they survived, continue to serve their interests.

Since 1992, some but not all associations have succeeded in finding a political base among enterprises, and parlaying that strength into lobbying the state for credits, privileges, and access. Politically inclined associations, such as the RSPP, wielded quite a bit of influence in the policy and personnel arena throughout 1992. Other associations and enterprises exerted influence on the Industrial Faction of the Parliament—in demanding investment credits for various sectors of the economy, as well as the indexation of working capital.

Why do enterprises join associations? Surveys and interviews with enterprises suggest that the majority of enterprises are members of some sort of association, and some are involved in more than one association. There are discrepancies, however, in the level of enterprise involvement; it appears that many enterprises initially joined associations without a clear idea of what benefits the associations might be able to deliver. Asked in a survey what they perceived as the main role associations would play in the transition, managers gave responses split evenly over three main functions: the provision of consultancy services, interest representation, and the re-creation of a command economy. The same survey indicated that one out of two respondents perceived associations to be the most effective means of exerting pressure on the state. (See Chapter 4 of this volume, "Attitudes of Enterprise Managers Toward Market Transition" by Irina Starodubrovskaya.)

There are indications that some enterprises may have been coerced into joining associations, or automatically retained their status as part of an association when they were cut loose from state controls, as in the oil production sector. While such tendencies do not appear to be prevalent at this time, there are indications that as some associations become active enough to extract exclusive privileges from the state (both federal and local), they will be able to discriminate effectively against enterprises that do not join.

It is not surprising that associations are continuing to define their objectives and to compete amongst themselves for member enterprises. Some winnowing of the field is inevitable. One activity that makes an association more likely to survive is if it provides needed services for its member enterprises in areas such as marketing or management. Such associations are typically fairly small, and do not hold or aspire to ownership stakes in their member enterprises. Over time, however, they may find it difficult to compete with consultant firms operating on a commercial basis.

Another practice that can make associations more viable is if they become vehicles for classic trust-like behavior by implementing agreements to fix prices or allocate markets. These associations may or may not own their member enterprises, although ownership would certainly strengthen enforcement. These associations might prove viable not only because they allow member enterprises to earn supernormal profits, but because they can engage in discriminatory behavior against defectors or newcomers to their markets. Such associations should be regulated by antimonopoly laws with direct provisions against price-fixing behavior.

The third characteristic of associations that could help them survive longer is some sort of ownership relationship between the member enterprises and the overarching organization. Associations that have organized on the basis of property ownership often are, or hope to become, something more than associations; these include groups of enterprises that aim to convert themselves into holding companies, joint-stock companies, or "diversified industrial groups." To the extent that these groups emerge by themselves in the absence of government support, it might be argued that an economy as big and complex as Russia's could come to sustain large and diversified industrial enterprises that are market and technological leaders in their sector, including in the international market.

In the context of an as-yet ambiguous institutional framework for private action, however, such groupings can easily aggregate the interests of enterprises who by themselves might not have sufficient political clout to be effective in lobbying the government for support. Political power in the enterprise sector depends on the size of the group or conglomerate that is lobbying, and the perceived social disruptions it can claim will result from restructuring. Therefore the government must be aware that such groups may tend to move the policy debate ever closer to a form of corporatist bargaining than otherwise.

This will become more apparent as the policy debate begins to broach issues of industrial policy and restructuring. Policies to provide support for intersectoral financial-industrial groups are being discussed in government circles; simultaneously some associations and holding companies appear to be receiving de facto responsibility for restructuring either by receiving permission to own controlling shares of enterprises in a particular sector, or by holding the state's shares of enterprises "in trust." These developments are particularly evident in the raw materials/energy areas.

Many associations, including some that are pursuing new activities, are still clearly extensions of ministerial or *glavk* structures. When the enterprise KAMAZ suffered serious damage in its production facilities as the result of a fire, the Ministry of the Economy not only assigned it funds from the government, but also instructed the producer association to which KAMAZ belonged to come up with contributions to assist the enterprise in rebuilding its facilities. Some producer associations, of course, such as those in the oil sector, are even more firmly rooted in the ministerial structure as they were established as associations as far back as 1965. This has left these associations with far greater levels of control over their member enterprises than associations that were established more recently.

Finally, many associations may find that the path to their survival lies in politics. Such industrial organizations may become the basis of future political parties—the RSPP and its involvement in Civic Union is a case in point. It is worth noting, however, that the political activities of enterprise associations abated toward the end of 1992 and the beginning of 1993. This may be attributable in part to their success in pursuing their agenda; many of their spokesmen became part of the government, and enterprises were receiving state support without having to put huge effort into lobbying.

In general, it seems that the future development of industrial associations will be along a path of intensive bargaining between the state and the "private" sector for political power and financial resources. As the number of associations decreases and those that remain become better organized, they will be better positioned to influence the state. In this context, the development of enterprise associations can be seen as a complementary response to the weakness of the state, and a necessary component of the tendency toward corporatism in the Russian economy. Not only are associations attempting to fill the vacuum left by the dramatic retreat of the state, but they also provide convenient counterparts for the state. In spite of its market rhetoric, a state with limited capacity has nonetheless found interacting with an at least minimally organized enterprise sector to be in its interest.[17] Corporatist arrangements may seem to be a useful short- to medium-term solution, but in the long run it is also possible that they may prove a deadly mix for a country emerging from a totalitarian regime with very weak traditions of autonomous civil society.

Policies For a More Effective State-Industry Relationship

Privatization has succeeded so far because enterprises have perceived it to be in their interest, and both erstwhile and existing sectoral ministries have thus been effectively stymied in their opposition. This may be due in part to the fact that in some ways privatization has so far not required enterprises or sectoral (ex-)ministries to change their behavior vis-a-vis each other; privatized or privatizing enterprises have continued to lobby for and receive support from the state. In other words, although privatization—the creation and enlargement of a sphere for private action—has proceeded in Russia, its necessary counterpart—the reduction and limitation of the sphere of state action—has not been as effectively implemented.

In the absence of an explicit plan for such a process, there are several causes for worry. First, there are indications that the current framework of support and protection (and the resulting lack of hard budget incentives) for state-owned enterprises may be extended to privatized enterprises as well.[18] Even under the best-case scenario when the government is prepared to exert financial discipline on privatized enterprises, enterprise dependence on the state may be perpetuated through discretionary use of the government's regulatory powers— e.g., its powers to dispense licenses, provide protection from international competition, etc. And given more than seventy years of dependence on the state, it is not unreasonable to assume that the demand and expectation for state intervention will be the rule, rather than the exception. While this system may be appropriate in the medium-term for SOEs, pending some rationalization and reduction of state support, applied to newly private enterprises it will not encourage the development of a private sector that regards itself as truly private and stands against excessive privileges, resources, and protection for the state sector.

Second, the tendency to allow the creation of holding companies (which closely mirror former administrative arrangements), or to allow associations to exercise the state's control function in trust, is developing in the absence of an explicit legal regime for corporate governance of SOEs. This further blurs the meaning of "private" and "public" interest. *Both of these developments foster ambiguities in the privatization process, which will counter even the best legal efforts at establishing clarity over the issues of ownership.*

These developments flow from the fear of some in government that if Russia's industrial structure comes apart, industry will not be competitive on the international market, and from a parallel desire to encourage the development of financial-industrial groups. They are also the result of the government's diminishing store of enticements to be offered to the enterprise sector. In particular, if the stabilization process proceeds, the government will have less and less to give away in terms of subsidies and privileges, and will have to rely increasingly on delegation of power. A delegation of power (such as giving shares in trust or allowing associations and holding companies to exercise the state's control function), however, establishes ever more direct access to state resources by blurring the boundaries of what constitutes state vs. private resources. A delegation of power will also tend to increase the political leverage of such holding companies and associations. If they are economically successful perhaps they will no longer credibly pressure the government for credits, but they will be in a good position to argue for privileges and cartel arrangements to protect their international position.

The third troubling consequence of the lag in limiting the sphere of state action is that the prevailing balance of power between the state and enterprises will work to preserve the current distortions of the economy. The distorted Russian price and trade regime creates artificial advantages for enterprises that might otherwise not be competitive. In addition, by recognizing particular industrial leaders or organizations as representing the interests of enterprises at large, the government may paradoxically lose the support (albeit so far rather tenuous) that it has from individual enterprise managers. The rise of financial-industrial groups will inevitably cause some managers to lose some of the control they have over their own enterprises. While the reformist policies of the government are today only weakly supported by enterprise managers at large, corporatist groupings might influence policies to be less reformist in return for more accountable support.

Finally, the non-transparent link between enterprises and the state can pose systemic dangers for the Russian economy. As Anders Aslund has noted:

> The state of reform in Russia can be summarized as a race between privatiza-
> tion and market development, on the one hand, and the rise of criminality and
> the transformation of the old elite into a new privilege group, on the other, while
> the inflation rate is a measurement of how the struggle proceeds. The higher it is,
> the better the old rent-seeking elite is doing.[19]

The very attributes of the Russian privatization program that made it so successful also give it the potential to bring the economy to a systemic crisis. By essentially giving away the state assets to those who happen to be in control of them, i.e., enterprise insiders, the state has achieved one of the most important objectives of privatization—the creation of a class of people who are intensely interested in the value of the assets they now own. Given more than seventy years of asset allocation by plan rather than by market, however, many of these assets will be worthless without a steady flow of state support, and this new class of "proprietors" is a powerful lobby for continued state intervention in the economy. In the short run, this lobby poses one of the greatest threats to the economy, as unchecked subsidies and direct credits edge the economy toward hyperinflation.[20] In the longer run, with a modicum of state authority, some of these demands may be resisted, but not all, and the Russian economy may end up in an unsatisfactory cycle of high inflation and periodic impositions of price controls, with all the attendant inefficiencies.

From the government's point of view, attempts at corporatist accommodation so far have been profoundly unsatisfactory. The inadequacy of the attempted corporatist arrangements lies in their impermanence, for a state with limited capacity is interested in minimizing the effort needed to arrive at and sustain compromises over policy. This impermanence is attributable to the institutional weakness of the enterprise sector. Viable corporatist arrangements require that the participants be able to deliver on the promises they make; so far, as discussed above, the Russian enterprise sector has been too weakly organized to deliver on its promises, and the state has not been strong enough to compel it to deliver. Moreover, successful—that is, relatively durable—corporatist arrangements would have carried their own risks in the Russian context; given such a weak state, the threat of state capture by non-state interests would have been high, and an inefficient, corrupt, and closed circle of political and economic interests the result.

At the same time, progress in reforms has not been achievable by "expanding the social basis of reform," or any maximization of social support for particular policies. Although the government has at times tried to bypass intermediary organizations, the gains have either been impossible to translate into support for specific policies, as for example in the referendum of April 1993, or the attempt has backfired, as in the December 1993 elections. This is not to say, however, that Russian culture or society is inimical to democracy, but that such a complex agenda of reforms cannot be implemented by recourse to populist and direct democracy.

The answer to this dilemma lies in part in recognizing that the political behavior of the enterprise sector in 1992 marked the outer limits of economic adjustment by the enterprises—that is, enterprises turned to politics when they encountered problems that they could not resolve economically. The only effective prophylactic against the development of an unhealthy set of relations between the state and the enterprise sector is the creation of an environment in which a critical mass of enterprises will be able to succeed without recourse to the state. The extent to which the enterprise sector influenced the course of macroeconomic policy in 1992 points to the persistent link between enterprise adjustment and macroeconomic stabilization. It also points to the range of political resources of the enterprise sector, which can be focused on different levels and branches of government. It is essential for Russian policymakers to examine the current balance of interests, both outside and within government, to develop a framework for industrial policy that includes the political as well as the economic objectives of the state.

In order to accomplish its economic objectives, the state must pursue policies which, if they do not prevent, at least discourage the enterprise sector from organizing to extract subsidies, privileges, and other powers from the state. *This will become ever more important as the balance of power between the state and the enterprise sector continues to shift against the state in the medium term.* The move toward a market system will, by transferring assets from the state sector, continue to empower new actors politically as well as economically.

The Russian government must also set clearer parameters for corporate governance. The governance of state enterprises will necessarily clarify the frame of reference for privatized enterprises, if only by default. As the discussion above may have indicated, it may be close to impossible under current circumstances to get consensus on an adequately reform-oriented scheme for corporate governance.

Notes

[1] Peter Katzenstein, *Between Power and Plenty* (Madison: University of Wisconsin Press, 1978), 17.

[2] Cf. Max Weber, *Economy and Society*, Guenther Roth and Claus Witich, eds. (Berkeley: University of California Press, 1978), v. I-II.

[3] Note not only Weber, but Adam Smith on state autonomy and capitalism, in particular *The Wealth of Nations*.

[4] The term as used here should be distinguished from the Western European sense of the word in which the emphasis is placed on the mediating role of the state between employers and labor.

[5] Richard Samuels, *The Business of the Japanese State* (Ithaca: Cornell University Press, 1987). The description is that of the "politics of reciprocal consent" of the Japanese economy put forward by Samuels as a challenge to the notion of an omniscient and omnipotent Japanese state.

[6] These new economic actors can be considered "private" only tentatively, given the tenuous, incomplete legal regime for property rights; furthermore, even if property rights were clear, the assumption by privatized enterprises that they are entitled to state support blurs dangerously the distinction between public and private property.

[7] Maxim Boycko, Andrei Schleifer, and Robert W. Vishny, "Property Rights, Soft Budget Constraints, and Privatization" (mimeo.), March 1993.

[8] There are distinctions to be drawn between types of insider control—worker-controlled vs. manager-controlled enterprises. While it is generally acknowledged that for a number of largely historic reasons in Russia, managers effectively control their workforce, it must be understood that enterprise managers are not wholly free in their behavior toward the workers. For example, surveys indicate that enterprise managers overwhelmingly prefer privatization Option 2, which gives management and workers control of the enterprise. In using this option, however, management appears to incur either explicit or implicit obligations toward workers, and is subsequently inhibited from laying them off, or cutting wages.

[9] See World Bank, *Crossing the Threshold of Structural Change*, Russia Country Economic Memorandum 1992, chapter 5.

[10] Boycko, Schleifer, and Vishny, 3.

[11] Boycko, Schleifer, and Vishny, 7.

[12] Formerly an official trade union. It has retained most of its assets (such as sanatoria, rest homes, and control over the Social Insurance Fund), and consequently still has the largest number of members and can make claims to being the most influential trade union. Following its abortive attempts to call up a strike in support of the Parliament in October 1993, however, its authority significantly eroded.

[13] First Deputy Prime Minister Viktor Shumeiko (formerly director of a defense industry enterprise in Krasnodar), Deputy Prime Minister Georgii Khizha (formerly chairman of a St. Petersburg enterprise association), and Deputy Prime Minister Viktor Chernomyrdin (formerly USSR Minister of the petroleum and fuels industry) were appointed to the Cabinet in May 1993. Chernomyrdin replaced Gaidar as Prime Minister in December of 1992, and Oleg Lobov (formerly second CPSU obkom secretary in Sverdlovsk, under Yeltsin) was appointed First Deputy Prime Minister as well as Minister of Economy in April 1993, followed by the appointment of Oleg Soskovets (formerly director of the Karaganda metallurgical combine) as First Deputy Prime Minister with responsibility over industry in

May of 1993. Appointments of this nature, moreover, were not restricted to the highest levels of government. Meanwhile, however, Khizha lost his position in May of 1993.

[14] Civic Union was a bloc of centrist political factions created in 1992, comprising, at various times, the political arm of the RSPP, the Renewal party, the *Smena* and Industrial factions of the Parliament, Nikolai Travkin's Democratic Party, and Vice-President Alexander Rutskoi's People's Party of Free Russia.

[15] Precise numbers of such organizations are difficult to arrive at, as not all forms of associations are regulated by law.

[16] "*Glavk*" is the abbreviation for *glavniy komitet*, a central board above enterprise level that was used under central planning to administer industry.

[17] This sentiment is clearly expressed in the government's concept paper for industrial groups, in which "the possibility for state organs to work with a small number of economic agents" is cited as one of the benefits of creating such industrial groupings.

[18] See in particular Article 17 of the new privatization program, included in Presidential Decree #2284.

[19] Anders Aslund, "Key Dilemmas in the Russian Economic Reform" (mimeo.), September 1993.

[20] This point is developed in William Easterly and Paulo Vieira da Cunha, "Financing the Storm: Macroeconomic Crisis in Russia 1992–1993" (mimeo.), October 1993.

Part III

Regional Analysis of Defense Industry Issues

7

Economic Performance and Policies in the Defense Industrial Regions of Russia

Clifford Gaddy

I. Introduction

Despite the attention that has been given to the problem of conversion of Russia's defense industry and to the nature of the country's military-industrial complex in general, relatively little seems to be known about how the defense industry affected the people who worked in the defense enterprises or lived in regions dominated by them. This is not to say that there is any shortage of conventional wisdom. For instance, it is usually taken for granted that the defense enterprises of the Soviet era possessed work forces that were more highly skilled, better educated, and better compensated than those in the rest of the economy, that these enterprises have suffered more from the transition to a market economy, and that—in part because of these difficulties—their managers and workers are bastions of opposition to the

Clifford Gaddy is a research associate at the Brookings Institution. An earlier version of this paper was presented at the meeting of the Tokyo Club Foundation for Global Studies in Washington, D.C. on September 30-October 1, 1993. The author expresses his appreciation to the participants of that meeting for thoughtful comments, and to the Tokyo Club Foundation for its financial support. He also thanks Melanie Allen of the Brookings Institution for excellent research assistance. In addition to helping compile and manage the database used in this analysis, she also directed the work of intern Alison Ney, whose contribution is gratefully acknowledged as well.

current reforms. In many cases, it is also assumed such statements apply not simply to the defense industries per se but also to the regions most dependent upon them. In large part, such statements, though widely accepted, have rested solely on anecdotal evidence. Rigorous statistical support for these contentions has been lacking.

This paper is an attempt to bring some new sources of information and a new approach to bear in the analysis of these issues. Recently available data on the Russian economy by its administrative subdivisions (the oblasts) now make it possible to perform cross-sectional statistical analysis of the economy in a way that was difficult before. Using these data, I have attempted to analyze the extent to which an area's involvement in the defense industry can explain its economic performance and the extent of its privileges under the old and new systems, its propensity toward reform in the recent period, and the way the region voted in the April 1993 referendum on the Yeltsin government and its program.

The rest of this paper is structured as follows: Section II presents the types and sources of the data used in the analyses, as well as the statistical methods employed. Section III utilizes data from the mid-1980s to test hypotheses about the economic status of the defense industrial regions on the threshold of the Gorbachev era. Section IV examines the economic performance of the defense regions in the period following the so-called Gaidar reforms of early 1992. Section V attempts to determine the extent to which defense regions may have differed from other regions in their willingness to embrace economic reform policies. Section VI presents an interpretation of the results of the April 1993 referendum with particular emphasis on differences in defense and non-defense regions.

II. Data and Methods

This study uses data of four different types from four sources. The first two are socioeconomic data about Russia's 70-odd oblasts. In the old Soviet Union, oblast-level data—either current or historical—were not easily available. Since the breakup of the Soviet Union, the Russian State Statistics Office has been publishing such data on economic performance by oblast, although on an infrequent and not particularly systematic basis. One such data set consists of historical statistics by oblast for the period 1965 through 1989. These data, only recently made generally accessible, provide a baseline for analyzing the pre-reform situation. The second set of data reports current economic performance by oblast. The third set consists of the oblast-level results of the April 1993 referendum. Finally, the fourth set of data, produced by the official Russian statistics agency, but hitherto unpublished, permits an estimate of the number of defense industry employees in each oblast of Russia.[1]

The method of analysis is multiple regression (ordinary least squares), taking the oblasts as units of observation. The data set has information for 73 of Russia's provincial administrative units.[2] The variables chosen for each particular part of this study are described in sections III-VI, below.

III. The VPK Under the Old System

It is usually assumed that the military-industrial complex (or the VPK, to use the Russian acronym) enjoyed special privileges under the pre-reform Soviet system. Not only did the defense enterprises have access to the best equipment and materials, but they also had the best workers. Assuming that—at least since the Stalin era—noncoercive means were employed to maintain this superior work force, one would expect to find that the defense industry employees themselves enjoyed a higher standard of living than average in Soviet Russia. To test this assertion, I examined the extent to which several measures of welfare and living standards in a region were associated with variables which measured that region's concentration of defense industry. In addition, I also examined the relationship between rates of labor turnover in industry and the size of the defense industry locally.

A. Choice of Variables

Welfare. The dependent variables in the regressions were various regional measures of welfare, grouped into five categories: (1) personal incomes and wages; (2) food consumption; (3) purchases of consumer goods; (4) housing; and (5) medical care. A description of the variables chosen to represent each of these is given below.

Defense Industry. The chief explanatory variable of interest in this and the following sections is regional concentration of defense industry in 1985. Two different measures of defense industry concentration were used. One is an absolute measure—the total number of defense employees in the oblast, labeled VPKTOT—and the other a relative one—the percentage of all industrial employees who worked in defense enterprises, or VPKPCT. Both measures refer to 1985.

I was especially interested in seeing whether or not regressions using the two defense industry variables would differ in their results. My supposition was that the presence of a substantial defense industry impacts a region's economy in two different ways. One, roughly speaking, is a direct, local, and principally economic impact, one that depends on the performance and behavior of defense enterprises in the area. To the extent that defense industries constituted a very large portion of all economic activity in a region, they would shape the local economy through that alone. But in addition, there is the role defense industry can play in influencing national policy toward the regions in which they are located. And here, it is not so much the relative size of defense industry locally that matters as its total size. A region with a very large number of defense employees may have been able to command relatively more centrally allocated resources than another region, even if in percentage terms the defense industry was not as dominant locally. In short, large total numbers confer political clout—in whatever form that is manifested. My hypothesis, then, is that VPKPCT (defense employment as a percentage of all manufacturing employment) would proxy for the direct, local impact, while VPKTOT (total defense employment) represented the overall political influence. To test this, each regression was run twice, once with each variable, and the results compared for the strength and significance of the coefficient estimates for VPKTOT and VPKPCT.

Control Variables. In addition to the defense industry variables, control variables in the regressions included the degree of urbanization of the region (URBAN), in order to separate the general effect of urban areas from defense industry regions (most of which were relatively urbanized), and (in the case of regressions of food consumption and consumer goods purchases) measured per capita personal income (INC85).[3] Descriptive statistics for all the variables are listed in Table 1 at the end of this report.

The data sets on which these analyses are based treat the cities of Moscow and St. Petersburg as equivalent to oblasts. For historical reasons as well as on account of their very large populations, these two cities—especially Moscow, as the political and administrative center of the Soviet empire—enjoyed special status in Russia. I wanted to be sure that the two metropolises did not unduly shape the picture for the country as a whole. Therefore, in addition to regressions using all 73 observations in the data set, I ran separate regressions on a reduced data set which omitted the cities of Moscow and St. Petersburg and the oblasts in which they are located.

In the following, Russia without Moscow and St. Petersburg is referred to as "the provinces." The tables for this section of the paper thus show four separate regressions for each dependent variable: regressions with and without Moscow and St. Petersburg, and regressions with the two alternative defense industry variables, VPKTOT and VPKPCT.

B. Econometric Estimates

The results of the regressions are presented in Table 2. The findings for each welfare variable are discussed below.

Wages and Income. The variable for wages [WAGE85] is the average monthly cash wage of employees in all sectors of the economy in 1985. The income variable [INC85] is annual cash income per capita (from official sources) in 1985.

Panels A and B of Table 2 present convincing evidence that Russia's defense industrial regions were not privileged when it came to official cash wages and total income. Controlling for the degree of urbanization of the oblasts, the VPKTOT variable has a significant negative effect on both average wage and per capita personal income. The results for VPKPCT are also fairly persuasive, with its negative effects on wages being somewhat stronger than on income in general. Overall, we conclude that *regions with large defense industry employment had lower wages and lower per capita official incomes than other urban areas.*

Food consumption. The variable chosen to represent the amount and quality of food consumed was kilograms of meat consumed per capita in 1985 [MEAT85]. As the regressions reported in Panel C show, the main determinant of meat consumption was income: where per capita incomes were high, so was consumption. Since defense industry regions had, as we have seen above, lower incomes on average, it might be expected that their meat consumption would also be lower. However, simple correlations between the meat consumption variable and the defense industry variables show that, on average, *meat consumption was not lower in defense regions than elsewhere.*[4]

Purchases of consumer goods. Purchases of two relatively common household appliances were chosen to represent spending by households on durable consumer goods: the number of washing machines [WASH84] and the number of vacuum cleaners [VAC84] per

106

100 households in 1984. Panels D and E of Table 2 show that in contrast to meat consumption, spending on durable consumer goods in the defense regions does not seem to have been higher than expected in relation to per capita incomes. Few of the coefficient estimates for the defense industry variables are statistically significant at conventional levels, but the signs are generally negative. Overall, the conclusion is that *households in defense regions purchased on average the same number of—or possibly fewer—vacuum cleaners and washing machines per family as compared to those in other urban areas with similar incomes.*

Thus, no special privilege accrued to the defense regions here. Durable goods purchases were driven by the degree of urbanization and levels of income, both in the metropolitan cities and in the provinces. (Curiously, though, the explanatory power of the same set of variables is much higher for vacuum cleaners than for washing machines. In particular, the regression for vacuum cleaner purchases shows a much stronger income effect, which is largely absent in the case of washing machines.)

Housing. Regressions were run to test the relationship between defense industry concentration and both the quantity and quality of housing available to the region's residents. The amount of housing space was measured by square meters of urban residential housing per capita in 1986 [HSG86]. The quality of housing was measured by the percentage of urban residential housing units equipped with indoor bathtubs [BATH86] and hot water [HTWTR86].

As Panel F of Table 2 (housing space) shows, the coefficient estimates for both the URBAN and INC85 variables are statistically significant in each of the four regressions. The signs of the estimates may seem puzzling, however—at least for the Westerner. There is, for instance, a positive correlation between the urbanization variable and the housing space variable: the greater the percentage of people in an oblast living in cities, the more living space they have. Assuming that a higher degree of urbanization generally means cities of larger size, this is perhaps not an expected result. Even more telling for the curious nature of the Soviet economic system is the finding that housing space was not positively correlated with personal incomes. In fact, the correlation is negative: the lower the population's income, the more housing space it had![5]

The results for the defense industry variables are ambiguous. The estimates for VPKTOT are not significantly different from zero. While those for VPKPCT tend to have a negative sign, they are only marginally significant. In short, on the basis of these statistics, *we reject the conclusion that defense industry regions had more housing than other areas with similar levels of urbanization and incomes.*

Turning to Panels G and H, however, we find tentative evidence that *defense areas may have had better quality housing.* At least as measured by the VPKTOT variable, defense areas tended to have a higher percentage of units with indoor baths than other urban areas of comparable income levels. (There is a similar tendency for hot water, but it is generally not statistically significant.) Overall, the results are not particularly strong, but again note that there is a negative correlation between the housing variable and income. This further suggests that defense industry regions—which have lower incomes—had better housing than the average urban area.

Medical care. Two variables (see Panels I and J) represented access to health and medical care: the number of physicians per 10,000 population [DOC85] and the number of hospital beds per 10,000 population in 1985 [BEDS85]. On balance, there is a negative trend for the defense industry variables in both these sets of regressions. It is to be noted that in the case of hospital beds, the explanatory power of the regression model is quite low (R-squares of 0.04 to 0.09). Nevertheless, the defense industry variables had a strongly or moderately significant negative effect in all cases. The conclusion, then, is *the defense areas did not enjoy privileged status in respect to medical care*, and may even have had lower standards than other regions.

Labor Turnover. One final set of regressions in this section goes beyond the measures of regional welfare to study the influence of defense industry concentration on the rate of labor turnover locally. The dependent variable (TURN85) measures the percentage of all industrial employees who left their companies during the year. Panel K shows that the VPKPCT variable has a significant negative impact on turnover. That is, *in regions where defense industry is a dominant employer, labor market stability was significantly higher.*

C. Discussion

As measured by the variables used in these regressions, it appears that if the defense industry areas enjoyed special privilege, it was not great. Our strongest finding is that the typical defense oblast had clearly lower cash wages and incomes than other oblasts. This in itself would appear to contradict the widespread perception that defense industries paid higher wages than other sectors.[6] But in addition, I found scant evidence of higher living standards as measured in other (nonpecuniary) terms. While the citizens of defense oblasts may have had a better quality of housing than other urban areas, I have failed to show that they consumed more meat, had more housing space, purchased more durable consumer goods, or had better access to medical care. At the same time, defense industrial regions had more stable labor markets.

The absence of measurable advantages in respect of living standards (and marked disadvantage in terms of incomes) in defense industrial regions raises the question of how such regions were able to retain the qualitatively better labor forces they are presumed to have had. There are (at least) five possible explanations. First, it has to be remembered that the statistical analyses above were based on mean values of the income and consumption variables for the entire region, not solely for defense industry employees. Thus, the question of whether hypotheses about living standards of defense industry employees can be extended to the regional labor force in general depends on the intra-regional distribution. It is possible that high-wage jobs in defense enterprises were more than outweighed by very low-wage positions in civilian industry, thus yielding a low mean wage (or other measures of living standards).

Secondly, I may have simply chosen the wrong variables in the analysis. That is, the things that made working in defense industry attractive are not being observed. Even in the West, and even in non-defense industries, about which there is more information, researchers often find that the intangible features of a workplace carry as much weight in job choice as measurable aspects such as the wage and working hours. For instance, the social prestige of working in the Soviet defense complex was by all indications quite high. Similarly, many skilled workers may have placed much weight on access to good equipment and supplies in an economy otherwise plagued by chronic shortages of both. For them, working in a defense plant would have simply represented the opportunity to do the job right.

A third possibility is that the variables used here are correct in principle, but my information about them is incomplete. The income variables, for instance, measure only official income and wages. Yet studies on the so-called second economy—the informal, or "black," economy—in the Soviet Union indicate that as much as 40 percent of household income was earned outside the state sector of the economy and was therefore not recorded in official statistics of the kind used here.[7] If residents of defense industry oblasts typically earned more income from the informal sector than citizens of other areas, this would change the results of the analyses above. (Although, of course, if they earned less informally, the findings above would be reinforced.) Similar questions can be raised about the other components of living standards. The variables used in these analyses measured purchases of washing machines and vacuum cleaners from the (official) retail sales network. Yet, many consumer goods were distributed to the population outside this network, and it is not unlikely that this practice was more prevalent in large defense companies and/or that the consumer goods distributed by defense plants were more desirable than those made available to other workers. (Defense industry accounted for a substantial portion of major consumer durables in the USSR.) Access to medical care, measured here by numbers of doctors and hospital beds, is not simply a quantitative issue. Workers in defense plants and their families might have enjoyed more efficient care through enterprise facilities. And so on.

A fourth possible answer to the question of the discrepancy between living standards and quality of labor may be that in fact defense industries did *not* have to provide incentives to retain their labor forces, since they did not have to compete for labor. This is a complicated issue, about which we have little information. The operation of labor markets in defense regions—like so much else about these cities—remains to be uncovered. There is some evidence that the labor markets in defense regions were restricted, with non-defense enterprises simply being denied entry except on very limited terms. For instance, a civilian plant that wanted to expand its work force had to apply for permission to the local (Communist Party) authorities, who in turn determined that the type of workers about to be hired were not needed in defense plants. This also happened explicitly with respect to graduating classes from the universities and engineering schools. In Soviet planners' jargon, the non-defense sector lived according to the "residual principle" with respect to labor just as it did with respect to other factors of production.[8]

A final possible answer to the apparent paradox posed above is that the defense labor force was *not* better. This flies in the face of so much conventional wisdom about the Soviet economy that it might seem frivolous even to consider it. Yet, as we have seen over the past few years, much of conventional wisdom about the workings and the purported achievements of the Soviet economic system has proved to be in need of revision. To my knowledge, there have been no published studies comparing the labor forces of defense and non-defense industries. On the other hand, much of what is reported anecdotally about the defense labor force can be traced back to representatives of the defense industrial complex themselves— individuals who, especially in the recent period of restricted budgets, have a clear incentive to exaggerate the threatened loss of human capital from their enterprises if they do not receive government support, etc.

Clearly, further research is needed to determine the relative quality of the defense labor force. As one provocative statistic, let me cite the fact that on a regional basis there is no correlation between the variable measuring the relative concentration of defense industry

(VPKPCT) and the percentage of the labor force with higher or specialized secondary education. Formal educational levels alone are, of course, only a partial measure of human capital, but I would have expected to see a positive relationship.[9]

There is one final observation that can be made on the basis of the econometric analysis in this section. One of the most significant and interesting results was that meat consumption in these regions was incommensurate with monetary earnings. That is, whereas everywhere else in the Soviet Union money mattered when it came to levels of consumption of this important food product, this was not the case in defense regions. It is tempting to conclude from this that the defense regions may have been more of a command-administrative economy than the rest of society, one in which a greater part of resources was allocated by central administrative decisions, not by individual choice. While it is true that the same pattern did not hold for the other two consumption goods studied, it would be worth further study to determine whether or not there are other important goods that parallel the case of meat. The question to be answered is whether the defense industrial regions constituted more of a non-monetary economy than the country as a whole.[10]

IV. Performance of the Defense Industry Regions Under the Gaidar Reforms

Just as it is the common view that the military-industrial complex was a privileged sector during the Soviet era, it is generally thought that the regions whose economies were dominated by arms manufacturers have suffered more than other areas during reform. One of the most drastic measures in Yegor Gaidar's January 1992 package of radical reforms was the slashing of the defense procurement budget. By the end of the year, domestic purchases of arms were down by 68 percent. At the same time, other centrally allocated funds became tighter, at least until about mid-year. What did this mean for the defense regions? To answer that question, I turn in this section to data on regional industrial performance, inflation, wages, personal income, and housing construction during the critical first half of 1992. Below, I report and discuss the results of similar kinds of regressions as carried out in the preceding section on historical data. Again, the key explanatory variables are VPKTOT and VPKPCT, together with the control variable for degree of urbanization (URBAN). (The descriptive statistics for these and other variables used are in Table 1.)

A. Choice of Variables and Findings

Industrial Performance. The two principal measures of economic performance for the first six months of 1992 are industrial output as a percentage of the corresponding period in 1991 [VOL92] and the change in real profits of industrial enterprises [RLPRF92]. Panels A and B of Table 3 show the regression results. The weak explanatory power of the model for these two variables is immediately apparent. The R-squares all remain below 0.08. Panel A shows that industrial output tended to be positively correlated with the degree of urbanization of the oblast, but that the presence or absence of large defense industry apparently had no impact. The change in real profits was even less systematic, varying almost randomly across oblasts of different degrees of urbanization and defense industry concentration. In sum, I conclude that *industrial performance in the first half of 1992 was no worse in the defense industrial regions than in others.*

Inflation. Inflation differed widely across the regions of Russia throughout 1992. The measure used here is the increase in prices of goods in the official (state-owned or newly privatized) retail sector in the first half of 1992. The average such increase for Russia as a whole was around 800 percent, with a range of 500-1,200 percent. The regression results reported in Panel C indicate that urban areas in general had higher inflation rates. But apart from that, *defense industrial concentration was not associated with higher or lower regional inflation rates.* (It is to be noted here that most of the inflation recorded in early 1992 was less a reflection of macroeconomic disequilibrium than regional policies with regard to price deregulation.)

Wages and Incomes. One phenomenon which was observed early in 1992 was increasing differentiation in wage levels among Russia's regions. By mid-1992, average industrial wages in the highest-paid oblast were nearly eight times higher than in the lowest-paid. (This compares to a ratio of only 3:1 in 1985.) In sharp contrast to the apparent lack of any connection between regional industrial performance and defense industry concentration, the picture of industrial wage development (Panels D and E) is a very definite one. Panel D (with WAGE92 as the dependent variable) shows that *defense industry oblasts (by both measures) had significantly lower nominal wage levels at mid-1992* than other areas with corresponding urban concentrations. (Normally, the more urban an area, the higher the nominal wage.)

Parallel with the increasing variation in nominal wage levels, there was also a huge regional variation in the rate of real wage growth in the first half of 1992. Measured real wages generally dropped quite sharply in the month of January owing to the sudden unleashing of a great deal of repressed inflation as prices were deregulated, but they quickly recovered—at least in industry. By June, real wages in industry were only slightly below the January level for the country as a whole. But regionally, real wage growth over the period varied from a low of -40 percent to a high of +70 percent. Where did the defense regions fall in this broad range? Panel E tells the story: *the defense regions had much lower real wage growth in the first half of 1992* than other regions. The coefficient estimates for VPKPCT show that for each additional percentage point in the ratio of defense employees to all manufacturing employees, real wage growth in the oblast was 0.7-0.8 percentage points lower.

While it would be interesting to see whether this trend held for the rest of 1992, figures for wage development for the entire year were not available for this report. Panel F, which reports the change in per capita *income* (i.e., all earnings, not just wages) for the entire year of 1992 [DINC1292], gives a milder picture than Panel E. The coefficient estimates for VPKTOT and VPKPCT are not significantly different from zero—i.e., average income growth for the year was not lower in defense regions than elsewhere. This may mean that the gloomy picture of wage development from the first half of 1992 had brightened somewhat by year-end, but not necessarily. The other possibility is that other forms of income helped compensate for the decline in wage income.

An interesting question about enterprise behavior poses itself when one compares the results in Panel B (industrial profits development) and Panel C (wage development). According to Russian law, profits are defined as revenues less costs of production [*sebestoimost'*]. A

111

certain part of wages is included in these costs of production, but only up to a specified ceiling (equal to four times the legal minimum wage). All amounts paid out in excess of that ceiling are charged to profits (and thereby become subject to the 32 percent profits tax). Since the base amount—the part of the payroll that is excluded from profits tax—is fairly low, in practice an enterprise cannot legally pay high wages without also reporting large profits. Empirically, this seems to be the case: in the data set, there is a highly significant positive correlation between profits and wages for Russia as a whole for the first half of 1992.

However, this positive correlation between profits and wages does *not* hold for defense regions. As we concluded above, the defense areas were no worse off than others in terms of profits in the first half of 1992. Yet they clearly fell behind the others in wage growth. This suggests that the defense enterprises may have been using their profits differently from other enterprises. Specifically, these enterprises may not have placed as high a priority on using revenues to pay wages. If so, that would be consistent with the possibility raised in the previous section regarding defense regions in the old system, namely, that they were less "monetary." In other words, employee benefits took the form of more non-cash benefits. It may well be that they are continuing even now to reward workers more with in-kind (non-monetary) benefits than with cash salaries.

Housing. One potentially good indicator of non-monetary benefits is residential housing construction. The variable chosen here is the change in residential housing (measured in square meters of housing space) completed in January–June 1992 as compared to the corresponding months of 1991 [HSG92]. For this period, completion rates dropped drastically all over Russia—by an average of 35 percent. The two principal sources of financing for housing construction in Russia are municipal budgets, funded largely through enterprise taxes, and enterprises' own funds.[11] We would therefore expect some connection between enterprise performance (profits) and construction. Panel G shows that this connection is absent: the coefficient estimate for the variable measuring real profits (RLPRF92) is not significantly different from zero. On the other hand, what does matter is defense industry, by both measures (VPKTOT and VPKPCT). These defense industry variables had a significant positive impact on new housing construction. Every percentage point of VPKPCT raised the change in housing completions by about half a percentage point (e.g., we would expect an oblast with 40 percent defense employment rather than 20 percent to show a 10 percentage point higher rate of housing construction).

The conclusion from the data seems then to be that in the tradeoff between using profits for higher wages or for social expenditures, the defense areas chose the latter. Once again, then, this would be consistent with what appears to be the tradition in Russia's defense-industrial complex. This is a subject worthy of future research, particularly to determine whether this policy may reflect the preferences of the work forces in the defense regions. If so, it could have important consequences in the future, as many of these enterprises are privatized with substantial employee ownership and influence. To the extent that the work forces of defense enterprises were self-selected, this means they may prefer a continuation of such in-kind components as opposed to more cash.

V. Regional Reform Policies and Defense Industry

One of the most widely accepted of all conventional wisdoms regarding Russian politics today is that the nation's military-industrial complex is a bastion of opposition to economic reform. Second perhaps only to the Supreme Soviet, the "defense-industrial lobby" has been blamed for wanting to preserve the old order. One way in which the defense industrialists might potentially exercise this allegedly retrogressive role would be by obstructing reform at the local level. If that is true, one should see differences in rates of reform among regions with greater or lesser concentrations of defense industry—a hypothesis that can be tested using the same approach as in earlier sections of this paper.

In principle, the regional approach lends itself well to a study of reform policies. Although the most well-known reform policies—the Gaidar macroeconomic stabilization effort of early 1992 and the ongoing mass privatization campaign headed by key reformer Anatoliy Chubais—have been initiated at the center, a great deal of the actual implementation of radical market-oriented reforms rests with oblasts and cities. Increasing public attention has also been directed to the regional component of reform. The case of Nizhny Novgorod is perhaps the best known, and it is suggestive in that the highly progressive Nizhny is one of Russia's main defense-industrial regions.[12] To determine whether Nizhny is an aberration among defense regions, or perhaps more representative than commonly thought, I decided to focus on two main areas of reform: price liberalization and privatization of state enterprises.

Price Policy. In an explicit decree in March 1992, the Russian federal government granted local governments the right to adopt their own policies regarding prices. From that point on, at the latest, much of the entire program of price deregulation—especially deregulation of retail prices—has depended on the regions. To my knowledge, there are no direct data on the degree of price subsidization in various regions. I therefore constructed an index of price subsidization as follows. Using published data on prices of selected food products in state stores and in private markets in the oblast capital cities, I computed the ratio of market to state prices for several food items. If we assume that the farmers' market [*rynok*] price is a free, market-clearing price, the difference between that price and the price in state stores—absent any other reasons for price differences—is attributable to subsidization of the state price.[13]

Panel H of Table 3 shows the results of a set of regressions which were run using the free market/state store ratio for beef [BFRATE] as the dependent variable. (Beef was the food for which there were most observations.)[14] The independent variables included, of course, the alternative defense industry variables, VPKTOT and VPKPCT, as well as control variables thought to affect the prices of beef. URBAN is the degree of urbanization. Two other variables were postulated to represent demand pressure: POP is the total population of the oblast and RLWGEINC is real wage growth in the first half of 1992.

From columns 1 and 2 of Panel H, it appears that the defense industry variables have a strong negative influence on the ratio in question, i.e., that there is a greater degree of price liberalization in the defense regions. It turns out, however, that this is a specious result, driven almost exclusively by the situation in Moscow and St. Petersburg. These two cities are clearly outliers when it comes to both food prices and several of the other variables. When they are dropped (cf. columns 3 and 4), not only does the general explanatory power of the regression drop drastically, but the defense industry variables lose all significance. The analysis thus provides no support for the thesis that price liberalization was less in defense regions. But it has to be stressed again that given the crude nature of the measure of price liberalization used here, any conclusions on the basis of these results must be very tentative. Better data are needed.

Privatization. Under the Russian government's ambitious program of privatization of state-owned enterprises in 1992, many small, medium-sized, and large enterprises have been put in the hands of private individuals. By the end of the year, the privatization of the larger enterprises (generally, those with more than 1,000 employees) had just begun. But the program of so-called small-scale privatization was well underway. Of a total of around 77,000 such small firms (generally defined as those with fewer than 200 employees, mainly in the retail trade and services), more than 27,000, or around 36 percent, had been privatized. Like price liberalization, this was a reform measure very much in the hands of the regions. Most of the small establishments were owned by municipal governments, and under the program, the sale was carried out by local bodies, with a great deal of local influence. Not surprisingly, the rate of privatization varied greatly by regions. While one oblast (Kaluga) managed to privatize essentially all of its 700 or so small enterprises by the end of the year, Tyumen' oblast had privatized fewer than 0.6 percent of its 1,500 firms.[15]

The results of regressions on a variable measuring the percentage of each region's small enterprises that had been privatized by the end of 1992 [PVTPCT] are shown in Panel I of Table 3. The results show that while the overall explanatory power of the models is low, there is the interesting result that privatization appears to have proceeded more rapidly in less urbanized oblasts (cf. the significant negative coefficient estimate for URBAN). The defense industry variables are not significantly different from zero in any of the four regressions, although the estimates are consistently positive in all. Thus, *the defense regions do not appear to have privatized more slowly than other regions.*

In sum, by these two measures of locally implemented market reform, areas of defense industrial concentration appeared as of mid-1992 to be no more or no less "anti-reform" than other areas in Russia. This, of course, is by no means conclusive evidence that the military-industrial lobby is not opposed to reform. All that can be stated on the basis of this analysis—and even this is tentative, given the crude nature of the price liberalization variable—is that if the defense lobby is anti-reform and if it indeed tried to block local implementation of key reform measures, it was generally unsuccessful in doing so.

VI. Results of the April 1993 Referendum

The preceding section examined local policies with respect to economic reform. The results concerning the role of defense industry were generally inconclusive. But even to the extent that I tentatively conclude that policies in defense regions did not differ from others, what was being reflected were the pro- and anti-reform attitudes of the most powerful local political forces, not the attitudes of the population as a whole. To the extent that they were elected at all, those policymakers have never really been required to defend their policy records before the electorate. The last general local elections in Russia were in the spring of 1990—when the USSR still existed and nearly two years before the reforms of the Gaidar government. It was not until the spring of 1993 that the population of Russia was given the opportunity to express its own views on the matter of reform.

For many observers, the results of the April referendum seemed surprising: a population that had allegedly suffered so much under the president and his program nevertheless voted in favor of both. Nationwide, Yeltsin received a 59 percent "yes" vote for himself personally and a narrower 53 percent for his program. (Since voter turnout was only 64 percent, however, he fell far short of the majority of registered voters which the parliamentary leader Khasbulatov had posed as the criterion for "victory.")[16] In the days and weeks after the referendum, a number of attempts were made to explain the results. Not all of these "theories" of Russian politics are easy to test. For instance, it was said that the reason the voters endorsed Yeltsin despite the hardships he has caused is that the Russian electorate is particularly sophisticated. Defying the conventional wisdom that people vote with their pocketbooks, Russians—the theory goes—looked beyond the short-term tribulations to see instead the long-term positive prospects promised by market reform. (A contrary view is to assume that Russians do vote with their pocketbooks. Hence, the majority of Russians, by voting for the incumbent Yeltsin, showed that they have already benefitted economically from his policies.)

Other explanations for the vote related it to regional trends, and some of these are more easily testable. One view, for instance, was that Yeltsin had weak support in the regions of Russia that have been displaying autonomous, even separatist tendencies. This would portend a threat to the integrity of the nation.[17] There were also those, including some influential figures in the circle around Yeltsin, who claimed that the most interesting regional pattern in the vote concerned the defense industrial regions. The vote, they said, showed that the strongest support for the president came precisely from those parts of the country with heavy concentrations of defense industry. A glance at a map of the election results tends to support this view: the highest pro-Yeltsin votes were in the Urals and several of the Far Eastern regions, areas where defense industry is particularly dominant.[18] One key Yeltsin adviser, Mikhail Malei, went so far as to declare that the vote demonstrated that the military-industrial complex was the "core of support" for Yeltsin. The policy implication, said Malei, is that Yeltsin must continue to pursue policies that benefit the defense industry.[19]

Using the types of data and the methods employed in the earlier sections of this paper, it is a relatively straightforward matter to test the assertion of Malei and others that defense regions supported Yeltsin. This section reports and discusses the results of regressions of the referendum vote on a set of possible explanatory factors which include not only defense industry concentration, but also other possible explanations.

A. Choice of Variables

Without pretending to undertake an exhaustive test of candidate explanatory theories, I proposed a set of regressions to study the impact of defense industry concentration on the vote, along with a number of other variables that might variously be regarded as control variables or as proxies for alternative theories of how regions voted in the April referendum.

These other variables include the region's (1) status as a republic; (2) age structure; (3) level of urbanization; (4) level of education; and (5) personal incomes.

Each of these, along with the variable to be explained—the referendum vote—is described in more detail below.

Voting Results. In regressions reported here, the dependent variable is the percentage of actual voters that voted "yes" on Question 1: "Do you have confidence in Boris Yeltsin?"[20] Regressions were also run using the vote on Question 2 ("Do you approve of Yeltsin's socioeconomic policy?"), but the qualitative results were very close to those on Question 1.

Defense Industry. As in earlier sections, the regressions for this section were run separately for two alternative measures of defense industry concentration, VPKTOT and VPKPCT. In contrast to the previous sections, however, the main discussion and tables report only the results for VPKTOT. In general, the VPKPCT variable performed quite poorly in the voting analysis. This is in itself an interesting result, and its implications will be discussed briefly below.[21]

To determine whether any effect apparently due to defense industry employment might actually be confounded with the effect of industrial employment of all kinds, a separate variable for total industrial employment was used (INDTOT).

Republics. To test whether the status of a region as a republic made a difference in the election results, the variable REPUBLIC was created. For 68 of the 72 observations, this is the equivalent of a dummy variable with a value of 1 for a republic and 0 otherwise. In the other four, it has a value between 0 and 1, reflecting the fact the status of some of their constituent units changed in the recent period.[22]

Age. It is often said that economic reform has divided the Russian population by generations: younger people more often tend to see the reform as an opportunity, while older people view it as a burden. Just where this "generational divide" goes, if there is one, is open to dispute. The dividing line I chose for the present analysis is the one between those still in active working age and those beyond retirement age. The variable OLD is the portion of the population of retirement age. Under current Russian labor law (as under the old Soviet system), men are eligible to retire at age 60 and women at age 55.

Urbanization and Education. URBAN is the same variable used in regressions in earlier sections of this report. It measures the percentage of the total population in the oblast that is classified as living in urban areas. HIGHERED measures the portion of the oblast labor force with higher or so-called "special secondary" education.

Income. Research from other countries has found strong correlations between economic indicators and aggregate voting behavior: the better-off economically a nation is, the more likely voters are to support the incumbent.[23] It is reasonable to at least entertain the possibility that this trend is true at the regional level as well. I therefore included a measure of local economic welfare. The variable used here is nominal per capita household income in the oblast in December 1992 (INC1292). It has to be noted that this is *official* monetary income and captures little, if any, of families' income derived outside the state sector of the economy or even through informal mechanisms from the state job.

B. Econometric Estimates

Table 4 reports statistical estimates for five separate models using the outcome of the vote on Question 1 (support for Yeltsin). Let us look first at the variables that turned out *not* to be important.

Republics, Education, and Age. Model (1) was designed to test whether the perception that the republics tended to vote against Yeltsin is correct. The correlation coefficient for the bivariate relationship between the REPUBLIC variable and the vote for Yeltsin (YES-1) does show a negative relationship but it is not significant (-0.2171). The multivariate regression results reinforce this finding: the coefficient estimate for REPUBLIC is not significantly different from zero, once other factors are controlled for. In fact, in no econometric specification of the voting model using multiple regressors did the REPUBLIC variable prove significant. In short, the status of a region as a republic simply did not matter in the referendum.

Model (2) presents the same model as (1) but without REPUBLIC. In both models (1) and (2), HIGHERED and OLD are insignificant. Anecdotal evidence and simple correlations had suggested that higher education would be a good candidate as an explanatory variable for the vote. (The correlation coefficient between HIGHERED and YES-1 is a highly significant +0.5532.) The fact that HIGHERED loses all significance in the regression analysis, however, suggests that education was serving as a proxy for other determinants, such as urbanization, higher incomes, and defense industry.

The age variable, OLD, though it has the expected negative sign, is insignificant at conventional levels.

Having removed REPUBLIC, HIGHERED, and OLD from contention as explanations for the pro-Yeltsin vote, we are left with three: urbanization (URBAN), personal income (INC1292),[24] and defense industry (VPKTOT). In models (1) and (2) all three are significant or very nearly significant.

Model (3) of Table 4 carries the analysis one step further. While it appears to be the case that total defense industrial employment did make a difference in the way regions voted in the referendum, can we be certain that this was an effect specifically associated with *defense* industry? Or might it be the case that large industrial employment of any kind in a region produced the same pattern of voting? To test this, model (3) includes as an explanatory variable INDTOT, which measures all industrial employment.

The results, shown in column (3) of Table 4, show that much of the effect ascribed by models (1) and (2) to defense industry may actually have come from industry. That is, once we control for total industrial employment, the significance of the coefficient estimate for VPKTOT drops substantially, although its size stays the same. On the other hand, it does not appear to be the case that industry alone serves as a strong explanatory factor, since the estimate for INDTOT itself remains small both in size and significance.

Gross Effects Versus Net Effects. The preceding discussion about the relative importance of large industrial employment in general and defense industrial employment in particular raises a fundamental point about the interpretation of the econometric results. Multivariate regression is an extremely useful tool to analyze the separate effects of several different factors acting simultaneously. By including such measures as urbanization, education, and total industrial employment along with defense industry size, we have been able to statistically sort out the distinct impact of each. But what if some of the set of factors used to explain the vote themselves are causally determined by others? For instance, we have established that high levels of urbanization and defense employment in a region had a positive influence on that region's pro-Yeltsin vote. At the same time, it might be argued that in many of Russia's regions the high level of urbanization itself is partly a result of the presence of a large defense industry. Statistics can show that there is a positive correlation between urbanization and defense industry. What statistics does not tell us is whether there is causality in this relationship and if so, in what direction it works. Here, we must rely on institutional knowledge. Many of Russia's large urban manufacturing centers were built up because the planners placed a concentration of large defense plants there, not the other way around. Once the plants were built, the workers came. The entire region then became more urban and better educated. This all goes to suggest that to fully appreciate the impact of defense industry, it might be better to drop the HIGHERED and URBAN variables from the model. This would allow the VPKTOT coefficient estimate to absorb their impacts and thereby reveal the gross effects of defense industry. That is, since the presence of defense industry is itself partially the reason for high urbanization and high educational levels, it is more accurate to look at that overall effect. The same can be argued for the effect of the INDTOT variable.[25]

Model (4) omits URBAN and HIGHERED but retains INDTOT. Finally, model (5) omits INDTOT as well. They thus reveal progressively more of the gross impact of VPKTOT. The results are as expected: VPKTOT grows in size and significance. I interpret the coefficient of VPKTOT in column (5) as an estimate of the full effect of defense industry on the vote. In this case, the coefficient is picking up all the effects of defense industry, including the indirect effects that could occur through the omitted other variables. Interpreting the difference between the VPKTOT coefficient in column (1) and that in column (5) as the magnitude of the indirect effects of defense industry suggests that such indirect effects are substantial, more than one-half the total effect.

Still, it is to be stressed that columns (1) and (5) both have meaning. Part of the interpretation of the effect on defense industry on the vote for Yeltsin depends on whether one believes that the impact on the vote mediated through the other variables (for instance, and perhaps especially, urbanization) would persist in the absence, or at least reduction, of total defense industry employment in the region. In the short term, the levels of urbanization and education, even if caused originally by defense industry, would remain. Thus, it may be that we should take seriously the isolated effect of defense industry as expressed in model (1). It may provide guidance about the attitudes of the populations of defense industry regions in the short term as the defense industry downsizes and/or converts, leaving the other variables relatively unchanged.

Total Defense Employment Versus Relative Concentration. Finally, one of the most important results of the statistical analysis is one not explicitly reported here. The defense variable chosen for the models reported in Table 4 is VPKTOT, or total defense employment. As pointed out earlier, regressions were also run using the alternative measure of VPKPCT, the percentage of the industrial work force in the oblast that worked in defense industry. As it turned out, VPKPCT performed very poorly. Although it, too, tended to have a positive sign, it lacked all significance. The finding that VPKTOT but not VPKPCT had an impact on the vote is important. It suggests that the driving mechanism is not the defense industry's dominant position in the local economy and society, but rather the lobbying power it commands on the national scale. This follows from my assumption that lobbying power is due not to the relative concentration of defense industry locally but to its total weight nationally. In other words, a small region with a heavy concentration of defense industries might be very dependent on the defense sector, but that does not mean that it can extract concessions from Moscow. Political clout comes from size and numbers.

C. Discussion

The basic message of this analysis of the referendum results is that (1) the status of a region as a republic seemed to make no difference in the vote; (2) the alleged "generation gap" did not manifest itself at the regional level; (3) areas with higher income levels had higher pro-Yeltsin votes, (i.e., in this sense at least, Russians did "vote with their wallets"); (4) urbanized regions were more pro-Yeltsin than others; and finally, (5) areas with large defense industry employment did indeed tend to give greater support to Yeltsin in the referendum than other areas.

Granting, then, that factors such as defense employment, incomes, and urbanization levels made a difference in the election, the next question is, how much of a difference? To answer that, we can look more closely at the size of the coefficient estimates in Table 4.

Defense Employment. The coefficient estimate of 0.0062 for VPKTOT in model (5) means that for each additional 10,000 defense employees in a region, we would expect an increase in the pro-Yeltsin vote of 0.62 percentage points. Expressed in terms of the elasticities familiar to economists, this implies an elasticity of 0.075, which may seem quite small. But another way to look at it is to ask how many votes was each additional defense worker "worth"? To calculate that, realize that on average, nearly 1,000,000 people voted per oblast. An increase of 0.62 percentage points represents 6,200 votes. Therefore, each defense employee was "worth" 6,200/10,000 = 0.62 votes for Yeltsin.

Monthly Income. The size of the coefficient estimate for per capita income (INC1292) in Table 4 ranges from 0.0077 to 0.0165. Thus, each additional 1,000 rubles per capita (the average monthly income in Russia in December 1992 was just under 10,000 rubles) meant on average a 0.8-1.7 percentage points' higher vote for Yeltsin, or 8,000–17,000 more votes per oblast.

Let us make the strong assumption that this income effect is the same no matter how the income was derived. Specifically, we assume that it does not matter if increased income reflects better economic conditions in the oblast or more artificial conditions—such as direct wage subsidies, tax concessions, or permissive export policies. That is, raising income levels is a policy option that could bring more votes—not a wild assumption. Then let us calculate: how much would a vote cost? The answer is, roughly 0.060–0.125 December 1992 rubles per month extra per citizen.[26] Six, or even twelve and a half kopecks, may sound ridiculously cheap (a kopeck, or one-hundredth of a ruble, is worth 1/1,000 of a U.S. cent). But remember that this is 0.06–0.125 ruble for *each* of the typical oblast's 2 million citizens, or 120–250,000 rubles, *for one vote total!* Again, assuming direct subsidies to a region (or its enterprises) have this effect, this means that the government could gain one additional percentage point in the result (10,000 votes) at a cost of an additional 1.2–2.5 billion December 1992 rubles or so per month. For the country as a whole, that would add up quickly: 90–187.5 billion extra per month for a one percentage point increase. (Strictly for the record, the actual increase in the Russian money supply in December 1992 was 337 billion rubles.)[27]

The Defense Regions Voted for Yeltsin, But Why?

Official government statistics report that total output (military and civilian) from Russia's defense plants was down 18 percent in 1992. Perhaps as many as 400,000 defense jobs were lost during the year.[28] According to the analysis reported in Section IV above ("Performance of the Defense Industrial Regions Under the Gaidar Reforms"), wages and wage growth in defense regions were considerably lower than in other areas in the first half of 1992. These are hardly the kinds of economic trends voters could be expected to endorse. Clearly, something else must have been happening in the defense regions to counterbalance these developments. Part of the explanation may lie in the finding from Section IV that higher non-cash benefits—housing was our example—did tend to compensate for monetary wages. But was this enough?

Another possibility is that the picture presented here for the first half of 1992 changed considerably in the following period. There is strong anecdotal evidence of a very large flow of funds into the defense industrial enterprises beginning in August–September 1992. Mikhail Malei, whose views cited in the introduction to this section are essentially vindicated by the present analysis, offers a case study of how regions were able to obtain these benefits through special contacts in Moscow. Malei, who has special ties to the Republic of Udmurtiya, was personally involved in making sure Yeltsin continued to lavish special benefits on "his" region literally until the eve of the referendum. On April 22 he and Yeltsin visited Udmurtiya, which has the distinction of having the most militarized economy of any region in Russia (57 percent of manufacturing employees traditionally worked in defense plants). They outlined a package of special benefits, later confirmed in a special executive decree, which included a promise that $250 million of funds obtained from foreign credits would be earmarked for the defense enterprises of Udmurtiya.[29]

On April 25, the population of Udmurtiya voted 56 percent in favor of Yeltsin. This was below the national average of 59 percent, and well below the vote in some of the other Urals oblasts such as Sverdlovsk and Perm. Does this mean that Malei's efforts on behalf of Udmurtiya were in vain? It is difficult to say, but it is worth looking not only at Sverdlovsk and Perm, but also at a couple of Udmurtiya's other neighbors that, like Udmurtiya, are minority-based republics with substantial defense industry employment. One, Bashkiriya, had fewer than 40 percent pro-Yeltsin votes. The other, Tatarstan, conducted a de facto boycott of the election. In the end, only 15 percent of its eligible voters gave Yeltsin their support.

Notes

[1] The historical statistics are from the Russian statistics agency's [Goskomstat's] "Pokazateli sotsial'nogo razvitiya avtonomnykh respublik, krayev i oblastey RSFSR" [Indicators of the social development of the autonomous republics, krays, and oblasts of the RSFSR], Russian State Committee on Statistics, Moscow, 1990. (This was originally a restricted document, with an initial press run of only 50 copies.) The recent statistics on performance are of the kind issued in, for instance, the appendix to Goskomstat's semi-annual economic report, "Ekonomicheskoye polozheniye Rossiyskoy Federatsii (dopolnitel'nyye dannyye) v I polugodii 1992 goda" [The economic situation in the Russian Federation (supplementary data) in the first half of 1992], Russian State Committee on Statistics, Moscow, 1992. The election data are from *Rossiskaya gazeta,* May 19, 1993. The figures for defense industry employment are for the year 1985 and are presented in Brenda Horrigan, "How Many People Worked in the Soviet Defense Industry?" [*RFE/RL Research Report,* 1:33 (21 August 1992), pp. 33-39. Her estimates are derived from figures in an unpublished document prepared by Goskomstat. That document includes figures for total industrial employment in each oblast, as well as a breakdown for each oblast by sectors of industry. The sum of the sectors, which otherwise appear to be an exhaustive classification of Soviet industry, do not, however, add up to the reported total. Horrigan attributes this unclassified residual to employment in defense industries.

[2] Although here and in the rest of this paper, I generally refer to these administrative subdivisions as "oblasts," Russia's constituent units are actually of three kinds: oblasts, krays (distinguished from oblasts in that all but one kray contained within it one or more lesser units, autonomous oblasts), and autonomous republics. In Soviet Russia there were 49 oblasts, 6 krays, and 16 autonomous republics. In addition, the large cities of Moscow and Leningrad were treated in the statistics separately from the oblasts. Today, the status of some of those units has changed. However, for most of this study the old units remain as the units of analysis.

I also speak of voting by oblast, even though technically speaking, Russia votes by electoral districts [*izbiratel'nyye okrugy*], of which there are 91. For the most part, these districts coincide with the political subdivisions. The exceptions are two electoral districts for the Ministry of Foreign Affairs and the Ministry of Defense. The ministries together accounted for 0.3 percent of eligible voters in the referendum and 0.5 percent of actual voters. They are not included in the analysis of Section VI.

[3] The URBAN variable follows the very liberal definition of an urban region used in official Russian statistics; that is, any town or village with 3,000 or more inhabitants. Alternative variables (e.g., the percentage of the region's population living in cities of 50,000 or more) were also tested, but none performed as well as the original URBAN. INC85 measures per capita nominal cash income from official sources. Obviously, it would be highly desirable to have a measure of *total* income, including income from non-official sources (private economic activity, moonlighting, etc.). Such data are, unfortunately, not available.

[4] Indeed, between VPKTOT and MEAT85, there is a significant *positive* correlation. (The correlation coefficients between MEAT85 and VPKTOT and VPKPCT, respectively, are 0.3746 and 0.0184). The multiple regression results in Panel C confirm that the typical region with large defense employment consumed more meat per capita than other urban areas *with the same levels of per capita cash incomes.*

Meat was chosen as the most desirable food of those available in the data set. But to

121

control for the possibility that other forms of protein (eggs, dairy products, fish) might substitute, I constructed a variable for the number of kilograms of animal protein per capita consumed annually, or PROT85. Although not reported here, the results were very similar to those for meat. The VPKTOT and VPKPCT variables were all significant, but slightly weaker than for MEAT85. Interestingly, URBAN—which was not significant for MEAT85— became quite significant. This implies that the meat versus alternative protein trade-off was operative in non-defense urban areas.

[5] The lack of a positive correlation between incomes and housing space is not surprising in light of the fact that rents in the Soviet Union were so low as to constitute a trivial portion of total household expenditures. The average family spent less than one percent of its income for rent. Comparable rent-to-income ratios in large cities in the West range from 16 percent in Tokyo and 18 percent in Munich to 21 percent in Paris and 23 percent in Washington, D.C.

The *negative* correlation between income and housing requires further explanation. In other work, I have proposed viewing the Soviet labor market as one based on a hedonic wage (an extension of the implicit market or hedonic wage theory pioneered by H. Gregg Lewis and Sherwin Rosen for a market economy). This model accounts for the present case well. The key is to realize that for many Soviet workers, housing was a benefit provided by the enterprise. In the Soviet version of the hedonic model, cash income and housing are two (of many) components in a bigger "wage bundle," and they will accordingly be subject to trade-offs against one another. (Equivalently, higher cash income may be thought of as a compensating differential for a relative lack of housing.) See C. Gaddy, "Pretending to Work and Pretending To Pay: A Hedonic Wage Approach to the Behavior of Soviet Workers and Managers," *Berkeley-Duke Occasional Papers on the Second Economy in the USSR*, Paper No. 24 (January 1991).

[6] As an example of an authoritative, and up-to-date, expression of this view, see the publication of the economics research arm of the Russian government, *Rossiya —1993. Ekonomicheskaya kon"yunktura* [Russia—1993. Economic performance], No. 3 (August), 1993, by the Center for the Study of Economic Performance, attached to the Council of Ministers and the Government of the Russian Federation. They write: "Earlier, the level of wages in the defense complex was substantially higher than in other sectors, something that facilitated the recruitment of highly-skilled labor into its enterprises" (p. 214).

[7] See, e.g., the various studies in the *Berkeley-Duke Occasional Papers on the Second Economy in the USSR*.

[8] The direct and indirect constraints on suppliers of labor should also be considered. Even though in a formal sense Soviet citizens had relatively broad freedom of job choice, they were subject to a number of significant restrictions. What is being measured in the regressions above are regional differences, and the assumption of the model is that job choice to some extent manifests itself in choice of region. However, the system of residence permits (*propiski*) prevented individuals from moving to some cities. (This system is still in effect in Russia today, although scheduled to be abolished.) Another obvious obstacle to mobility was the housing shortages. The real question is the nature of the Soviet labor market, in particular the extent to which defense industries in search of more or better labor would have needed to compete with non-defense regions or whether they could count on local supply.

[9] For VPKPCT and the variable for higher education (HIGHERED), the correlation coefficient in question was +0.0503. This is not significant at any conventional level. Interestingly,

a significant positive correlation does exist between higher education and total defense employment (VPKTOT). It might also be noted that a similar analysis of approximately the same variables for the United States does show a strong positive correlation between rates of educational achievement and defense employment. The correlation coefficient between the ratio of a state's defense employment to total manufacturing employment, on the one hand, and the percentage of its citizens over 25 with some college education, on the other, is +0.4514. The U.S. statistic is significant at the 0.001 level for a one-tailed test.

[10] The importance of monetization of an economy is not to be underestimated. To the extent that money in the hands of an individual empowers that person to make more free choices (even if some of those choices have to be made illegally; e.g., by trade on black markets), he or she can achieve a higher level of welfare at lower levels of consumption measured in volume of goods than if goods are allocated by administrative rationing of some kind. Freedom of choice is not merely a psychological issue; it has economic value.

[11] Most of spending on housing and other components of the "social sphere" comes directly from enterprises rather than government. In Chelyabinsk, for instance, enterprises account for fully 66 percent of all social spending. The central government accounts for 14 percent, and the local government 20 percent.

[12] Measured by total number of defense employees (the VPKTOT measure used in this report), Nizhnyy Novgorod ranks fourth among Russia's regions, behind only Sverdlovsk oblast and the Moscow and St. Petersburg regions.

[13] It should be noted that in only one oblast was the market/state price ratio equal to one, even though about one-third of the oblasts in Russia have no direct price subsidies on food. There are several other reasons why the prices diverge, in addition to subsidization of the state prices. First, even where there are no direct price subsidies, indirect subsidies of the state sector may keep its prices lower. The state sector may be enjoying the benefit of subsidized (price-controlled) inputs such as feed grain, etc. (On the other hand, since many of the inputs to the private sector come legally or illegally from the state sector, the difference may not be that great.) Second, private market prices respond more rapidly to market pressure. At the retail stage, prices in state food stores are still subject to profit ceilings and are based on historical costs of inputs. Free market prices may be changed daily. Finally, it is widely acknowledged that there are quality differences in the food sold in state stores and in the market: the markets sell a higher grade.

Despite all these additional factors, however, if we can assume that they are relatively constant across oblasts, the ratio of free market to state prices remains a valid measure of *relative* price subsidization.

[14] The variable is the mean ratio of free market to state store prices for beef in the capital city of each oblast for four time periods from August to November 1992. The prices were published in the agricultural weekly newspaper, *Krest'yanskiye vedomosti*.

[15] The privatization data used in this analysis are from the Russian State Committee for the Management of State Property (GKI).

[16] There were four questions in all on the referendum ballot:

1) Do you have confidence in the President of the Russian Federation, B. N. Yeltsin?

2) Do you approve of the socio-economic policy carried out by the President of the Russian Federation and the Government of the Russian Federation in 1992?

3) Do you consider it necessary to conduct early elections for President of the Russian Federation?

4)   Do you consider it necessary to conduct early elections for Peoples' Deputies of the Russian Federation?

[17] The political scientist Boris Pugachov, for instance, dramatically played up this danger in his commentary on the referendum, "Urok dlya vlasti" [Lesson for the authorities], in *Rossiskaya gazeta*, May 19, 1993: 2-3. He wrote: "The referendum has revealed a total crisis in the depths of Russian society; ... it has revealed a fall in the authority of the central power and a widening crisis of confidence in its institutions (especially disturbing is the development of this process in the republics)."

[18] Such a map, though incomplete, was published in the *Financial Times* of April 28, 1993 on page 2.

[19] Malei, a former deputy prime minister, was Yeltsin's special adviser on defense conversion issues. He was recently named head of a newly created Interdepartmental Commission on Scientific-Technical Problems of the Defense Industry. His comments on the referendum results were made, among other occasions, in public and private meetings in Washington, D.C., in May 1993.

[20] An alternative to using the direct percentage of the vote as the dependent variable is to use a log-odds transformation. (E.g., the log-odds of a percentage "yes" vote would be ln [(% yes)/ (1 — % yes)].) This ensures that the dependent variable is not limited and prevents a result in which one might predict results more than 100 percent or under 0 percent. When, as in the present case, most observations lie in the range of, say, 20 to 80 percent, there is little practical advantage to using a log-odds transformation. On the other hand, there is a disadvantage in that the interpretation of the coefficient estimates requires several more steps of calculation. I did in fact run all regressions reported in the paper using this alternative specification. The model's fit was only marginally better, and all the qualitative results were the same as those reported here.

[21] Another difference from previous sections is that the results reported here do not include separate regressions with and without Moscow and St. Petersburg. As we saw earlier, there were in several cases major differences when the two metropolises were included or excluded. For the referendum, I actually did run all regressions without Moscow and St. Petersburg, but in no case did their exclusion change the results more than very slightly.

[22] Four of Russia's present republics were promoted to republic status only after the Soviet period. They were earlier autonomous regions within other units—i.e., they did not have the status of "autonomous republics" in the Soviet era. As a result, there is in some cases a problem of lack of separate data. For example, the present-day Republic of Khakassiya was earlier an "autonomous oblast" within Krasnoyarsk kray, and its data were included in that kray. In the present report, Khakassiya is not treated separately but is subsumed under Krasnoyarsk. However, to account for the fact that to the extent that status as a republic matters, Krasnoyarsk, which includes a republic, will be affected, I gave Krasnoyarsk a value for the REPUBLIC variable which is equal to the percentage of eligible voters in Krasnoyarsk which come from Khakassiya (388,000/2,527,000 = .153). The same was done for Krasnodar, Altay, and Stavropol' krays (which included, respectively, what are now the republics of Adygeya, Gorno-Altay, and Karachay-Cherkessiya).

[23] See, for instance, Michael S. Lewis-Beck and Tom W. Rice, *Forecasting Elections,* Washington, D.C.: CQ Press, 1992. Lewis-Beck and Rice point out, however, that this does not mean that individuals "vote with their pocketbooks."

[24] A number of different variants of an income variable were tested. All of them, it is to be

noted, refer only to "official" income—see note 3 above. The one reported in Table 4 is a variable which measures nominal income; that is, income not adjusted for the high (and varying) rates of inflation in Russia. I also used changes in nominal and real income over various periods. All produced the same general results, but it is interesting that the one which performed best was for the nominal income level. The fact that Russians' voting behavior was apparently influenced more by their current nominal income than by the real increase over the past year or several years suggests that this may be at least one area in which the money illusion works in Russia.

[25] To state all of this a bit more formally, let us posit a voting model in which the percentage of "yes" votes for Yeltsin (YES-1) is a function of defense industry employment (VPKTOT) and other variables:

$$\text{YES-1} = f(\text{VPKTOT}, X) + u,$$

where X is a vector of other covariates (urbanization, age, education, income, etc.) and u is a stochastic error, assumed to satisfy

$$E(u\text{-VPKTOT}, X) = 0.$$

Then the fundamental point about the risk of understating the total effect of VPKTOT when it is itself a structural determinant of some of the components of X can be seen by looking at the model above. The total effect of VPKTOT is $df/d\text{VPKTOT}$. Consider how $E(f\text{-VPKTOT}, X)$ varies with VPKTOT:

$$dE(f\text{-VPK}, X)/d\text{VPKTOT} = f_{\text{VPKTOT}} + f_x d X/d\text{VPKTOT}.$$

This equation emphasizes that the total effects of VPKTOT on the vote are not given simply by the partial derivative f_{VPKTOT} that holds all else constant but rather by the total derivative that allows X to vary in response to variations in VPKTOT. Thus, both the direct (f_{VPKTOT}) and indirect ($f_x d X/d\text{VPKTOT}$) channels of influence must be admitted as possibilities if the purpose of the investigation is to determine the overall political effect of defense industry employment.

[26] 1,000 rubles/8,000 votes = 0.125 rubles per vote. 1,000 rubles/17,000 votes = 0.06 rubles per vote.

[27] *Rossiya — 1993: Ekonomicheskaya kon"yunktura,* No. 1 (February, 1993, p. 28).

[28] *Rossiya — 1993: Ekonomicheskaya kon"yunktura,* No. 1 (February, 1993, p. 157).

[29] For more details and background on the Yeltsin government's special attention to Udmurtiya, and its possible role as a pilot project for other regions, see the section in C. Gaddy and Melanie L. Allen, "Russian Arms Sales Abroad: Policy, Practice, and Prospects," *Brookings Discussion Papers,* Brookings Institution, September 1993.

Table 1. Descriptive Statistics for All Variables

Variable	Description	Mean	Standard Deviation	Minimum	Maximum
VPKTOT	Total defense industry employment in 1985 (thousands)	74.19	79.97	0.00	350.00
VPKPCT	Defense industry employment as a fraction of all manufacturing employment in 1985	0.23	0.13	0.00	0.57
INDTOT	Total manufacturing employment in 1985 (thousands)	285.09	234.68	10.78	1,083.09
URBAN	Fraction of population living in urban areas	0.70	0.12	0.42	1.00
INC85	Per capita income in 1985 (rubles/year)	1,749.70	480.46	975	3,711
WAGE85	Average wage in 1985 (rubles/month)	206.35	56.93	146.30	440.40
MEAT85	Per capita meat consumption in 1985 (kg/year)	63.15	10.91	34.00	102.00
WASH84	Washing machines per 100 households in 1984	79.12	8.02	57.00	93.00
VAC84	Vacuum cleaners per 100 households in 1984	58.21	7.28	35.00	80.00
HSG86	Square meters of residential housing per 100 persons in 1986	917	88	650	1,070
BATH86	Number of indoor baths per 100 housing units in 1986	78	9	53	98
HTWTR86	Number of housing units with hot running water per 100 units in 1986	66	15	12	95
DOC85	Physicians per 10,000 population in 1985	41.44	11.65	27.90	104.30
BEDS85	Hospital beds per 10,000 population in 1985	137.38	12.13	104.60	184.50
TURN85*	Number of workers who changed jobs in 1985 per 100 workers	14.05	4.04	7.10	29.40
VOL92	Industrial output for first half of 1992 as a fraction of first half of 1991	0.86	0.06	0.67	0.99
RLPRF92	Change in real (inflation-adjusted) enterprise profits in industry in first half of 1992 as compared to first half of 1991	0.04	0.36	-0.62	0.92
GDS92	Ratio of retail price index on goods in first half of 1992 to same index for first half of 1991	9.03	1.07	6.05	13.15
WAGE92	Average wage in industry in June 1992 (rubles/month)	3,291.86	1,855.30	1,453.00	11,269.00
RLWGEINC	Change in average real wage in industry in first half of 1992	-0.08	0.21	-0.40	0.71
DINC1292	Percentage change in nominal per capita income from January to December 1992	1,170.12	251.57	287.40	2,121.30
HSG92	Housing construction in first half of 1992 as a fraction of first half of 1991	0.65	0.20	0.32	1.22
BFRATE	Ratio of state store price of beef to private market price in November 1992	1.50	0.44	1.00	3.65
POP	Total population (thousands)	1,967	1,482	282	8,678

126

Table 1. Descriptive Statistics for All Variables (cont.)

Variable	Description	Mean	Standard Deviation	Minimum	Maximum
PRVPCT	Fraction of small state enterprises privatized as of January 1993	0.39	0.23	0.006	100.00
TURNOUT	Fraction of eligible voters actually voting in April 1993 referendum	.65	.07	.23	.78
YES-1	Fraction of voters voting "yes" on Question 1 (support for Yeltsin) in April 1993 referendum	0.57	0.12	0.14	0.84
HIGHERED	Fraction of labor force with some post-secondary education	0.29	0.03	0.25	0.42
OLD	Fraction of population over working age	0.18	0.05	0.04	0.26
INC1292	Nominal per capita income in December 1992 (thousands of rubles/month)	9.580	4.043	1.322	24.695
REPUBLIC	Index variable. Equal to 1 for sixteen republics, 0 for ordinary oblasts, and a fraction between 0 and 1 for four krays which contain republics	0.23	0.41	0.00	1.00

*This figure includes only workers who left their jobs on their own initiative or who were fired for violations of labor discipline. It does not include so-called planned turnover, such as men drafted into the armed forces, women on maternity leave, or workers transferred to other jobs by their employers.

Table 2. The Russian Defense Industrial Regions in the Mid-1980s

A. Average Wage (Rubles/Month) in 1985 [WAGE85]

	Including Moscow, St. Petersburg		Provinces Only	
VPKTOT	-0.371		-0.348	
	[4.67]		[3.87]	
VPKPCT		-89.375		-84.406
		[1.85]		[1.75]
URBAN	311.866	192.654	321.854	249.242
	[5.74]	[3.65]	[5.60]	[4.27]
R-square	0.35	0.18	0.35	0.24

B. Per Capita Personal Income (Rubles/Year) in 1985 [INC85]

	Including Moscow, St. Petersburg		Provinces Only	
VPKTOT	-2.209		-2.661	
	[3.42]		[3.92]	
VPKPCT		-553.214		-517.326
		[1.48]		[1.41]
URBAN	2977.583	2269.849	2734.694	2171.98
	[6.74]	[5.56]	[6.32]	[4.89]
R-square	0.39	0.31	0.40	0.28

C. Per Capita Meat Consumption (Kilograms/Year) in 1985 [MEAT85]

	Including Moscow, St. Petersburg		Provinces Only	
VPKTOT	0.045		0.028	
	[3.86]		[2.29]	
VPKPCT		5.84		5.341
		[0.90]		[0.93]
URBAN	10.625	31.091	7.980	17.576
	[1.13]	[3.72]	[0.89]	[2.20]
INC85	0.015	0.013	0.015	0.013
	[7.65]	[6.16]	[7.38]	[6.92]
R-square	0.68	0.62	0.61	0.59

D. Number of Washing Machines Per 100 Households in 1984 [WASH84]

	Including Moscow, St. Petersburg		Provinces Only	
VPKTOT	-0.016		0.017	
	[1.12]		[1.25]	
VPKPCT		-7.774		-5.189
		[1.04]		[0.83]
URBAN	12.717	6.392	15.288	22.716
	[1.07]	[0.66]	[1.53]	[2.60]
INC85	0.002	0.002	0.005	0.003
	[0.67]	[0.99]	[2.00]	[1.45]
R-square	0.06	0.06	0.23	0.22

E. Number of Vacuum Cleaners Per 100 Households in 1984 [VAC84]

	Including Moscow, St. Petersburg		Provinces Only	
VPKTOT	0.002		-0.002	
	[0.21]		[0.16]	
VPKPCT		-8.995		-8.847
		[1.94]		[1.93]
URBAN	22.097	24.943	20.264	21.266
	[2.92]	[4.17]	[2.67]	[3.33]
INC85	0.007	0.007	0.008	0.007
	[4.50]	[4.49]	[4.57]	[4.89]
R-square	0.54	0.56	0.52	0.54

F. Housing Area (Square Meters/100 Population) in 1986 [HSG86]

	Including Moscow, St. Petersburg		Provinces Only	
VPKTOT	0.098		0.056	
	[0.66]		[0.35]	
VPKPCT		-107.110		-123.601
		[1.43]		[1.73]
URBAN	283.147	353.874	299.428	301.084
	[2.35]	[3.66]	[2.54]	[3.02]
INC85	-0.083	-0.095	-0.107	-0.110
	[3.27]	[4.04]	[4.03]	[4.63]
R-square	0.20	0.22	0.23	0.26

G. Baths Per 100 Urban Housing Units in 1986 [BATH86]

	Including Moscow, St. Petersburg		Provinces Only	
VPKTOT	0.041		0.034	
	[2.67]		[1.92]	
VPKPCT		9.475		8.835
		[1.15]		[1.08]
URBAN	16.102	34.221	18.195	29.426
	[1.28]	[3.23]	[1.41]	[2.58]
INC85	-0.002	-0.004	-0.003	-0.005
	[0.81]	[1.67]	[1.17]	[1.97]
R-square	0.23	0.16	0.16	0.13

H. Hot Water Per 100 Urban Housing Units in 1986 [HTWTR86]

	Including Moscow, St. Petersburg		Provinces Only	
VPKTOT	0.042		0.028	
	[1.65]		[0.95]	
VPKPCT		10.972		10.080
		[0.84]		[0.76]
URBAN	33.523	51.547	37.431	45.975
	[1.63]	[3.05]	[1.76]	[2.50]
INC85	-0.005	-0.007	-0.008	-0.008
	[1.15]	[1.72]	[1.59]	[2.06]
R-square	0.16	0.14	0.12	0.12

I. Number of Doctors Per 10,000 Population in 1985 [DOC85]

	Including Moscow, St. Petersburg		Provinces Only	
VPKTOT	0.010		-0.03	
	[0.62]		[2.41]	
VPKPCT		-2.389		-4.923
		[0.26]		[0.77]
URBAN	51.259	55.018	32.869	26.493
	[4.48]	[5.52]	[4.15]	[3.43]
R-square	0.31	0.30	0.22	0.16

J. Number of Hospital Beds Per 10,000 Population in 1985 [BEDS85]

	Including Moscow, St. Petersburg		Provinces Only	
VPKTOT	-0.053		-0.045	
	[2.64]		[2.02]	
VPKPCT		-18.86		-17.640
		[1.69]		[1.57]
URBAN	20.631	4.246	22.132	13.100
	[1.51]	[0.35]	[1.54]	[0.96]
R-square	0.09	0.04	0.07	0.05

K. Employee Turnover in Industry (Percent/Year) in 1985 [TURN]

	Including Moscow, St. Petersburg		Provinces Only	
VPKTOT	-0.007		-0.008	
	[1.14]		[1.20]	
VPKPCT		-7.787		-8.046
		[2.59]		[2.63]
URBAN	-17.133	-18.663	-18.114	-19.321
	[4.37]	[5.70]	[4.42]	[5.23]
R-square	0.33	0.37	0.30	0.35

Note: N=73 for columns 1 and 2 of each panel and N=69 for columns 3 and 4, which omit the observations for the cities of Moscow and St. Petersburg and Moscow and Leningrad oblasts. Absolute values of t-statistics are shown in brackets. Each equation also contains an intercept.

Table 3. The Russian Defense Industrial Regions: Performance and Policies in 1992

A. Industrial Output, First Half 1992 as Percentage of First Half 1991 [VOL92]

	Including Moscow, St. Petersburg		Provinces Only	
VPKTOT	0.000		0.000	
	[0.68]		[0.08]	
VPKPCT		-0.079		-0.043
		[1.35]		[0.77]
URBAN	0.107	0.080	0.148	0.153
	[1.49]	[1.21]	[2.03]	[2.24]
R-square	0.03	0.05	0.07	0.08

B. Percent Change in Real Profits in Industry, First Half of 1992 [RLPRF92]

	Including Moscow, St. Petersburg		Provinces Only	
VPKTOT	0.000		0.001	
	[0.16]		[0.94]	
VPKPCT		-0.251		-0.382
		[0.70]		[1.13]
URBAN	-0.275	-0.155	-0.123	0.045
	[0.65]	[0.38]	[0.28]	[0.11]
R-square	0.01	0.01	0.01	0.02

C. Retail Inflation, First Half of 1992 [GDS92]

	Including Moscow, St. Petersburg		Provinces Only	
VPKTOT	0.000		0.000	
	[0.03]		[0.35]	
VPKPCT		0.842		0.711
		[0.83]		[0.74]
URBAN	3.027	1.852	3.358	3.467
	[2.55]	[1.63]	[2.69]	[2.97]
R-square	0.11	0.06	0.12	0.13

D. Nominal Wage in Industry (Rubles/Month), June 1992 [WAGE92]

	Including Moscow, St. Petersburg		Provinces Only	
VPKTOT	-11.954		-10.913	
	[4.54]		[3.60]	
VPKPCT		-4817.970		-3648.656
		[2.99]		[2.31]
URBAN	9151.435	4436.339	9584.127	7373.810
	[4.99]	[2.45]	[4.95]	[3.86]
R-square	0.30	0.18	0.30	0.23

E. Percent Change in Real Wages in Industry, First Half of 1992 [RLWGEINC]

	Including Moscow, St. Petersburg		Provinces Only	
VPKTOT	-0.001		-0.001	
	[3.57]		[2.71]	
VPKPCT		-0.817		-0.719
		[4.20]		[4.09]
URBAN	0.541	0.313	0.606	0.423
	[2.37]	[1.43]	[2.51]	[1.99]
R-square	0.16	0.24	0.13	0.23

F. Percent Change in Per Capita Nominal Income, January to December 1992 [DINC1292]

	Including Moscow, St. Petersburg		Provinces Only	
VPKTOT	-0.681		-0.054	
	[1.73]		[0.13]	
VPKPCT		-237.114		-49.075
		[1.04]		[0.25]
URBAN	1055.069	615.181	1254.120	1245.250
	[3.92]	[2.41]	[4.87]	[5.15]
R-square	0.18	0.10	0.29	0.29

133

G. Housing Construction, January to June 1992 as Percent of January to June 1991 [HSG92]

	Including Moscow, St. Petersburg		Provinces Only	
VPKTOT	0.001		0.001	
	[3.04]		[3.94]	
VPKPCT		0.507		0.503
		[2.69]		[2.94]
RLPRF92	0.038	0.043	0.002	0.054
	[0.64]	[0.64]	[0.03]	[0.87]
URBAN	0.287	0.535	0.412	0.670
	[1.37]	[2.54]	[1.97]	[3.27]
R-square	0.23	0.20	0.27	0.24

H. Ratio of State to Private Market Price of Beef, November 1992 [BFRATE]

	Including Moscow, St. Petersburg		Provinces Only	
VPKTOT	-0.002		-0.001	
	[2.23]		[1.23]	
VPKPCT		-0.899		-0.486
		[2.13]		[1.30]
RLWGEINC	-0.501	-0.480	-0.102	-0.099
	[2.01]	[1.94]	[0.44]	[0.44]
URBAN	1.52	1.156	0.837	0.668
	[3.06]	[2.54]	[1.85]	[1.62]
POP85	0.018	0.001	0.000	0.000
R-square	0.30	0.30	0.06	0.06

I. Percentage of Enterprises Privatized as of January 1993 [PRVPCT]

	Including Moscow, St. Petersburg		Provinces Only	
VPKTOT	0.049		0.058	
	[1.28]		[1.39]	
VPKPCT		21.274		24.243
		[1.10]		[1.17]
URBAN	-58.219	-38.062	-58.269	-45.499
	[2.21]	[1.60]	[2.13]	[1.76]
R-square	0.07	0.05	0.07	0.07

Note: N=73 for columns 1 and 2 of each panel and N=69 for columns 3 and 4, which omit the observations for the cities of Moscow and St. Petersburg and Moscow and Leningrad oblasts, for all panels except Panel I (privatization). For Panel I N=69 observations for columns 1 and 2 and N=67 for columns 3 and 4. Absolute values of t-statistics are shown in brackets. Each equation also contains an intercept.

135

Table 4. The Determinants of Oblast-Level Votes for Yeltsin

Independent Variable	Model 1	Model 2	Model 3	Model 4	Model 5
VPKTOT	0.00026	0.00025	0.00025	0.00041	0.00062
	(1.64)	(1.63)	(0.89)	(1.34)	(4.35)
INDTOT	—	—	0.00000	0.00007	—
			(0.01)	(0.78)	
URBAN	0.4834	0.4948	0.4944	—	—
	(3.18)	(3.47)	(3.36)		
HIGHERED	0.1470	0.1328	0.1333	—	—
	(0.32)	(0.29)	(0.29)		
OLD	-0.2887	-0.2605	-0.2614	-0.1634	-0.0975
	(0.98)	(0.98)	(0.94)	(0.55)	(0.34)
INC1292	0.0077	0.0078	0.0078	0.0157	0.0165
	(1.99)	(2.10)	(2.06)	(4.31)	(4.75)
REPUBLIC	-0.0068	—	—	—	—
	(0.23)				
R-square	0.57	0.57	0.57	0.45	0.45

Notes: Absolute values of t-scores are reported in parentheses. Each column reports the results of an ordinary least squares (OLS) regression where the dependent variable is the percentage of "yes" votes on Question 1 (support for Yeltsin) in the April 25 referendum. Each equation also contains an intercept.

The coefficient estimates may be used to calculate how the pro-Yeltsin vote would be expected to vary as the values of the independent variables change. For example, the estimate for VPKTOT is the model's prediction of how many percentage points difference in the pro-Yeltsin vote there would be between two otherwise similar oblasts in which one has more defense employees than the other. Thus, model 5 says that for each additional 1,000 defense employees, the pro-Yeltsin vote would be expected to be 0.062 percentage points higher.

8

Conversion of Russian Defense Industries: A Macroeconomic and Regional Perspective

Jacques Sapir

This paper is a study of the conversion process in Russia from both a macroeconomic and a regional point of view, in the context of the global economic reshaping of Russia. Specifically, it addresses how to devise a true stabilization policy and what might be a sensible economic policy for the next five to ten years.

Part 1 focuses upon the nature and problems of conversion and its macroeconomic implications. After defining the size and specifics of conversion in Russia, the paper investigates the nature of capital needs; the problem of recoupment time is discussed. A discussion follows of the relationship between the conversion process and macroeconomic policies from both supply and demand sides.

Part 2 addresses the problem Russia faces of regional economic disintegration, first recalling economic trends toward regional segmentation predating the transition process and the effect of the first six months of 1992 upon this segmentation. This section then investigates the relation between the relatively high share of the military-industrial complex in industrial production and the process of regional economic differentiation, and proceeds to analyze the regional nature of Russian inflation and conversion.

Part 3 explores ways out of the current situation. Conversion and stabilization can be made compatible; the nature of the economic policy required to accomplish this is analyzed, as well as the kind of Western assistance that would be most effective in this process.

Jacques Sapir is an assistant professor at the Centre d'Études des Modes d'Industrialisation, École des Hautes Études en Sciences Sociales, Paris.

I. Conversion Problems and Macroeconomic Implications

When Soviet or Russian conversion is discussed, it is frequently forgotten that conversion was not invented by Gorbachev. As a matter of fact, the Soviet government launched a program of conversion in the early to mid-sixties. Some plants producing outdated products (like airplane engines of late thirties technology) were transformed to produce civilian products. Western assistance was sought and obtained. It is thus extremely important to put the current process in its actual context.

An Institutional and Historical Perspective on Conversion

What we might call the military-industrial sector of the former Soviet economy consisted of three concentric circles.[1] The first circle consisted of ministries and the State Committee for Defense Industry. By 1988, there were eight ministries and the State Committee for the Dissemination of Technical Information. The second circle consisted of ministries with activities that were closely related to defense needs, such as atomic energy or civil aviation. The third circle was the factories supplying the first two circles.

This whole structure was under the control of the Military-Industrial Committee or VPK. A measure of control was also exercised by the military committee of Gosplan, and by an ad hoc department of the Central Committee of the Communist Party of the Soviet Union (CPSU). Hereafter the VPK sector will be used as a measure of the military-industrial sector.

Approximately 22 million people were employed by the Soviet Union VPK sector, and 7.6 million by the MOOP. This does not mean that every employee was committed to the production of weapons.[2] A large proportion of these workers were employed in civilian production. One can estimate the actual number of workers engaged in direct military production at between 4.7 and 5 million.[3] Many consumer goods (e.g., consumer electronics and appliances) were completely or largely produced by the VPK sector.[4] More basic products, however, including 8 percent of steel production, 26 percent of numerically controlled machine tools, and 15 percent of agricultural tractors were also produced under the VPK aegis.[5]

By the end of the eighties Russia comprised 72.5 percent of VPK-related employment, and 73 percent of defense enterprises. This ratio was higher for the aerospace industry (86 percent) and ground forces weaponry production; and was distinctly lower for shipbuilding and electronics, which were concentrated in the Baltic states and Byelorussia.[6]

This distribution was affected but not significantly changed by the disintegration of the Soviet Union. When the USSR finally collapsed, it was clear that some parts of the VPK sector had been moved to Russia. However, the other newly independent states still controlled a portion of this sector.[7] The Russian government was able to reach agreement with Central Asian countries and Belarus. To some extent, we can view the current Russian VPK sector as a kind of multinational complex, as some design and engineering facilities located in Russia are still linked to production plants in Uzbekistan and Kazakhstan.[8] This new situation is obviously very important; as the CIS is stillborn, the conversion process will be linked to bilateral political agreements where the Russian influence will be quite important.

The Soviet military-industrial sector has frequently been viewed by the West as the most favored economic sector of the country, since the VPK received the lion's share of investment and skilled people. However, the very size of this sector made it futile to attempt to isolate it from the rest of the economy.[9] To a large extent, this sector was not immune to the problems of the Soviet economy, which was not a command system in its purest form but a combination of priorities and bargaining, with shortages and overinvestment that entailed some deep microeconomic consequences.[10] The sector generated a specific technological culture,[11] i.e. a particular way of solving technical problems and a specific form of innovation. This led to a "style,"[12] both in management and in actual products. All attempts to create a structure responsive to the customer through a system of military supervisors inside enterprises failed; the system was unable to ensure the Soviet military establishment the level of quality it desired.[13]

In 1966, the Soviet government launched a program to convert some outdated military plants to civilian production in Ufa and Izhevsk. Agreements were reached with some foreign companies like Liebherr, ZF, and the French state-owned group Renault. The latter company was in charge of the complete retooling of Izhmash in Izhevsk (Udmurtia), to make it a producer of automobiles (the Moskvich 412). This was as much a diversification process as a conversion process and involved an extended network of French and German subcontractors. As a result, in the seventies, Izhmash became one of the Soviet Union's main automobile production plants.[14]

Thus some experience of conversion was already at hand. It may be argued, however, that the economic and institutional context then was very different from the current one. While some specific points (mainly how to optimize lateral technology transfers) are probably still relevant, conversion dynamics are now significantly different than in the sixties and seventies.

The New Conversion Process

What was in the sixties the result of a policy implemented through the usual channels of the Soviet economy is now a painful process of reaction and adaptation to three different shocks.

First, the VPK sector has had to adapt to tremendous demand shock. Since 1989, the defense budget has been severely curtailed, with a particular budget crunch in the last months of 1991 and in 1992. The attempt to reduce the budget deficit was, of course, extremely important in this process. Defense expenditures were estimated at between 16 and 17 percent of the state budget during the eighties, falling to 15.8 percent in 1988 and 14.5 percent in 1990.[15] By the end of 1991, Russia had to cope with both a budget deficit of around 20 percent of the GNP and the disintegration of the Soviet Union, leaving a much reduced fiscal base and, of course, much reduced military needs. The crunch was then unavoidable; cuts across the board were much more extensive than previously planned or implemented. They induced a bigger shock than anticipated for the defense industry, as operation and maintenance could not be curtailed on the same level as other items. Another problem was the cost of repositioning forces leaving Eastern Europe, and later, the CIS countries. Procurements and R&D were dramatically reduced to such an extent that a total collapse of the military-related industrial base was feared. In reality, things eased by the second half of 1992. Nonetheless, procurements and R&D have been reduced by a factor of 70 percent and 35 percent respectively.

139

Table 1. Expenditures for the different branches of the Soviet armed forces as a percentage of expenditures in 1988.

	1989	1990	1991
Ground forces	84%	76%	62%
Tactical air forces	86%	70%	55%
Navy, tactical	102%	91%	72%
Strategic offensive forces	86%	85%	65%
Strategic defensive forces	98%	96%	95%
Space	68%	66%	51%
Total	89%	81%	68%

Sources: Unattributed document of the Defense Intelligence Agency, "Moscow's Defense Spending Cuts Accelerate," Washington, June 1992, and "Statement for the Record of Ms. Kathleen Horste, Special Assistant for Russia/Eurasia, Defense Intelligence Agency, to the Joint Economic Committee of the U.S. Congress," June 8, 1992.

The second shock was a supply shock. The wholesale price liberalization of January 1992 destroyed at once all price references for enterprises without enabling a new coherent price structure to emerge in the vertical industrial chain. A process of bargaining began in which the size of mobilization stocks was an important factor as well as the non- or low-divisible and non- or low-substitutable nature of some industrial goods. Supply links were interrupted and relative prices fluctuated widely, preventing plant managers from beginning internal restructuring. In addition, wholesale prices were largely driven by energy prices;[16] wholesale price inflation was not directly induced by monetary aggregates but was closely linked to a cost-push movement generated by highly rigid microeconomic production functions.[17]

This situation was aggravated further by the near collapse of the internal payment system.[18] Part of the huge interenterprise debt was due to payment lags; but they created a true insolvency problem and some enterprises had to delay payments as they were waiting for their own money. By the second half of 1992, two answers emerged. The first one was simply a return to barter or quasi-barter trade, grounded on 1984 relative prices. By the end of 1992, it was estimated that 40 percent of interenterprise trade was under barter conditions.[19] This situation was predominant in the VPK sector, where old links were rebuilt. Nonetheless, it impaired to a considerable extent diversification of suppliers or clients and the conversion process itself.

The second answer was the implementation of a "cash in advance" system for intraregional trade.[20] This further intensified the trend toward barter, and induced some enterprises to internalize production that had previously been subcontracted.

To some extent the collapse of the Union had comparable effects. Payments were severely affected, supply links interrupted, and barter flourished. Here again, former VPK links were crucial in assisting the rebuilding of trade, mainly on a barter basis. However, there was also a trend to "Russianize" some products, particularly when Ukrainian or Baltic subcontractors had been involved. Links with enterprises in Belarus, Kazakhstan, and Uzbekistan seem to have survived.

The third shock was an institutional one, following the dissolution of the traditional production ministry apparatus and of the VPK itself by 1992. Some parts of industry that reported to the VPK previously were handed over to the Ministry of the Economy. At the same time, the Ministry of Defense tried to retain some control through committees answering directly to deputy minister Andrei Kokoshin. The previously close-knit network disintegrated, although close relationships between enterprise managers and defense ministry officials still operate informally. Uncertainties in the political sphere and concerning some aspects of the reform process (mainly privatization) have created a high-risk environment both for enterprise managers and for foreign investors. The old Soviet system was largely characterized by a complementary ensemble of formal and informal rules. Its disintegration has cast doubts not only upon the formal level, but also upon the nature of the mix between formal and informal rules. Since 1991–1992, there has been a clear move back to close institutional links at the regional and local level. Although this created some local pockets of stable information, it also generated a trend of extreme regionalization of both the economy and the decision process. Decision-implementing was always quite regionalized in the Former Soviet Union.[21] By the summer of 1992, decision-making became regionalized.

Since it was not coordinated at a national level, the creation of these pockets of largely institutional stability has produced more uncertainties and generated much greater inefficiencies in economic and institutional information-gathering. The use of bilateral links, both between the enterprises themselves and between enterprises and local authorities, became systematic by 1992.[22] This obviously helped to stabilize the economic situation, but at a cost. By the end of 1992, the Russian economy was more and more a type of "cellular economy."[23]

The very factors that made conversion both urgent and mandatory were impeding its implementation to a greater extent than forecasted (see Figure 1). It is beyond doubt that the VPK sector suffered less than the civilian economy during 1992.[24] Direct armament production was badly hit, but it was just a portion of this sector. What's more, the very nature of the VPK system enabled bilateral links and informal networks to be built or reactivated much more quickly than in the rest of the economy. Nevertheless the combination of these three shocks has slowed the conversion process.

Conversion and Restructuring

Different paths for conversion and restructuring were possible, each with its own constraints. The easiest way to achieve conversion is to make use of civilian production technologies and facilities. This is generally aided by previous experience in civilian production and, of course, by the existence of strong demand. Such a process can be quick, requiring very little new investment (at least in the short term), and is then compatible with decentralized financing.

Figure 1

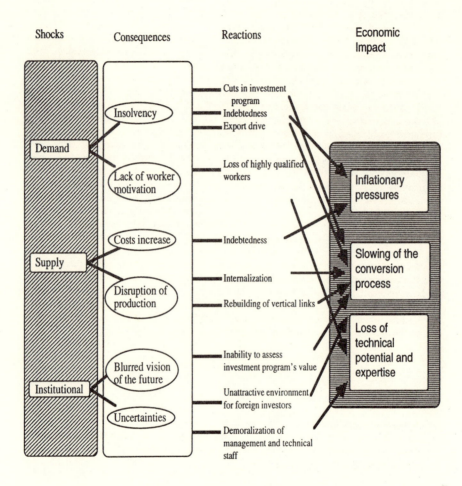

When direct conversion is not possible, diversification can be achieved. Relying on civilian-related technologies, experience in civilian production, and expectations of a good market, enterprises can first try to diversify and then switch completely to new products. However, they will need to retool and retrain part of the workforce, which takes considerable time and financing. Retooling means heavy investment, and retraining is costly too. Before diversification can become effective, the day-to-day life of the enterprise must be financed. The crude approach of temporarily closing down and laying off employees cannot work unless unemployment benefits are provided.

Nevertheless, closing down may be the only solution if technologies at hand are too narrowly specialized and future market expectations are only fair to poor. But since military plants are generally quite large, this could raise serious regional unemployment problems. It would then probably be necessary not only to pay unemployment benefits but also to implement regional economic assistance by launching a massive retraining program, developing infrastructures to attract new activities, and providing plants with tax breaks.

These three different paths highlight different problems related to industrial restructuring. The most obvious, but not necessarily the most important, problem is the overstaffing of a majority of enterprises. This situation has not been generated by any political bias. It was induced either by an excess in final demand for some goods or by substitution of labor for capital in an attempt to gain flexibility in a shortage-prone environment.

This environment has also led to an internalization process. Enterprises have long favored reducing dependence upon external supplies as far as possible. It was of course impossible to achieve complete autarchy. Nonetheless, former Soviet enterprises have developed many industrial activities peripheral to their main production. These activities, if unable to protect the enterprise against an absolute shortage (as demonstrated during the first half of 1992 when supplies were sometimes interrupted), have at least enabled them to manage lags and relative shortage situations. They are the productive equivalent of hoarding stocks, and are also detrimental to efficient operation, as opposed to effective operation.

The shortage-prone environment, combined with internalization, gave birth to a specific technological culture. Soviet enterprises, particularly in the VPK sector, have been innovative. But innovation was focused on gaining more productive flexibility, reducing the impact of low-quality supplies, and making good use of extant capacities. It was production-driven innovation, not market-driven innovation.

A fourth problem lies in the social responsibilities assumed by Soviet enterprises. This can be thought of as the social equivalent of production internalization. Large enterprises were, and still are, relatively self-sufficient social systems. Not only does this burden their operation costs but it means that closing down would deprive workers not only of their wages but also of a considerable range of social benefits. Thus, there is a strong incentive to keep enterprises running.

Ownership is also a serious problem, because the quick degradation of state legitimacy and the confusion surrounding the privatization process (including various unconventional schemes of ownership) are weakening the principal/agent relationship.

For all of these reasons, conversion will be costly. Retooling, retraining programs, and infrastructure development all need financing, as do unemployment benefits and the transfer of social welfare facilities from enterprise ownership, which are absolute preconditions for labor market flexibility.

This creates a contradiction between macroeconomic stabilization and financing conversion. The more the conversion process is delayed, the more subsidies burden the state budget. But to speed up conversion, we have to alleviate the supply shock and find ways to raise the needed capital. These two goals are inconsistent with a "shock therapy" approach to stabilization.

The potential conflict is between enterprises and public authorities competing for the available capital. It is not linked to ownership. Private or state-owned, enterprises will need to raise capital for retooling and diversification. But infrastructure development and transfer of the social support system from enterprises to the public sector will lead to a considerable demand for capital from public authorities.

Financing Conversion

The most important problem, then, is how to finance the conversion process, and particularly how to finance it quickly to reduce macroeconomic destabilizing pressures and political horse-trading. Internal savings will not provide a complete answer. Neither income distribution nor political uncertainties favor a rapid expansion of savings. It has been argued that the 1991-92 depression has induced only a relative decrease in per capita income, more or less to the 1985 level.[25] However, these figures completely underestimate the new distribution pattern generated by the Russian economic policy.

By April 1993, it was apparent that a great majority of the population of the Russian Federation was living under the average income level, which was greatly skewed by a small group of around two million people with more than 27 percent of income. What this distribution means is that there is no longer a middle-income class in Russia. The consequence for the formation of savings is obvious. Given the ownership situation in Russia, if such a small group accounts for such a large share of income, this could only be explained by massive profits earned in speculation. It is well known that such speculators are not likely to save or invest in highly uncertain situations. They usually prefer to use their wealth in conspicuous spending, or to protect it in foreign banks or in gold.

The rest of the population is probably too impoverished to provide an adequate savings base. Official data suggest that in many regions per capita income exceeds per capita expenditures by a wide margin. Such a conclusion may not take into account regional rationing or the effects of other local price control mechanisms. Actual savings, therefore, are probably considerably lower than these data suggest.

A strong middle class is a prerequisite for a large savings ratio, but the trend is toward elimination of the middle class. Income policy could be an important part of any policy aimed at generating investment capital.

Foreign investments are another potential solution. Such investment is inhibited by the understandable political reluctance of the Russian government to open up the assets of some very sensitive enterprises, and by the reluctance of investors due to legal and political uncertainties prevailing in Russia.

Even if these problems could be solved in the near future, two other factors would limit foreign investment in the Russian defense sector. The first is the size of the economic crisis in the wealthier market economies (West Germany, Japan). The ability of these countries to invest is limited by their own need for investment and their significant investment programs in other countries. The second factor is that other sectors of the Russian economy offer faster returns on investment and will therefore attract the lion's share of foreign investment.

An export drive could provide some funds. It is apparent that such a policy has been chosen by the Russian government, which has tried everything to expand exports of arms, other industrial products, and non-finished goods. But here again problems are quite significant. Major arms deals could be embarrassing for Western governments. Even putting political considerations aside, countries such as the United States, Great Britain, and France

Figure 2. Per capita income distribution in rubles as of April 1993

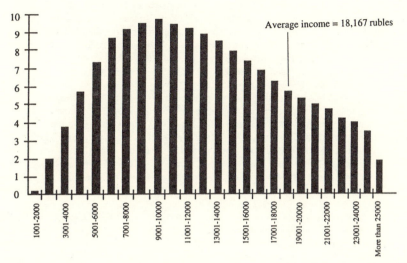

Source: Goskomstat Rossii, *O Razvitii Ekonomicheskikh Reform v Rossiiskoi Federatsii (yanvar'-mai 1993 goda)*, 1993, Moscow.

Figure 3. Russian per capita income as of April 1993

Gini's curve

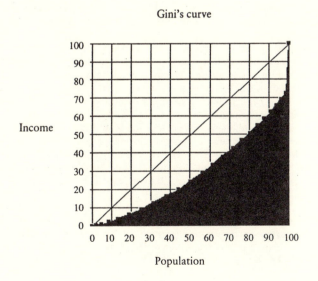

are also facing a demand crunch induced by defense budget reductions and are competing fiercely on foreign markets. The Russian argument that part of the U.S. anti-proliferation rhetoric is no more than a kind of protectionism cannot be completely denied.

Arms sales are not the only problem. The VPK sector has strong export capacity in industrial raw and semi-raw materials. A major Russian export drive could destabilize world markets as was the case in the aluminum market. Since Western economies will be depressed for the next two or three years, Russian export potential is bleak.

It may seem like a good idea, in the abstract, to boost some exports, such as oil, gas, and raw materials, and use the revenues to reconstruct a decaying industry, but this strategy will run into serious practical problems. Some raw material markets are already severely depressed. Intra-OPEC competition does not bode well for oil and gas, not to mention the fact that Russian extraction conditions lead to higher prices and great investment needs. An export strategy would make sense only if G24 economies were on a fast-growth track for the next decade or more. The Russian population is not at the same standard of living as in some OPEC countries. If, to achieve such an export strategy, industry has to be savaged, then demand for imported consumer goods would strongly conflict with demand for imported capital goods. One of the painful lessons of the last twenty years is that such a situation would lead nowhere but to an economic and social crisis.

Internal savings and foreign investments would be the best solution, but it is doubtful that they will provide enough funds to speed up the current rate of conversion. The problem will probably be more how to sustain this pace for the next five or ten years, and to avoid slowing down or even a partial reversal.

Channeling available funds toward conversion will raise the problem of time until return on investment. The more uncertain the environment the more investors will seek a rapid return. This could significantly reduce the availability of capital as industrial diversification will certainly not lead to early profits. We have here the second potential conflict, linked to the relative time scales of investors' criteria and of industrial restructuring.

Efficient and well-developed equity and financial markets, which will take considerable time to establish in Russia, could soften this conflict to some extent, but they cannot make it disappear.

Two issues then arise. First, it is not obvious that conversion in a troubled and uncertain transition environment is compatible with decentralized financing. Decentralized finance involves the ability of any agent to accumulate enough income above operating capital requirements to fund expansion. Centralized finance through governmental subsidies could take two different forms: stock markets and institutional intermediation through a highly concentrated banking sector, closely linked with the Central Bank.

Financial and stock markets could theoretically collect and centralize savings on a mass scale, enabling enterprises to find easy sources of capital for expansion. Simultaneously, they could provide for enterprise guidance through the very movement of stock value. Such a role requires a very stable institutional environment, however, combined with extremely experienced operators and a good degree of prudent control. If these preconditions cannot be met, speculative markets could be destabilizing.

Institutional intermediation between capital supply and demand could mitigate the problem of recoupment time much more efficiently than emerging and highly unstable financial markets. There is a strong argument here favoring the development in Russia of a kind of overdraft (or bank credit) economy, according to the Japanese, German, or French pattern, and not of a financial market economy as in Great Britain and the United States. But institutional intermediation cannot be a complete substitute for decentralized financing. The second question is then how to provide enough incentive to attract capital to finance conversion.

The Limits of the Supply-Side Approach to Conversion, and the Merits of the Demand-Side Approach

It could be argued that it is meaningless to devote much attention to conversion. After all, we could hope that with true price signals, competition, and private ownership, the market economy will do the job. The notorious failure of the planned approach of conversion doesn't speak well for any particular economic policy. There is a strong argument that price liberalization combined with trade liberalization will make domestic relative prices approach world relative prices, which will stimulate competition; this process, it is argued, is more than enough to achieve restructuring and then conversion.

It could even be argued that since the "cash in advance" system burdens the buyer's side with a new uncertainty (of whether the paid-for supplies will be delivered as contracted) it could create more or less the same effect as shortages as far as enterprises are concerned.

Actual economies differ from a theoretically perfect world. If some imperfections are institutionally generated, others result from the very nature of industrial activities. Even modern macroeconomic approaches are grounded on simplistic assumptions of divisibility and substitutability. Modern microeconomics has cast doubt on these assumptions as well.

It must be acknowledged that hoping for such a large industrial sector as the VPK to switch to civilian production, when internal demand is greatly depressed, is a contradiction in terms. Boosting internal demand will minimize export drive, allow enterprises to think long-term, and allow for quick profits.

Say's law, the assumption that supply will create its own demand, does not take into account that supply restructuring and adjustments are not necessarily on the same time scale as demand evolutions. The most important problem obviously lies in the speed of the supply-side adjustment to new constraints.

If the economy consisted primarily of small and medium manufacturing enterprises working with a low capital intensity and producing short-cycle products, as in the late eighteenth and early nineteenth centuries, such a vision of nearly instantaneous adjustment would not be wrong. Even if enterprises were unable to adapt, it would be fairly simple for entrepreneurs to raise capital to create new enterprises to take advantage of opportunities. In that case, the Hayek-Schumpeter paradigm of free economy and creative destruction could be amply justified.

The situation is quite different, however, when production is done by large enterprises, which should be understood as organizations with specific forms of rationality. In this situation new constraints are felt by rises in prices and costs, and adjustment implies partial or total reconstruction of the enterprise's technological basis. Closing down creates its own problems. More often than not it does not really free labor and capital, as workers will need retraining and machine tools cannot easily be applied to new productive uses. Massive unemployment, created by closing down large enterprises, also generates a local depression effect, which is not an incentive for the creation of new enterprises. Labor mobility could in part offset this problem, but it would require cheap and readily available housing and social welfare facilities not linked to the enterprise or local authorities. Any such linkage will

147

restrict this mobility. Adapting to new constraints will mean raising capital on a much larger scale than before. Supply-side flexibility in this context is equivalent to the availability of large investments.

However, in an economy strongly biased toward large enterprises, where capital is scarce, supply-side rigidity would foil any attempt to restructure using relative-price constraints. The time lag between price changes and production changes would prevent relative prices from efficiently doing their job. This has been amply demonstrated by the Cobweb theorem. The Cobweb is a clear alternative to a Keynesian approach to price rigidities.[26] It implies the necessity of a flexible microeconomic approach. Free relative prices do not lead to equilibrium. Worse, they could lead to a complete collapse of production, or generate such severe bottlenecks that restructuring would be impossible, and trap the economy in a downward spiral.

At best, enterprises would be able to implement the necessary restructuring, but they would have to accumulate huge debts to finance that restructuring as well as their day-to-day operation before the process would be fruitful. Interest on this debt would destroy their profitability. We would then be brought back to the worst-case situation. Debt consolidation or subsidies for enterprises during restructuring might be solutions, but neither of these alternatives would help macroeconomic stabilization, because either the banking sector would be heavily burdened by bad loans, or the budget deficit would be significantly increased.

The bottom line is that in a fully industrialized system dominated by large and mainly internalized enterprises, capital is required to accelerate adjustment. If money is readily available, quick adjustment strategies can be chosen; if not, adjustment has to be spread over a long period.

If we look to different implications of large industrial plant operation, other problems arise. The so-called "Big Bang" approach to transition was grounded on the assumption that relative prices were the main tool to achieve industrial restructuring. [27] The sequence of price liberalization-privatization-restructuring was justified by this assumption, which implied that it would foolish to attempt any restructuring before achieving "true" relative prices. This line of reasoning implicitly views prices as efficient vectors of the information needed for supply-side adjustment, independent of the microeconomic consequences of shortage intensities.

It is doubtful, however, that prices are capturing all the information needed in interenterprise trade. This problem is obviously much more important when technological culture is more strongly biased toward internalization than in Western economies. In such a situation it is quite doubtful that free relative prices could lead to an efficient equilibrium, even where markets are complete.[28]

Furthermore, the information conveyed by prices is not always clear. Enterprises, or networks of closely related enterprises, are better understood as organizations where knowledge is collective and channeled through informal means.[29] Destruction of the organization, either by closing down enterprises or destroying networks, does not free information: each sector of the organization owns just a part of the total, which is without meaning unless all parts are brought together. In fact this brings up an interesting paradox. If all information and knowledge could be explicit, which is a basic assumption of the "Big Bang" approach, one cannot understand why central planning did not work, because in this situation planning is more efficient than markets. If part of the information and knowledge is implicit, as suggested by Hayek, then planning is inefficient. But if uncertainty extends to the very framework of economic activity (which is undoubtedly the situation during the transition), then market iteration is even less efficient.[30]

There are some very strong theoretical arguments for the view that the supply-side approach to industrial restructuring that has been implicitly or explicitly the basis of "Big Bang" or "shock therapy" strategies is not well-founded. The relevance of this result for conversion is obvious.

Not only is a stable and dynamic internal market an absolute precondition for large-scale conversion, but supply adjustment cannot be achieved by market means alone. Some form of coordination between demand and supply policies has to be achieved.

A New Macroeconomic Agenda?

It is undeniable that the macroeconomic context has given considerable urgency to conversion and at the same time created a very unfavorable context for it. On the other hand, any delay of conversion will exacerbate macroeconomic destabilizing pressures. Conversion, and the industrial restructuring it entails, is an integral part of any stabilization program. A microeconomic approach to this process shows that many common assumptions concerning transition and stabilization in Russia are unsound. Likewise, it highlights the necessity of combining supply-side restructuring with demand enhancement.

Financing conversion will be one of the most difficult problems to solve. With financial markets in their very infancy, relying on decentralized financing for restructuring and credit restriction for stabilization can lead only to a bigger depression with very strong internal pressures for a major export drive, not to mention nasty political implications.[31] Some type of institutional intermediation system that could be patterned upon post-war Japanese or French experiences is clearly needed. At the same time, public expenditures have to be maintained to assure the development of social and technical infrastructures to counteract the trend toward internalization, and capital must be raised for retooling and diversification.

This situation requires a resolute break with the approaches to macroeconomic policy and institution-building that have been dominant in Russian government circles. As a matter of fact, there is one good argument supporting the Big Bang approach: Russia did not have the administration needed to implement a gradual transition. The so-called shock therapy, in other words, was no more than a survival strategy that had to be implemented to allow the government enough time to reorganize.

If this is true, one may wonder if, by setting clearly unreachable targets (e.g., a fast reduction of the budget deficit and ruble stabilization), this strategy was not undermining its main goal by destroying government credibility. Reputation is never built by Stalinist slogans such as "There is no fortress the Bolsheviks can't storm."[32] Reputation is built by results, and results are obtained not only through sound decisions but through sound implementation.[33] Gradualism might have been extremely difficult to implement, but by setting realistic goals and establishing legitimacy it could have been a dynamically self-improving process. The Big Bang approach has led only to social and political confrontation, and further weakening of central government authority and legitimacy. This last problem is certainly the most important one and therefore the next part of this paper is devoted to the economic disintegration process.

II. Conversion Problems and the Process of Economic Disintegration

Setting the Scene

As discussed above, conversion has a distinct regional impact. In general, enterprises related to the VPK sector are large and concentrated in certain regions. Recall that "region" can mean either one of the very large "economic regions" (such as the North, the Northwest or the Urals), or one of the 88 administrative regions ("oblasts") of Russia. Hereafter the former will be called zones, and the latter, regions.

Regions were always an important part of the Soviet structure. Behind a formal centralized system was one that was quite decentralized, where regional authorities had some decision-implementing power.[34] This resulted mainly from the very nature of Soviet planning; it was generated by informal links between local administrative authorities, large enterprise managers, and even local military commanders,[35] links that were an absolute necessity in managing resource allocation in a shortage-prone environment.[36]

The economic crisis has accentuated the relevance of these links. Each step toward the disintegration of the Soviet system was also a step toward the strengthening of these links. By 1990 or 1991, economic segmentation, which has been quite obvious between the former Soviet republics, also became a problem for regions. Prices, incomes, and the intensity of shortages frequently fluctuate wildly from one region to another.[37]

Yeltsin initially advocated regional autonomy in order to undermine Gorbachev's power. After the failed 1991 putsch he tried to implement a new administrative system with governors and presidential representatives.[38] The continuous degradation of the economic situation, however, prevented any administrative stabilization. Former regional bosses were still quite active and frequently powerful since the power bases—the abilities to control and allocate resources—were unchanged. At the same time, regions tried to unite themselves in new associations usually on a broader basis than the old economic zones.

The reforms of 1992 led to a new level in regional segmentation. The confusion induced by price liberalization prompted a return to bilateral links between enterprises and an increased reliance on economic cooperation on a local basis. The ill-fated attempt at credit control provided regions with good arguments to claim their sovereignty,[39] and provoked some regions, like Krasnoyarsk, to print their own currency.[40] Moscow had no option but to mellow.

Another extremely important problem was related to the allocation of fiscal revenues between central and local authorities. This division of funds is organized on the basis of taxes, and the revenue split has to be bargained between the relevant actors. This system was in effect under the Soviet system, and is still working with the new Russian VAT. It would be hard to devise a more effective way to split up the country. Not only does this process lead to antagonism between central and local powers, but it also creates competition between local powers. As a result, local authorities have been able to get some resources, enabling them to have largely autonomous economic policies, while the central budget was deprived of most of its capabilities.

By summer 1992, regions were progressively gaining in decision-making authority, and economic differences among them increased to a considerable extent.[41] Of course, this two-pronged process of economic differentiation and political autonomy had a considerable influence on every aspect of economic policy, including conversion.

Regional Differentiation and the Concentration of Defense Industry

Economic depression has been substantially regionally differentiated[42] although every region and economic zone has suffered. There have been specific intervening factors, such as the quasi-civil war situation in the Northern Caucasus. Border trade, mainly with China in the Far Eastern economic zone, or with Finland in the Northern zone, has provided some shelter against depression. Raw materials extraction has been another significant regionalizing factor.

Goskomstat figures (see Figure 4) show that depression is much greater where consumer industries were predominant, such as around Moscow (the Central Region). They also show a shift of economic activity to the east. A new zone, including the Urals, Western Siberia, and part of the Volga region (or Trans-Volga), got the upper hand in 1992 and early 1993. If we

Figure 4. Depression and regional concentration of the VPK

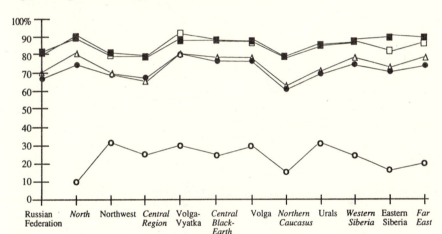

	Industrial production during the first ten months of 1992 as a percentage of the same period in 1991
■	Industrial production during the first ten months of 1992 as a percentage of the same period in 1991
□	Industrial production during the first five months of 1993 as a percentage of the same period in 1992
△	Industrial production during the first five months of 1993 as a percentage of the same period in 1991
●	Industrial production during the first five months of 1993 as a percentage of the same period in 1990
○	The VPK share of industrial employment

Sources: Goskomstat Rossii, *O Razvitii Ekonomicheskikh Reform v Rossiiskoi Federatsii (yanvar'-dekabr' 1992 goda* and *yanvar'-mai 1993 goda)*, January 1993 and June 1993, Moscow.

151

Figure 5.
The relative impact of depression compared to the relative weight of the VPK sector.

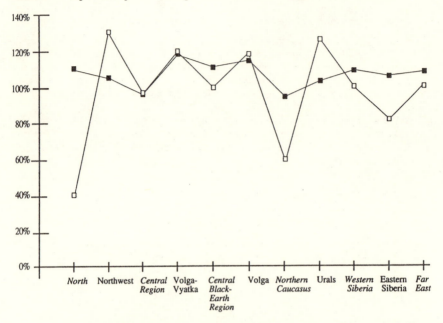

— ■ — Industrial production for each region in the first five months of 1993, compared with
the same period in 1990, as a percentage of the average for the Russian Federation

— □ — The VPK share of industrial employment in each region as a percentage of the
average for the Russian Federation

Source: Goskomstat Rossii, *O Razvitii Ekonomicheskikh Reform v Rossiiskoi Federatsii* (*yanvar'-mai 1993 goda*), June 1993, Moscow.

take into account the relative success of the Far East, it becomes obvious that the part of
Russia which is between St. Petersburg and the Moscow zone is now relatively impoverished
and underdeveloped.

What is striking is the close correlation between resilience in the face of economic
depression and the concentration of the VPK sector (see Figure 5).

Since arms production declined sharply during 1992, this situation is even more interesting. It can only mean that civilian production has shown a considerable level of resilience,
and that the old VPK infrastructure has been effective in fighting the confusion. It also means
that managers of large enterprises are a political force to be reckoned with (their influence
can also be seen in the prominence of Volsky's Union of Industrialists and Entrepreneurs).
Lastly, it means that politically, regional authorities in Russia's eastern areas had considerable leverage when dealing with Moscow.

Figure 6. Income levels by economic zone

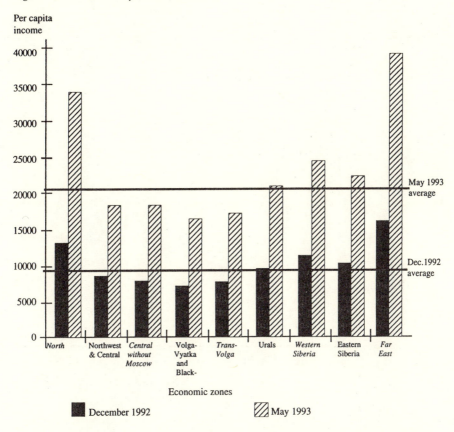

Per capita income

Economic zones

■ December 1992   ▨ May 1993

Source: Goskomstat Rossii, *O Razvitii Ekonomicheskikh Reform v Rossiiskoi Federatsii* (*yanvar'-mai 1993 goda*), June 1993, Moscow.

But regional economic differentiation does not stop at production. Differentiation is also evident in prices, incomes, and institutional changes. Six months after the "Big Bang" of January 1992, prices were still wildly different from one region to another. Part of this segmentation is political, as local authorities are maintaining price controls and subsidies. However, part of it is merely technical. Deficiencies of infrastructure, such as movement of goods or payments from one region to another, are giving birth to a kind of cellular economy. Privatization also varies widely, not only between zones but also between regions.[43]

At the same time, because of the very different regional impact of the depression, per-capita incomes also differ. These sharp income differentiations roughly correspond to sectoral differences. Inside each different zone there are also striking differences between individual regions.

As a matter of fact, the relation of expenditures to income, on a regional basis, does not show what could be expected in a true market economy (see Figure 7).

Figure 7. Distribution of Regions by Income vs. Expenditure

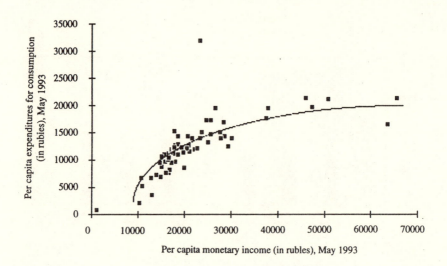

Goskomstat Rossii, *O Razvitii Ekonomicheskikh Reform v Rossiiskoi Federatsii (yanvar'-mai 1993 goda),* June 1993, Moscow.

The curve is much flatter than would be expected from Keynesian economics. Deposit rates are negative, financial markets are in their infancy and plagued by very serious uncertainties (not to mention highly illegal operations), and the use of foreign currencies as a savings medium is restricted to some cities. From a neoclassical point of view, these factors could lead to a major goods-buying drive (not only for direct consumption but for hoarding as well) and thus a steeper curve.

Three basic cases could be forecast given the reasoning we used to try to find a relation between a proxy of the marginal saving propensity[44] and income level. 1) If the Russian economy had been a market economy, the usual curve would have been found. 2) Based on what has been said about segmentation, a segmented market economy could be possible.

Then, nominal differences in income would not prevent actual income equalization; the regional price structures would act as a tool of equalization in segmented markets. A nearly horizontal curve could then be anticipated. 3) With the survival of quantity rationing it would be impossible to find some goods regardless of saving. A vertical curve would then be expected.

Figure 8. Marginal saving propensity vs. regional income levels.

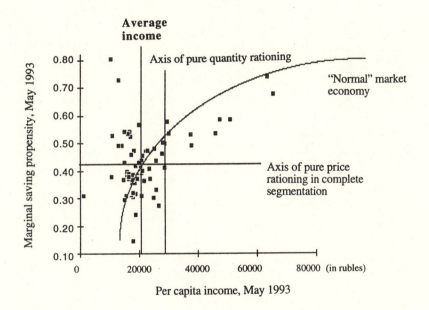

Per capita income, May 1993

The cloud obtained in figure 8 displays a kind of mix of the last two cases. Obviously there are still many regions where we can suspect quantity rationing. On the other hand there are some regions where segmented market theory applies.

Attempts to correlate by various methods (e.g., linear and polynomial) do not provide good results until 21 regions (28 percent of the initial sample of 75) are omitted. By doing this, we tried to minimize the effects of what we have called either the local command economy or the local segmented one.

We found that a non-negligible number of regions, mainly in the central and eastern parts of the country, display characteristics incompatible with any form of a market economy. Moreover, others display effects of market segmentation.

This suggests that the transition to the market economy was still partial by May 1993, and only really effective in the western part of the country, the very place where the depression has been the worst. Economic zones known for high levels of VPK influence are notoriously included among those where regions are least marketized. However, there are also regions where defense-related industry has been important but which seem quite marketized.

Table 2. Marginal saving propensity to per capita income correlation.

	Initial sample		Modified sample	
	Linear regression $Y = Ax + C$	Polynomial regression $Y = Ax + Bx2 + C$	Linear regression	Polynomial regression
R	0.466	0.504	0.834	0.844
R2	0.199	0.254	0.695	0.713
R2 adjusted	0.188	0.233	0.689	0.702
DW	1.503	1.656	1.383	1.432
A	4.839 E-06	(-) 4.564E-06	7.72E-06	1.42E-05
B		1.39E-10		(-) 8.838E-11
C	0.323	0.446	0.227	0.135

Finally, there are also significant regional differences in actual income levels, and case one is also in fact partly valid. The situation in May 1993 does not seem to be very different from December 1992.

Regional Dynamics

If we look at the different regional situations in Russia, three distinct kinds of economic dynamics appear to be at work.

The first is what could be called a depressed local market economy. In some regions market relations have made their mark. Prices are actually free, barter is very infrequently used, and microeconomic adjustment is beginning. In general, these regions are among the more depressed, with both extremely low and extremely high income groups. Privatization is well under way and new entrepreneurs are flourishing. Wages in state-owned enterprises and administration are extremely low, to the point where workers take outside jobs. The social system is decaying fast, both in terms of benefits and infrastructure, because of very tight local public budgets.

Because of the depression, however, trading is still more rewarding than production, and speculation remains quite active in these regions. The brutal fall of actual incomes also provides a basis for illegal market operations, from contraband (particularly interesting because of the undervaluation of the ruble) to prostitution and drug trafficking. Moscow is a good example of this situation. Another possibility is a flourishing border trade propelled by rapidly expanding foreign demand. This is probably the situation on the Russo-Chinese border and in the Far East.

The second kind of regional economy is what could be called a raw material producer/ rent-seeking economy. Where raw materials (oil, gas, diamonds, etc.) can be exported, a constant inflow of foreign currency helps to sustain local economic activities. State enterprises are commercialized but not really privatized; nonetheless they are able to pay relatively high wages and to provide fairly developed social services. This type of region generally trades by barter system with others, trying to exert the maximum influence relative to the worth of its raw products. But such regions are still highly dependent on industrial goods, if only to continue extraction of raw materials. Foreign investment is sought, partly as a way to offset dependency on other industrial regions. Economic relations are not those of a pure market economy, as export-induced income leads to expanding local budgets and large local subsidies.

These regions try to keep for themselves the rent generated by their extraction activities and they favor a large devaluation of the ruble since they receive foreign currency.

Table 3. Characteristics of the three different regional economies.

	Rent-seeking regional economy	Local command economy	Local market economy
Relation inside the productive system	Mainly multilateral, but from oligopolistic or monopolistic situations	Mainly bilateral, with a strong emphasis on bargaining (implicit) and technical dependencies.	Multilateral with both supply and demand optimistic
Labor market	Seller's market with a strong demand for highly qualified workers.	Internal markets with strong polarization from the enterprise social role, and strong influence of implicit knowledge.	Buyer's market, with growing unemployment.
Supply characteristics	Large irreversibility effects due to long range investments. Non divisible investments. Natural resources a dominant factor.	Large investments needed with both low divisibility and strong irreversibility effects. Technological culture extremely relevant.	Extremely flexible, with low investments, highly divisible, and fairly easy labor-to-capital substitution.
Demand characteristics	Low elasticity, foreign demand important or even dominant.	Internal demand mainly, with low to moderate elasticity. Supplier-buyer link extremely important.	Internal demand with very high elasticity.
Prices	Determined by world prices; rent situations and subsidies for retail prices.	Financing variables for big industrial organizations. Mainly bargained prices in barter trade. Subsidies predominant in retail prices.	True market prices.

157

The third situation could be called a local command economy. In regions dominated by big industrial enterprises, institutional reforms have developed very little. Wholesale prices are mainly former Soviet prices, and barter is the dominant form of trade, with bilateral links the rule and not the exception. Retail prices are frequently controlled, and the internal distribution system of big enterprises is still working. These enterprises are accumulating large interenterprise debts, and, because of their social (and hence political) influence, local authorities avoid antagonizing them when they do not cooperate in reform. Largely independent, even if still state-owned, these big enterprises are making some attempts at restructuring. But they mainly seek to preserve favorable positions as producers of non- or low-substitutable goods in their relations with the two other kinds of regions.

These different regional dynamics are not only leading to different regional rates of inflation, but also setting the pace of the national inflation. Increasingly, attempts to maximize rent and income are decisive in this process. Such a situation obviously has crucial consequences for enterprises trying to convert.

Toward Regional Conversion Dynamics?

Differences among the regional environments highlight the possibility of different strategies for conversion. The local command economy, and even to some extent the rent-seeking economy provide the opportunity to slow down or even stall the conversion process. Strong pressure on the central government to allow a policy of free arms export is a highly probable solution in these regions, but it does not mean that there will be no diversification. If possible, enterprise managers will try to expand their economic and power bases by making good use of available production capacity. But this diversification will be induced less by a true search for market opportunities than by a search for bilateral links between an enterprise and a supplier, or even between an enterprise and local authorities. Conversion, if implemented as industrial diversification, will be quite close to the old conversion process already described.

The regions with a local market economy, on the other hand, will have strong incentives to close down unprofitable enterprises—true conversion. Since a quick shift to civilian production is rarely possible, partial or complete closing down will be the most frequent solution after a transition period during which enterprises will be idle. Even if formal closing can be avoided, a portion of the workforce will leave and join those engaged in survival or speculative activities. Emigration, for engineers and even highly skilled technicians, could emerge as a solution. This situation is obviously not positive from the perspective of either the Russian or Western governments. The potential loss in technological abilities is of course feared by the Russian government; but the impact of a major migration of defense specialists is also feared by Western powers.

The local rent-seeking economy could, however, provide some incentive to diversification. Local authorities will be eager to reduce their technical dependence on other regions. They could channel funds earned by exporting raw materials to finance the diversification process. The nasty side of what could otherwise be an interesting trend is that it would clearly denote an implicit secessionist move by some regions. Even if this does not occur, we could then see a process of complete autonomous segmented development, inducing duplication of production facilities and, sometimes, local trade tariffs.

On the whole, regional differentiation will not help the transition process. It might even add new sources of conflict and fuel political and economic tensions. Disturbance of the terms of trade between regions will seriously affect any economic calculus for investment projects linked to conversion. Market segmentation will reduce opportunities and incentives. At the same time, if conversion slows significantly and is distorted by regional dynamics, production sector rigidity would remain high with obvious consequences for inflation and regional disintegration itself. Here again we see how the conversion and macroeconomic processes interact.

Regional differentiation of conversion threatens an already segmented Russian economy. Adoption of differentiated conversion strategies, if not coordinated, could only exacerbate economic conflicts between regions. Conversion could then become another pressure toward the progressive disintegration of Russia.

III. Ways Out: How To Reorganize Conversion Policy

Goals and Context

The current situation suggests some important goals for any Russian government. Macroeconomic stabilization is obviously one goal, but the experience of the last 18 months proves that it cannot be achieved without building market structures and infrastructures. Contrary to some assumptions, and for various reasons ranging from the very nature of the Russian production system to the sheer size of the country, market building cannot be a spontaneous phenomenon.

The state is absolutely critical to developing these structures and infrastructures from both an economic and an institutional point of view. Reducing budget expenditures too quickly for the sake of deficit reduction could be self-destructive if it impairs market development and state legitimacy, and thus prevents stabilization.

Another extremely important priority is Russia's future economic development. So large a systemic change would be very path-dependent. Russian authorities must assess what strategies can remain open for the next twenty years. A strategy based on raw materials is probably not feasible, not to mention its social, distributional, and political implications, but going back to the old rule is a dead end. To protect industrial capacities and, at the same time, achieve enough diversification and flexibility of the VPK sector is probably the only viable approach.

One of the main short-term goals of any sensible conversion policy is reducing the budget burden. This requires significant reduction of budget subsidies as either direct or indirect unemployment benefits. The main goals would be improving industrial flexibility, accelerating microeconomic adjustment, and enabling restructuring to create profitable enterprises.

Preserving the national technological potential is also a legitimate Russian goal. This would entail a commitment to preserve R&D departments, and to avoid massive emigration of scientists and engineers. This goal may not be compatible with a fast and complete reduction of subsidies.

Modernization of Russian industrial structures might also require substantial input from converted military enterprises. Clearly this modernization could be done by importing a significant amount of Western investment goods, but in the current context limits on imports might make sense, at least temporarily. In this approach, stabilization and industrial restructuring could conflict.

A stringent stabilization policy could significantly slow conversion, since demand would be too low and investment nonexistent. This policy would also probably exacerbate regional differentiation. Results would be counterproductive. The VPK sector would then probably be able to get enough subsidies to weaken any anti-inflationist policy. Regional differentiation would also fuel inflation and destroy all macroeconomic tools available to the central government.

A sensible stabilization policy would coordinate stabilization, industrial restructuring, and economic homogenization (this does not mean that all regions would have to follow exactly the same approach). Centralization is an empty dream in a country like Russia. But the general approach has to remain. Indeed, industrial restructuring and conversion are obviously the most important parts of this, and homogenization is the best way to cope with the inflation problem.

Macroeconomic Policy

The main priority of macroeconomic policy should be to switch from conflict-induced inflation to growth-related inflation. A stabilizing framework to manage repartition conflicts is the most important tool to devise. It could be linked to a cost and income policy, but the most important point would be the regulation of some critical prices. If barter trade and bilateral links are as developed as we have reason to think, then we have to admit that the price liberalization of 1992 has been a partial failure. It would of course be madness to return to control of retail prices, but industrial prices are entirely different. For some critical products, prices would be better determined through formal negotiations between enterprises and their governments. Agreements would then provide ceiling and bottom limits for six-month to three-year periods, in exchange for formal commitments by enterprises to implement internal restructuring programs, the scope of which would be coordinated at the national level. Such a procedure has been used with tremendous success not only in France following World War II, but also in the EEC (for restructuring of the steel industry).

Subsidies would not be eliminated; such a commitment today would lack any credibility and quickly erode the reputation of any government. However, subsidies and long-term credits would be managed through agreements similar to those described above and would be strictly related to microeconomic restructuring. This policy could be much more efficient than raising interest rates when financial markets are still in their infancy. A high interest rate policy is not stabilizing, as Poland's experience shows, but utterly destructive for the emergent private sector.[45]

Public budgets must be maintained to provide for welfare services previously derived from budgets of enterprises, because the labor market could not function efficiently without them.

Last, but not least, convertibility would be assessed in light of the ability of the Russian government to implement control over exchange rates. If the Russian government is able to do so, there is no reason why the ruble could not be convertible. If it is unable, until such control could be implemented, it would be better to go back to administrative exchange rates since anything is better than a wildly speculating narrow market.

This macroeconomic policy, complemented by an income policy and a revamping of taxation, could produce the kind of framework needed to implement restructuring on a larger scale. It would certainly not halt inflation, but that goal is clearly unrealistic at this time. However, by stabilizing microeconomic behaviors, the policy would help stabilize the level of inflation, providing time to develop the tools to reduce it to a more reasonable level (by Western standards). It must not be forgotten that inflation was quite high in France during the "glorious 30 years," i.e., during the economic boom of 1945–1975.

Industrial Policy

Since the sequence by which liberalization precedes restructuring is based on faulty assumptions, an industrial policy is needed to expedite conversion. It is obviously critical not to confuse such a policy with central planning. Industrial policy is to be thought of as a set of goals and rules enabling the coordination of local decision-making, without interfering with implementation. The experience of newly industrialized Asian countries is a good argument for such a policy combining traditional macroeconomic tools and specific institutional ones.[46]

Industrial restructuring must first be coordinated to avoid either overshooting or anomalous behavior from some regions. Production and productivity targets have to be determined on a nationwide level. Investment programs have to be prepared to cope with regional depression caused by downsizing enterprises. One goal of such an industrial policy is to provide a framework for territorial management, and to alleviate interregional conflicts. Supply-side restructuring implies a combined system of enterprise tax reduction and levying of import taxes to shelter industries during the restructuring phase.

Financial systems must be devised to insure the channeling of funds and to handle the problem of time until return on investment. These systems will manage credit distribution under the aegis of national branch agreements. They will initially provide low-cost credit but with strict restructuring commitments and progressively evolve toward higher interest rates in close coordination with emerging financial markets.

Before any true privatization can be implemented it is critical to reestablish the principal/ agent relationship. This requires the creation of holding structures, transregional and possibly transnational (across CIS borders). These financial-industrial groups would be parties to the agreements already mentioned. They would have to be free to buy shares in privatized enterprises to create industrial synergies. The holding system could then be used for partial privatization. It would be less sensitive for the Russian government to allow foreign enterprises to buy shares of these holding structures than of specific enterprises.

The demand side of this policy would involve developing a medium-range investment program at the national or regional level. Not only is such infrastructure-building (or rebuilding) badly needed, but it could provide a stable enough market to allow for better capital recoupment time. This would not be so different from policies implemented in Japan, Korea, or Taiwan.

This industrial policy would also have to provide clear rules and guidelines for international cooperation. Foreign investors need to know their rights and the priorities of the

Russian government. This cannot be left to regional authorities. By making public the broad outlines of an integrated program, for restructuring, demand, and financial institutions, Russian authorities would provide precisely the kind of stable environment foreign investors are waiting for. Such a policy could significantly reduce the level of uncertainty more than a commitment to unrealistic (albeit pleasant-sounding) goals. The guarantee of negotiated targets with managers of large enterprises and regional leaders would give credibility to such a program that iron proclamations from Moscow could never provide.

Western Assistance

The problem of conversion and restructuring is now quite politically sensitive. Some inside the Russian administration are deeply convinced that Western policy is to de-industrialize Russia, keeping it as a producer of raw materials. At the same time, some in the West are afraid of a potential rebuilding of a strong military-industrial apparatus in Russia.

In fact, obvious common goals exist toward which cooperation could be developed. If it is a legitimate goal for any Russian government to preserve the technological capabilities of its industry, it is also a goal for Western governments to avoid the economic disintegration of Russian industry, even if military related, which could lead to serious proliferation problems, not to mention social unrest and political destabilization of the country. It is worth every dollar it takes to ensure a true conversion process that will neither degenerate into a major arms export drive nor lead to massive economic collapse.

There is also no doubt that Western assistance to conversion could be much more efficient if coordinated with an integrated industrial policy. In the spirit of the Marshall Plan, Western assistance could fund part of a program to rebuild infrastructure, ameliorating the budget deficit problem. Western assistance could also have a tremendous effect by helping to stabilize and expand intra-CIS trade and CIS-Eastern Europe trade.

Opening markets is another obvious option, but no Western government is ready to do this, given the threat of major exports and dumping. That is why it is so important to help the Russian government sustain and develop internal demand. It is the best guarantee against any export dumping policy.

Some complementarities should be explored. While Western companies usually have more expertise in marketing, internal organization, and management, and lead in some technological sectors, the Russian technological potential is not to be underestimated. Joint ventures could exploit these complementarities and provide a stable basis for cooperation. Technology transfer restrictions of all sorts have to be abolished for this to happen.

Western assistance cannot be the panacea for Russian ills. But it can help to reduce inevitable conflicts among legitimate goals of an integrated economic policy. Medium- to long-term public assistance, like the Marshall Plan, would undoubtedly provide a clear signal for private investors.

Notes

[1] "Pravitel'stvo strany: ego funktsii, polnomostiya, otvetsvennost," *Pravitel'stvennyi Vestnik* 18 (1989): 23. Groupe d'Etudes et de Recherches sur la Stratégie Soviétique (GERSS), "La conversion des industries de défense en URSS," *Economie Prospective Internationale* 47 (1991) 3rd quarter. J. Sapir, *Les bases futures de la puissance militaire russe*, Cahiers d'Études Stratégiques 16, Groupe de Sociologie de la Défense-Centre Interdisciplinaire de Recherche sur la Paix et d'Etudes Stratégiques (GSD-CIRPES), Paris, 1993.

[2] A. Ozhegov, Y. Rogovsky, and J. Jaremenko, "Konversiya oboronnoi promyshlennosti i preobrazovanie ekonomiki SSSR," *Kommunist* 1 (1991): 54-64.

[3] J. Cooper, *The Soviet Defence Industry: Conversion and Reform* (London: Royal Institute for International Affairs, 1991).

[4] *Vestnik Statistiki* 5 (1989).

[5] J. Cooper, *The Soviet Defence....*

[6] GERSS, "Reconversion Industrielle" in J. Sapir, Gen. R. Ernould and D. Pineye (eds.), *La décomposition de l'armée soviétique*, Cahiers de la Fondation pour les Études de Défense Nationale 45, Paris (1992). J. Cooper, *Defence Industry Conversion in the East: The Relevance of Western Experience*, NATO colloquium, Brussels, April 1992.

[7] J. Sapir, "L'avenir des forces armée en Russie (1)," *L'Armement* 38 (July–August 1993): 8-17.

[8] J. H. Monnier, "L'industrie de défense en Russie," *L'Armement* 38 (July–August 1993): 98-109.

[9] J.Sapir, *The Soviet Military System* (Cambridge: Polity Press, 1991).

[10] C. Davis, *Interdependence of the Defense and Civilian Sectors in the Contemporary Soviet Economy*, papers given at the American Association for the Advancement of Slavic Studies convention, 1989, Chicago. D. M. Kemme, "The Chronic Excess Demand Hypothesis," in C. Davis and W. Charemza (eds.), *Models of Disequilibrium and Shortages in Centrally Planned Economies* (London: Chapman & Hall, 1989). J. Sapir, *L'économie mobilisée* (Paris: La Découverte, 1990).

[11] J. Sapir, *Les bases futures...*, 72-77.

[12] As defined by S. R. Barant, in "The Influence of Russian Tradition on the Political Style of Soviet Elite," *Political Science Quarterly* 102, no. 2 (1989): 273-293.

[13] L. Badgett, *Defeated by a Maze: The Soviet Economy and its Defense Industrial Sector* (Santa Monica, CA: The RAND Corporation, 1988). P. Almquist, "Soviet Military Acquisition: From a Seller's Market to a Buyer's," in S. Clarck (ed.), *The Soviet Military Factor In a Changing World* (Boulder, CO: Westview Press, 1991). T. Malleret, *Les transferts de technologie non négociés de l'ouest à destination de l'URSS et leur contribution au potentiel militaire soviétique* (Paris: École des Hautes Études en Sciences Sociales, 1992).

[14] GERSS, "Reconversion industrielle," 269-273.

[15] S. Alexashenko, *The Budgetary System of the USSR*, (Brussels: EEC Economic Committee, November 1991).

[16] E. Vigdorchik, V. Volkonskii, E. Gurvich, G. Kantorovich and E. Jarkin, *Liberalizatsiya tsen v Rossii: itogi 1992 goda* 6 (Moscow: Ekspertnyi Institut, Rossiskii Soyuz Promyshlennikov i Predprinimatelei, January 1993).

[17] J. Sapir, "Formes et natures de l'inflation," *Economie Internationale* 54, 2nd quarter (1993): 25-66.

[18] C. de Boissieu, D. Cohen and G .de Pontbriand, "Gérer la dette interentreprises,"

Economie Internationale 54, 2nd quarter (1993): 105-120.

[19] See J. Sapir, "Formes et natures de l'inflation,"*Economie Internationale* 54, 2nd quarter (1993): 25-66, and *The Russian Economic Barometer* 4 (1992): 1-19, 37.

[20] Discussion with Russian economists and with C. de Boissieu, September 1993.

[21] A. Avtorkhanov, *The Communist Party Apparatus* (Chicago: Henry Regnery Company, 1966). J. Hough, *The Soviet Prefects* (Cambridge: Harvard University Press, 1969).

[22] I. Boeva, T. Dolgopiatova and V. Shironin, "Gosudarstvenniye Predpriyatiya v 1991-1992," *Ekonomicheskie problemy i povedinie* (Moscow: Institute of Economic Policy, 1992).

[23] J.Sapir, "Marchés régionaux ou régionalisation du marché?" in R. Berton-Hogge (ed.), *La Fin de l'URSS* (Paris: La Documentation Française, 1992).

[24] J.Sapir, *La Russie un an après*, working paper, Centre d'Études des Modes d'Industrialisatión, École des Hautes Études en Sciences Sociales, Paris, January 1993.

[25] V. Koen and S. Philips, *Price Liberalization in Russia, the Early Record*, IMF Working Paper, Washington D.C., November 1992.

[26] M. Ezekiel, "The Cobweb Theorem," *Quarterly Journal of Economics* 2 (February 1938): 255-280.

[27] D. Lipton and J. Sachs, "Creating a Market Economy in Eastern Europe: The Case of Poland," *Brookings Papers on Economic Activity* 1, 1990.

[28] S.J. Grossman and J.E. Stiglitz, "On the Impossibility of Informationally Efficient Markets," *American Economic Review* 70 (June 1980): 393-408. J. Green, "The Non-Existence of Informational Equilibria," *The Review of Economic Studies* 44 (1977): 451-463. J. S. Jordan and R. Radner, "Rational Expectations in Microeconomic Models: An Overview," *Journal of Economic Theory* 26 (1982): 201-223.

[29] D. Foray, "Repères pour une économie des organisations de recherche-développement," *Revue d'Economie Politique* 101, no. 5 (1991): 790-808. J. L. Gaffard, *Economie industrielle et de l'innovation* (Paris: Dalloz, 1990). B.J. Loasby, *Choice, Complexity and Ignorance. An Inquiry into Economic Theory and the Practice of Decision-Making* (Cambridge: Cambridge University Press, 1976). E. Penrose, *The Growth of the Firm* (Oxford: Basil Blackwell, 1968).

[30] A. Orlean, "Pour une approche cognitive des conventions économiques," *Revue Economique* 40, no. 2 (March 1989): 241-272.

[31] G. Calvo and J. Frenkel, "From Centrally Planned to Market Economies: The Road from CPE to PCPE," *IMF Staff Papers*, June 1991.

[32] Here I am thinking explicitly about comments made by Russian "liberals," most notably Fyodorov's comments after the defeat of Rutskoi and Khasbulatov: "We have crushed the rebellion, we will crush the inflation."

[33] G.W.Breslauer, *Khrushchev and Brezhnev as Leaders: Building Authority in Soviet Politics* (Berkeley, CA: University of California Press, 1982). See also D.M. Kreps and R. Wilson, "Reputation and Imperfect Information," *Journal of Economic Theory* 27 (1982): 253-279.

[34] D. Bahry, *Outside Moscow: Power Politics and Budgetary Policy in the Soviet Republics* (New York: Columbia University Press, 1987).

[35] S. Zamascikov, *Political Organizations in the Soviet Armed Forces* (Falls Church, VA: Delphic Associates, 1982).

[36] J. Sapir, "La dimension fédérale de la crise de l'Union soviétique," *Economie prospective internationale* , no. 46, 2nd quarter (1991).

[37] J. Sapir, "Marchés régionaux ou régionalisation du marché? L'éclatement de l'espace économique ex-soviétique," in R. Berton-Hogge (ed.), *La Fin de l'URSS - Héritages d'un Empire* (Paris: La Documentation Française, 1992).

[38] A. Gazier, "Les régions russes du 'Centre-Terres Noires': des pouvoirs locaux en transitions ou en opposition?" in *Revue d'Études Comparatives Est Ouest* 24, no. 1 (1993): 131-158.

[39] *Delovaya Sibir*, 28 March–April 3, 1992. *Sibirskaya gazeta*, April 6-12, 1992.

[40] *Izvestiya*, July 22, 1992: 2.

[41] J. Radvanyi, "La Russie minée par ses régions?" in *Revue d'Études Comparatives Est Ouest* 24, no. 1 (1993): 57-68.

[42] J. Sapir, "Différences économiques régionales, transition et politique de stabilisation en Russie" in *Revue d'Études Comparatives Est Ouest* 24, no. 1 (1993): 5-56.

[43] J. Sapir, "Différences," 5-56.

[44] The marginal saving propensity is defined as the ratio of income minus expenditures for consumption goods to income.

[45] Y. Zlotowski, "Politique monétaire et thérapie de choc en Pologne: les limites de l'expérience 1990-1991" in *Economie Prospective Internationale*, no. 53, 1st quarter (1993).

[46] C. Johnson, *MITI and the Japanese Miracle* (Stanford, CA: Stanford University Press, 1982). L. Jones and I. Sakong, *Government, Business and Entrepreneurship in Economic Development: the Korean Case* (Cambridge, MA: Harvard University Press, 1980). K. S. Kim and M. Roemer, *Growth and Structural Transformations. Studies in the Modernization of the Republic of Korea: 1945-1975* (Cambridge, MA: Harvard University Press, 1979). D. I. Okimoto, T. Sugano, and F. B. Weinstein, *Competitive Edge* (Stanford, CA: Stanford University Press,1984). R. Wade, *Governing the Market. Economic Theory and the Role of Government in East Asian Industrialization* (Princeton, N.J.: Princeton University Press,1990).

Part IV

Transition to the Market at the Enterprise Level

9

A Case Study of Russian Defense Conversion and Employee Ownership: The Saratov Aviation Plant

John A. Battilega

Introduction

In 1991 the Soviet government turned ownership of the Saratov Aviation Plant (SAP) over to the enterprise's workforce, thus making it the first enterprise of its size to be privatized.[1] In February 1993, the enterprise completed its transition to an employee-owned joint-stock company. The experiences of this enterprise provide important insights into the issues and problems faced by other Russian enterprises attempting defense conversion and privatization, especially through the employee ownership option.

This paper discusses the experiences of the Saratov Aviation Plant in its transition from a state-owned plant producing 55 percent defense products to an employee-owned joint-stock company using, in 1992, about 6 percent of production capacity for the defense industry. The paper briefly reviews the history of the plant, and then discusses the sequence of events and activities which led from early privatization under special conditions granted by the Soviet government to full incorporation as a closed joint-stock company. The paper considers the role played in this process by Western assistance. Finally, the paper identifies several issues and obstacles experienced by the Saratov Aviation Plant that will probably also surface in all Russian enterprises undergoing similar transformations.

John Battilega is a corporate vice president at Science Applications International Corporation.

The focus of this paper is the period from 1989, when the Saratov Aviation Plant first began defense conversion, to February 1993, when the plant became a joint-stock company.[2] A subsequent paper, in progress, will concentrate on the newly privatized plant's first year of operations.

History and Organization

The Saratov Aviation Plant is located in the city of Saratov, about 600 kilometers southeast of Moscow,[3] and is one of three former large defense enterprises located in that city. The plant was founded in 1931 during the first Five Year Plan, initially to make agricultural machinery. In 1938, to meet war needs, the plant began to produce fighter aircraft designed by the Yakovlev Design Bureau. Between 1941 and 1945, SAP manufactured more than 13,000 airplanes, 23 percent of the fighters produced by Soviet industry. The Yak–1 and the Yak–3 became mainstays of the Russian army during World War II. Since then, the plant has continued to develop military aviation products. More than fifteen basic types of aircraft and helicopters and more than forty modifications have been produced, including the Yak–11, LA–15, MiG–15, and Yak–25 fighters, the Yak–27 reconnaissance plane, and several military helicopters. The plant also produced naval cruise missiles.

In addition to military aviation products, the Saratov Aviation Plant produces commercial aircraft for both domestic and foreign uses. The Yak–40 is a small, light, passenger airplane intended for short-haul routes. From 1965 to 1984, SAP produced and delivered more than 1000 Yak–40 aircraft to the Soviet Union and to 21 other countries. In 1984, the plant began producing the mid-size Yak–42 aircraft, which exists in several versions. The Yak–42 has been sold to Aeroflot, as well as to many Eastern European countries, Cuba, and China. SAP also produces spare parts for Yak–40 and Yak–42 aircraft, and provides a variety of aviation-related training, maintenance, and air-delivery services.

SAP also produces non-aviation consumer products. These include kitchenware (spoons, kettles, teapots, pans), bicycles and tricycles, children's toys, sports training equipment, agricultural equipment, and machines for packing powder products. The total production volume of consumer goods for 1991 was valued at approximately 15 billion rubles in late 1991 prices.

The Saratov Aviation Plant currently employs approximately 13,000 workers and occupies about four million square feet of production space. Operations are divided into 57 different production shops/units operating in fifteen separate physical plants. SAP, like many major Russian enterprises, owns facilities to accommodate the social needs of its workers. These facilities include four collective farms, which produce food sold to SAP workers; about 350 large apartment complexes located close to the plant; and health care, child care, and educational facilities.[4]

Defense Conversion

In 1988, approximately 55 percent of SAP's production capacity was dedicated to military products. At that time, the general director, Alexander Yermishin, made a decision to convert production from military products to civilian aircraft and consumer goods.[5] Since then, production lines for two types of fighter planes and two types of cruise missiles have been phased out, and the capacity of the plant has been shifted to the production of improved versions of the Yak–42 civilian passenger plane. In 1992, only 6 percent of SAP's production capacity was devoted to military support equipment, with the remainder dedicated to commercial aviation products and non-aviation consumer goods.

An important part of SAP's defense conversion strategy is expansion of commercial aircraft production, both in volume and in product lines. In 1991, SAP sold Yak–42 aircraft to Cuba and China, and received strong interest from Italy, Iran, Israel, Egypt, Yugoslavia, and other countries. Technical and economic estimates by Russian research institutions suggested that a significant global market exists for the type of light and medium aircraft SAP can produce. As a result, over the next ten years SAP plans to increase production of the Yak–42 aircraft (as well as produce new versions), to reopen the production line for the Yak–40 aircraft, and, when financing is available for production equipment, to produce a third aircraft, the T–401. The T–401 is a small, six-passenger airplane suitable for corporate use, and also for patrols. SAP plans to expand its plant capacity to be able to produce approximately 50 Yak–42, 300 Yak–40, and 250 T–401 aircraft per year by the year 2000. In addition, SAP plans to increase its production capacity for consumer goods, with the goal of an annual sales volume of approximately 31 billion rubles in late 1991 prices.

In order to meet these objectives, SAP developed and has started to execute a comprehensive plant modernization and development plan.[6] Production machinery for military aircraft has been destroyed, and new machinery is being installed in its place. An independent assembly complex and an additional mechanical plant have already been built, and a separate agro-industrial firm has been formed. Over the last two years, modern computer-controlled machinery has been introduced into production shops, completely financed by hard currency generated by SAP. In addition, the State Scientific and Technical Committee has developed a comprehensive plan for SAP to fully automate many aspects of aircraft production as soon as investment capital can be secured. Detailed financial plans to the year 2000 have been prepared for discussion with potential investors.

New SAP marketing staffs have been hired and are being trained in order to make SAP less dependent on the Ministry of Aviation Industry for foreign aircraft sales. Arrangements have been made with research institutes in Ukraine to develop better software for production scheduling, and to help streamline the internal management process. SAP also has a staffing plan, and expects to expand its workforce by 5000 employees by the year 2000. SAP management estimates that it will take seven to ten years to complete its expansion plans and achieve fully profitable operation as a privatized corporation. SAP is aggressively pursuing joint ventures with foreign firms worldwide, and is also attempting to secure investment loans from international funding sources.

Finally, SAP management has taken steps to gain experience in market-based operations. In early 1991, five of the specialized production units were made independent legal entities and allowed to operate as separate small enterprises, serving SAP aircraft production needs but also producing consumer goods for independent sales.[7] This step gave SAP managers experience producing and selling consumer goods at market prices.

Formation of a Collective Enterprise

Part of the SAP strategy has been privatization involving employee ownership. As a first step, SAP representatives negotiated with the Soviet government for plant ownership by the workforce in the form of a collective enterprise.[8] The process of transition from a state to a collective enterprise began in 1988,[9] with the official authority to proceed eventually granted in 1991. Resolution 19 of the Council of Ministers of the USSR, dated 10 January 1991, granted the SAP workforce outright ownership of selected assets of the plant.[10] These assets included: a) the collective farms, housing complexes, and health care and educational facilities that served the workers; b) those production facilities whose value had depreciated by at least 70 percent; and c) any new production facilities acquired as a result of profits generated after the plant began to operate under collective ownership. These assets were considered to account for 54 percent of the enterprise's worth. The workforce was also to be allowed to purchase the remaining assets of the plant, with payment on an installment schedule. The first payment was due in the first half of 1991; subsequent payments were not scheduled.

To determine the cost of the portion to be purchased, the plant was valued using standard formulas provided by the Ministry of Aviation Industry.[11] This method assessed the value of SAP assets at 250 million rubles in early 1991 prices. The Soviet government transferred 54 percent of SAP to the collective enterprise outright, and sold it the remaining 46 percent for the book value as assessed by the formula. Thus the collective enterprise incurred a debt of 115 million rubles to the Soviet government (which was later transferred intact to the Russian government).

SAP management[12] then decided to divide the ownership of the collective enterprise into shares, valued at the time at one ruble each, that were distributed as follows: 46 percent was reserved as a guarantee against the debt from the government, 30 percent (which was equal to the formula-assessed value of the housing complexes) was reserved for further economic separation of the housing assets from the main aircraft production, 6 percent was held in reserve to use as special incentives; and 18 percent was distributed directly to the SAP labor force. Each employee was given 500 shares, plus an additional number based on a formula which considered length of service, professional qualifications, and five-year salary history. Individual share certificates were not issued; instead, the number of shares received was recorded in each employee's workbook. No formal internal market for trading shares was established, but employees were free to buy and sell from each other at whatever price they could negotiate. Employees were also offered the opportunity to buy additional shares from the SAP reserve for one ruble each, and were given two additional shares for every one purchased, subject to a minimum purchase of 400 rubles and a maximum purchase of 4000 rubles. By this method, SAP collected 1.1 million of the 1.5 million rubles due to the government on the first installment, and was able to make the first payment to the state in 1991.

The Transition to Full Employee Ownership

In 1991, SAP management decided to move as quickly as possible from the collective ownership structure to that of an employee-owned joint-stock company, for several reasons. They believed that the joint-stock company would: a) give employees a greater sense of ownership than the collective enterprise did, thus motivating them and increasing productivity; b) provide a means of obtaining investment capital from the employees and possibly from other sources for plant modernization, product development, and marketing; c) provide a recruiting incentive for new employees from the Saratov region; and, most of all, d) provide a better financial basis for the firm and its workers to help compensate for the inadequate external economic infrastructure. These beliefs were reinforced by the success of the experiment in which five SAP production shops operated as separate small-enterprise legal entities, enabling them to receive their economic profits directly, and distribute these to their workers.

Securing Western Help

As a part of its conversion and privatization strategy, the Saratov Aviation Plant aggressively pursued help from the West in many areas. The primary source of help was a collaborative project on defense conversion between the Institute of United States and Canadian Studies (ISKAN) of the Russian Academy of Sciences, and Stanford University's Center for International Security and Arms Control (CISAC) in the United States. During 1991, ISKAN and CISAC arranged for executives of Soviet enterprises undergoing defense conversion to visit the United States and meet with counterparts from American defense enterprises.[13] Alexander Yermishin participated in some of these meetings, and discussed his objectives with representatives from CISAC.

As a result of these discussions, CISAC agreed to arrange for a team of American specialists to provide technical assistance to the Saratov Aviation Plant in its transition to a Western-style employee-owned corporation.[14] In addition to CISAC and ISKAN, the project team included the Science Applications International Corporation (SAIC), a large U.S. employee-owned corporation that itself is undergoing defense conversion, and the Foundation for Enterprise Development (FED), a U.S. nonprofit organization that specializes in the establishment of employee stock ownership programs (ESOPs).

In December 1991, Yermishin discussed the status and objectives of the Saratov Aviation Plant with members of the CISAC team, and invited the team to participate in a meeting of senior SAP managers to be held at Saratov in January 1992. The purpose of that meeting was to review the progress of the plant over the last year, and to discuss issues associated with the transition to full employee ownership and to a Western-style operation. Nine people from the CISAC team participated in the meetings, which were held over a three-week period.[15] About 25 SAP managers participated.

During the meetings, SAP managers discussed the current status of collective ownership, the attitudes of the workers, production and facility expansion plans, organizational structure, personnel management issues, quality control problems, and current financial planning and management methods. They discussed their approach with the CISAC team, and asked many questions about what they saw as the main issues associated with the transition to a privatized, employee-owned, decentralized company.

The CISAC team responded with discussions and lectures on a wide range of subjects. These included basic concepts of stock ownership; alternative forms of employee ownership; corporate management structures; Western cost accounting terminology and methods; financial planning, reporting, and management methods (including income and balance sheets); decentralized management structures; personnel management; administrative structures; employee incentives (including bonuses, fringe benefits, and profit sharing); stock valuation methods; internal stock markets; corporate charters and bylaws; and the relationship between tax structures and incentive structures. SAIC was used as a specific example of how these issues had been addressed in a U.S. employee-owned corporation. Several internal SAIC policy and procedures documents, along with corporate legal documents, were provided to SAP managers for reference. SAP also videotaped all of the lectures for subsequent use with other SAP employees.

During the third week, SAP managers divided into five working groups, each of which focused on one of the following areas: future production plans, financial planning, management, personnel, and legal documents necessary for the transition to a joint-stock company. The objective was to prepare a set of documents to be the basis for SAP's transition from a collective enterprise to a U.S.-style, employee-owned, privatized joint-stock company. The members of the CISAC team were divided among the working groups to answer questions as required. At the end of the week, the working groups submitted their reports. The management, financial, and personnel groups decided to adopt the main elements of Western corporate structure and decentralized financial planning and personnel management. The stock and charter group was not able to complete its work because of difficulty understanding basic stock concepts, corporate charters and bylaws, and how to form a Western-style employee-owned corporation within current Russian law.

In April 1992, four senior SAP managers came to the United States to meet with the CISAC team to discuss progress that had been made since January.[16] The meetings were held over the course of a week at the SAIC facilities in McLean, Virginia.[17] A major focus of discussion was a set of six draft documents SAP managers considered to be essential to their progress. The documents were being developed for an employee meeting planned for June 1992, at which employees would formally authorize a new joint-stock company to replace the collective ownership structure, along with the implementation of revised corporate management, financial planning, and personnel methods. Three of the documents were required by current Russian law: a charter, a founding contract, and bylaws (or "decree") of the shareholders. Three others had been developed as management documents: bylaws of the board of directors, bylaws of the chairman of the board, and bylaws of the committees/officers. The "founding contract" is unique to Russian law, with no equivalent required for the establishment of an American corporation. The charter does have an American counter-part. The other four documents normally would be contained in the bylaws of an American company.

The structure and contents of the draft legal documents demonstrated a significant evolution in the understanding of SAP managers about the concept of a Western-style corporation. In the January sessions, many SAP managers believed that charter documents must contain the details of all aspects of company structure and operations, and that those details must be voted upon by the employee-owners. The later draft documents reflected an improved understanding of the real purposes, and inherent simplicity, of charter documents, and of the differences between the responsibilities of a corporate board of directors and a corporate management council responsible for company operations.

Several other subjects were discussed in some detail. These included corporate manage-ment procedures, personnel management, financial and stock accounting computer systems, corporate financial and administrative staff structures, stock valuation and distribution methods, incentives, and industrial security procedures.[18] With the exception of industrial security, all of these subjects had been discussed at the January meetings in Saratov, but the SAP managers raised new specific questions that surfaced when they tried to apply the information they had received earlier.

Forming a Joint-Stock Company

As a result of the April sessions, SAP managers made final revisions to the draft legal documents and to the operational and financial procedures. In May 1992, SAP retired its debt note outstanding with the Russian government and received a full certificate of ownership in exchange, thus becoming the first fully privatized defense enterprise of its size in Russia. SAP had planned to complete the final transformation to an employee-owned joint-stock company in June; however, continuing changes to Russian law prolonged this process.[19]

In July, as an interim step, SAP made the transition from collective ownership to a partnership with limited liabilities. This change was necessary because of a new Russian law that would prohibit collective ownership. Over the latter half of 1992, SAP continued to prepare the necessary legal documents for transition to a joint-stock company. The firm developed procedures for distributing full ownership to the employees and pensioners, created an initial board of directors,[20] refined the new management structure, and created procedures for stock accounting[21] and for the operations of an internal market.[22] SAP leadership also initiated a massive program to communicate with, educate, and discuss the proposed change with the SAP workers,[23] and continued to discuss the proposed changes with the local trade unions.

SAP management particularly focused its attention on two difficult issues. The first was distribution of ownership in the new joint-stock company, a complex issue for several reasons. First, the original share distribution to the employees in 1991 excluded the assets used to secure the outstanding note to the Soviet government. Once SAP repaid the debt, the 115 million one-ruble shares corresponding to this portion of the plant had to be distributed.

175

Second, SAP had performed a more refined plant valuation than the one done in 1990. This new valuation reflected not only a more accurate estimate of the market value of SAP assets, but also the financial growth that had occurred in 1991 and 1992. Third, procedures were needed for distributing ownership between current long-term employees, current recent hires, employees about to retire, and pensioners, so that each group would feel it was being treated fairly. Finally, Russian law required that the full ownership of the company be distributed to the employee-owners as a part of the incorporation process. As a result, the shares previously held as a management reserve for incentive programs also had to be distributed.

The second critical issue that required special attention was that involving roles, rights, and responsibilities of the five small enterprises that had been created in 1991 as independent legal entities. These enterprises savored their independence, but were also necessary parts of the main aircraft manufacturing production chain. SAP senior management concentrated on these two issues in order to work out compromises acceptable to all parties. In addition, there was continuing concern about whether to incorporate as a closed or an open joint-stock company. In the end, the final decision was to incorporate as a closed-stock company in order to gain some experience with stock company operations,[24] while reserving the option to become an open-stock company at some time in the future.

In October, a conference of SAP worker delegates approved a process for distribution of property and for the establishment of the management structure of the new joint-stock company. The final charter documents and management and ownership structure were presented to a congress of the SAP employees on February 6, 1993.[25] The change in ownership structure was approved by a 95 percent vote. Alexander Yermishin, general director, was elected to the new board of directors by a 98 percent vote, and subsequently was elected chairman of the board. Three other new board members received the minimum 75 percent vote required by Russian law. The sixth of February marked the culmination of a process that began in 1989 and was groundbreaking in Russia in many respects. It had taken more than two years in a period of extraordinary political and economic turbulence, but SAP had finally become a fully employee-owned joint-stock corporation.

Business Operations During the Process of Privatization

SAP's transformation to a privatized employee-owned joint-stock company took place concurrently with the transformation of the enterprise from a command-economic to a market-economic mode of business operations. In retrospect, it is apparent that SAP leaders' aggressiveness in moving into market-based business practices had a direct and favorable influence on the attitudes of the workers facing a totally unfamiliar form of ownership. Conversely, the fact that SAP was moving aggressively to become a privatized employee-owned company made employees willing to work harder to stabilize business operations. Finally, the combination of these two phenomena also made a positive impression on SAP's external suppliers, as well as on others in the Saratov region and in Russia.

As 1992 began, SAP confronted many problems associated with the transformation to market-based operations. According to Yermishin, principal challenges included finding reliable suppliers (taking into account time, quality, and cost reliability); obtaining a fair economic valuation of SAP in order to make good investment decisions; establishing SAP's social welfare sector (housing, farm, education, and health facilities) on a self-supporting basis so as not to handicap the aircraft sector; understanding and complying with international aircraft quality control standards; obtaining marketing help; improving production efficiency; and training SAP managers at all levels in Western-style corporate operations, privatization, conversion, and employee-ownership principles.[26]

V. Gorbunov, vice director, identified the additional problems of SAP's lack of modern production technology based on computer-aided design/computer-aided manufacturing (CAD/CAM) methods, and a parallel lack of modern information processing systems. Gorbunov agreed with Yermishin on the need for managerial experience in market-based corporate operations.[27]

SAP's director of personnel, Y. Kovshov, pointed out such specific problem areas as the difficulty in retaining highly skilled workers, the need for adequate housing, the necessity of a wage scale consistent with those of other Saratov enterprises, and the lack of an internal labor market within SAP.[28]

The CISAC team observed other issues as well. On the computer front, SAP did not have modern financial planning and accounting software systems, or modern production scheduling software. Dealings with SAP suppliers suffered from the lack of competition and incentives for the suppliers. With the market and the economy unstable, the firm needed surrogate measures of profitability and performance to guide financial planning. In order to complete production on existing foreign aircraft contracts, SAP needed cash; the CISAC team felt the firm should negotiate with state marketing organs for progress payments on the contracts in order to minimize the credit needed from local financial institutions. The CISAC advisors also saw a need to review employee fringe benefits versus individual employee responsibilities, and a need for education and training in Western cost-accounting methods. Finally, they advocated retaining independent financial and legal advisory firms familiar with both Western methods and practices and the current state of Russian law.

By October 1992, SAP had made substantial progress in most of its major problem areas. It now had more than 1600 reliable suppliers. SAP explained to the management of each supplier what it was trying to do, and offered a share in the SAP profits if supplies were delivered on time. The suppliers seemed eager to be a part of the SAP team. SAP also had continued to modernize plant facilities; modern production machinery now stood in the bays where cruise missiles used to be produced, bays that had been empty in January. The ten months from January to October also saw the acquisition of more than 160 modern computers, which were partially linked in a local area network supporting the mechanical preparation of the production plant.[29]

SAP also made some needed management changes by electing an executive director, analogous to the chief operating officer of a Western corporation, to run the company on a day-to-day basis,[30] and by establishing the new position of deputy director for sales to handle both domestic and international sales. Other progress involved steps toward the separation of the ownership and operations of some of the social welfare facilities from that of the aircraft company.[31]

During 1992, SAP also substantially improved its economic situation. During that year, overall production in Russia declined by 20 percent, but SAP production increased by 30 percent, and profits increased by 50 percent.[32] SAP also established good relations with China, India, Cuba, Israel, and other nations, and is continuing to cultivate those relationships. The general aircraft development plan prepared two years earlier proceeded according to schedule.[33] Foreign investment in general modernization did not yet materialize, but investors in Europe agreed to finance the development of specific new aircraft projects.[34] One SAP-developed idea for a new aircraft design—a "flying plate" based on screening and hovering effects—received serious attention abroad as a major new development project. The plant did well enough to add a second shift of 2000 workers. The one negative component to the SAP economic picture was in the sale of consumer goods: kitchen products continued to sell, but sales of toys and other consumer goods decreased.

SAP has also been able to improve the conditions of its workers. The average salary, which had been 900 rubles/month in January, was approximately 6000 rubles/month by October, and was tied to an inflation index based on prices of goods in the local Saratov market.[35] A basic automated personnel management system was also developed. Furthermore, SAP began to focus on other important issues, such as environmental problems.[36] At the end of 1992, the Saratov Aviation Plant was one of only two former defense industries in Saratov in good financial condition. The move to privatize via employee ownership certainly had a direct effect on this situation.

Issues and Obstacles

During the privatization of the Saratov Aviation Plant, several important issues and some obstacles surfaced. Although most problems have been successfully overcome by SAP, they are similar to issues that will face other enterprises attempting to privatize through employee ownership. Given SAP's experience, we can group the major issues involved in privatization through employee ownership into five main areas.

1) Conceptual Understanding

Discussions of transition to a joint-stock company revealed a lack of understanding among managers and employees of many of the basic concepts behind a market-based stock corporation.[37] These included the very idea of a corporation, stock, stock valuation, the relationship of stock value to profitability and growth, stock issuance, stock dilution, and stock liquidity. A second set of conceptual issues focused on governance, and included the role and responsibilities of a corporate board of directors (versus the management council responsible for day-to-day operations), the purpose of shareholders' meetings, shareholders' voting rights and responsibilities, and the basic idea of "one share, one vote" (as opposed to "one shareholder, one vote"). A third set of conceptual issues concerned corporate legal documents (charter and bylaws) and the difference between those documents and documents that describe day-to-day corporate operations and production development plans. Both managers and workers must receive significant training, with explanation of many new concepts, in order for privatization to succeed.[38]

2) Trust

SAP managers expressed concern that transition to an employee-owned joint-stock company may not actually result in the distribution of the profits to the employees and managers. They also were anxious about insuring that employee-owners would have sufficient say in company operations, and that they would have the power to replace the board of directors. These concerns illustrate a cultural issue that SAP managers had to confront as a part of the transition to employee-ownership: they had learned their jobs under the Soviet system, which eroded trust in authority. Workers and managers did not trust the government, the legal system, or enterprise management.

SAP managers found, however, that trust is an essential requirement of a Western-style joint-stock company. The stockholders must believe that the elected board of directors will act in their best interests. They must be comfortable delegating their authority to others to vote on their behalf, with the overarching good of the stockholders as the guiding principle. The stockholders must also trust that the legal system will provide them with a means of resolving disagreements fairly. Employee ownership makes this basic issue more immediate because the employee-owners are also subject to the day-to-day problems of running a company. The employees must trust that company management will successfully deal with day-to-day problems and create a long-term strategy. Finally, the employee-owners must trust that profits and rewards will be distributed to them fairly and in accordance with established procedures.

It will take time, some positive experiences, and substantial education and training to instill the necessary trust in Russian society that will permit the routine operation of employee-owned joint-stock companies. Until trust is established, employees will probably be wary of this form of ownership, and will need a careful and deliberate system of involvement and feedback from management in order to be fully supportive.

3) Employee Expectations

In several instances, employees expected that employee ownership would mean maximum control and immediate personal profit, which led them to advocate short-sighted policies. Many SAP employees wanted to keep ownership solely in the hands of employees because they feared outsiders. SAP managers, however, saw the need for selective foreign investment in order to attract foreign capital. There was also conflict over the shares that were withheld from the workforce as a corporate reserve for future incentives. Many SAP managers and employees felt that these shares should be distributed immediately. Some SAP employees and managers also pushed to dispose of shares withheld for revenue in order to meet current economic problems associated with inflation, rather than retaining them for their long-term growth potential.

The managers of the five small enterprises that had previously been granted legal independence demonstrated another clash of interests resulting from inappropriate expectations of the new structure. They wanted to retain financial independence so that they could distribute their profits directly to their workers. SAP management called for the return of their revenues to SAP; their reward for financially sound management would be additional ownership shares in SAP, or simply an increase in the value of stock already owned.

4) Procedures and Operations

There were several issues SAP encountered concerning the mechanics of transition to and operation of an employee-owned joint-stock company. Difficult new tasks included creating procedures for the initial distribution of ownership; establishing stock programs and ownership plans to provide different classes of incentives; creating and operating an internal market for trading stock; electing an initial board of directors; defining and carrying out operational duties of the board; learning and executing the mechanics of stockholder meetings and votes; creating a bonus, incentive, and profit-sharing system for rewarding employees for increased productivity; and drafting a full disclosure statement for stockholders explaining the risks and potential rewards associated with stock ownership.

5) Law

Several issues surfaced with regard to Russian law.[39] At the beginning of 1992, extant laws raised a number of problems for SAP. The most basic of these was the issue of SAP's legal status as a collective enterprise. Collective property was not a long-standing form of property in the Soviet Union. It was introduced by the USSR Law on Property (March 1990) as a halfway step toward the creation of real private property, which was completed by the Russian Law on Property of December 1990. Neither this law nor the Russian Law on Enterprises and Entrepreneurship, also passed in December 1990, mentioned collective property. The legal status of a "collective enterprise" was therefore ambiguous.

By 1992, there were also legal difficulties in implementing SAP's plan to become a fully employee-owned joint-stock company. The Russian government's draft privatization plans limited the fraction of employee ownership permitted to an enterprise.[40] The draft laws applied only to state and municipal enterprises about to be privatized, however; because the Saratov Aviation Plant was fully privatized by May 1992, it did not fit into either category. Also, there were legal ambiguities concerning the procedural requirements for transfer of ownership from a privatized collective enterprise to a joint-stock company. Finally, the legal structure was incomplete and did not regulate security exchanges, enforce the corporate right of first refusal of stock repurchase,[41] define procedures for establishing an employee-owned closed joint-stock company with foreign investment, or determine legal forms for a corporate charter and bylaws.[42]

180

As 1992 progressed, some of these legal ambiguities were clarified, and new ones appeared. In July, SAP moved from collective ownership to the form of a "partnership with limited responsibilities" as the result of an imminent Russian law that threatened to outlaw the collective form of ownership. At the same time, new regulations affected the process of transition to a joint-stock company and created new requirements for stock company formation, housing, and asset valuation. The net impact of these regulations was to delay the process by several months. Perhaps most importantly, the Russian legal requirement for transferring all ownership to employees upon incorporation as a joint-stock company prevented SAP from immediately establishing ESOPs and other forms of stock-based worker incentive programs, which are a principal advantage of employee ownership.

Conclusion

Over the last three years, the Saratov Aviation Plant has made the transition from a Soviet state-owned defense enterprise to a Russian privatized employee-owned joint-stock company producing commercial aviation and consumer products, with minor support to defense requirements. The progress made in 1992 has resulted in an enterprise whose position is looked upon favorably by its employees, its suppliers, and its customers, in contrast to similar enterprises. In his address to the delegates at the February 1993 meeting at which SAP became a fully privatized joint-stock company, General Director Yermishin enumerated some of the company's major achievements in 1992. More than 8000 employees purchased shares in the new joint-stock company, the plant's economic activity increased by 15 percent over the previous year, and 1992 was the first year since 1976 that there was an increase in the size of the workforce. The quality of products also improved, and the enterprise initiated new programs aimed at improving the housing conditions of its workers. In addition, the enterprise began the production of two new aircraft types, acquired new modern machinery for some of its production shops, and purchased a substantial number of new computers to support both technical and management requirements.

SAP still faces many challenges in market-driven operations. Success will depend on the degree to which SAP can resolve these issues and still execute the firm's development plan in the midst of the turbulent Russian economy.

The experience of the Saratov Aviation Plant provides a number of important lessons for other enterprises in Russia. In particular, the principal lesson from this experience seems to be the importance of senior management initiative. SAP's managers worked to find solutions to problems at the enterprise level without waiting for the overall economic, legal, and political situation to stabilize, and they were willing to proceed incrementally into unfamiliar areas in order to gain the necessary experience The Saratov Aviation Plant experience suggests that enterprises that adopt this kind of attitude will probably undergo defense conversion and privatization much more successfully than those that do not. The SAP experience also suggests that with proper explanations, training, and employee involvement, employee ownership can be an excellent option for privatization.

SAP's experience also identified the following general areas that should be addressed by any Russian enterprise attempting a similar endeavor.

181

1) Education

Substantial education and training is essential for both enterprise management and workers on the principles and structure of market-based corporations, on stock concepts and mechanics, and on the relationship of financial standing to stock values. This training is needed to make individuals comfortable with new ideas and to counter attitudes that carry over from the Communist system. Workers must learn the difference between the short-term and long-term value of stock, and should be encouraged to view stock in terms of its long-range benefits, a view that will be easier to encourage as the Russian economy stabilizes.

Education should also address the social welfare sector, evaluating state/enterprise responsibility versus individual responsibility for these benefits, and illustrating how such policy choices affect wage structure and enterprise profits. It can also be useful to describe the democratic system of checks and balances that protects individuals' rights, promotes trust of institutions, and provides established procedures for resolving disagreements. Finally, employees should be taught how to balance employee-ownership rights and responsibilities in order to ensure that the employee-ownership structure remains viable.[43] Such awareness will depend largely on experience as well as education.

2) Improved Valuation Methods

Russian accounting practices differ significantly from Western practices. When combined with the instability of the Russian economy and the inconvertibility of the ruble on the international market, it becomes very difficult to get a fair market assessment of an enterprise's assets. Some buyouts have been negotiated based on depreciation schedules for equipment and formula values of assets, but there is no established means for assessing intangible values such as goodwill, market position, and technological advantages. Until these issues are resolved, a standard and comprehensive method should be devised to establish a fair initial buyout price, and to allow periodic revaluation of the company.

3) Russian Legal Structure

Russian law must be adapted to allow enterprises to privatize via employee-ownership until a full legal and economic infrastructure is established. Employee stock ownership programs and other incentive stock programs must be given legal status as part of the initial creation of the joint-stock company. If these alternatives were available from the outset, employee-ownership would be more attractive due to additional incentives that could be used by enterprise management to increase the value and profits of the enterprise.

4) Assistance with Daily Operations

Practical experience with the mechanics of operating an employee-owned privatized corporation will take time. Western counterpart firms can contribute greatly by sharing their experiences and solutions to typical problems as the details of operations are put into practice.

Notes

[1] A. Yevreinov, "Saratov: Moving Toward the Future," *Soviet Life* (September 1991): 20.

[2] This paper is an adaptation, with minor revisions, of an earlier paper by the author published as Chapter Four of M. McFaul (ed.), "Can the Russian Military-Industrial Complex Be Privatized? Evaluating the Experiment in Employee Ownership at the Saratov Aviation Plant," A Report of the Defense Conversion Project of the Center for International Security and Arms Control (Stanford, CA: Stanford University, May 1993).

[3] Details on SAP history and product lines are from *Collective Enterprise* "Saratov Aviation Plant" (Saratov, 1991), 1-2; and the brochure, *Collective Enterprise, Saratov Aviation Plant* (Saratov, 1991), 1-4.

[4] Factual information not otherwise attributed was collected over the course of numerous meetings with SAP managers, at SAP in Saratov in January 1992, at SAIC facilities in McLean, Virginia in April 1992, and back at SAP in Saratov in October 1992 and February 1993.

[5] Alexander Yermishin, author's interview, Saratov, January, 1992.

[6] *Aviation Production Development of Collective Enterprise "Saratov Aviation Plant" Under Conditions of Economic Reform* (Saratov, 1991).

[7] At the time this step was taken, aircraft prices were state-regulated, and separate enterprises had to be formed to sell products at market prices. Since then, this requirement has been relaxed.

[8] A "collective enterprise" is not state-owned, but neither is it fully employee-owned in the Western sense. The term denotes collective ownership by the labor force. The Western concept of an employee-owned company involves a corporate legal entity, with shares of stock that account for the current value of all corporate assets, and are issued to the employees as stockholders, who are thus the owners. This type of structure is known as a "stock company" under Russian law, and is sharply distinct from a collective enterprise.

[9] Yevreinov, 20.

[10] "Council of Ministers of the USSR Resolution on Conversion of Saratov Aviation Plant and Saratov Electro-Aggregate Production Association into Collective Enterprises," in *Aviation Production ... Under Conditions of Economic Reform*.

[11] The formulas used did not attempt to reflect current world market value of SAP assets. Nevertheless, the formula valuation did give SAP management some basis for further distribution of ownership to the individual employees.

[12] Corporate governance at Saratov Aviation Plant is currently based on an annual company conference of delegates selected as representatives by work units (some as small as five employees). A total of 576 delegates was chosen for the first conference, and these delegates then voted for a nine-person Board of Directors, who in turn elected Alexander Yermishin as president and chairman of the board.

[13] David Bernstein and Katherine Smith, "Collaborative Project on Soviet Defense Conversion," May 1991 Project Status Report of the Center for International Security and Arms Control (Stanford, CA: Stanford University, 1991).

[14] The Saratov Aviation Plant is the first Russian enterprise to be selected as a case study for a project funded by the Carnegie Corporation of New York. The purpose of the project is to gather empirical evidence to be used to formulate models for successful defense conversion within Russia; these models could be used by other enterprises and also assist in policymaking within the Russian and U.S. governments. There were two principal reasons SAP was

chosen: the manager is a young, dynamic, Western-style businessman who is strongly motivated and committed to conversion; and privatization began early (the state had turned ownership over to the employees before the August 1991 coup attempt against the Soviet government). For further insights into both points, see Galina Batsanova, "Alexander Yermishin: An Unidentified Flying Opportunist," *Delovie Lyudi*, May 1993: 76–78.

[15] Participants on the CISAC team included the Assistant to the Directors of CISAC (D. Bernstein), a practicing lawyer and specialist in Soviet labor law from the University of California, Berkeley (K. Hendley), two senior executives from SAIC (J. Battilega and M. Tobriner), a senior financial specialist from SAIC (S. Cosentino), two Associate Directors from the Foundation for Enterprise Development (R. Bernstein and D. Binns), a senior management specialist from ISKAN (Y. Ushanov), and an Assistant Professor of Finance from Moscow State University, at the time a visiting fellow at CISAC (T. Krylova).

[16] The visitors were V. Gorbunov, Vice Director and Chief Operation Officer, M. Mordvinkin, Chief Financial Officer, Y. Kovshov, Director of Personnel, and S. Sotov, Head of Industrial Security.

[17] All personnel from the CISAC team who visited Saratov in January were present at this meeting except for Y. Ushanov from ISKAN, who was replaced by G. Kochetkov. New participants included another research associate from CISAC (M. McFaul), a number of SAIC managers, and legal, financial, and personnel specialists, who provided discussions in specific areas of SAP interest.

[18] Many new industrial security problems confront SAP. These include not only the physical security of SAP commercial products and facilities, but also a range of intellectual security issues: intellectual property rights, airplane design rights, nondisclosure issues in subcontracts, team projects and joint ventures with other commercial enterprises, SAP-proprietary information, and patent rights.

[19] By October, SAP increased the size of its legal staff, and was contemplating hiring an independent legal firm to help with its transition problems and with the general legal issues associated with market-economic operations.

[20] Procedures had to be developed to nominate and present an initial slate of candidates to the workers. Since Russian law required approval by three quarters of the stockholders, the enterprise set up a procedure for a large slate of candidates to be narrowed down progressively until the required number were elected with the necessary majority.

[21] SAP assigned a financial manager to the job of developing an internal stock accounting system and of working out the mechanics of stock trades. A basic computer system was also developed to assist in this process.

[22] SAP's initial approach was to create a true internal market by which shares would be traded on a monthly basis, with supply and demand determining the price of the stock each month. This approach allowed the internal market to proceed, but made stock prices susceptible to the inordinate impact of trading a small number of shares in a given month. The relative insensitivity to this kind of anomaly is one of the advantages of the formula approach to establishing the stock price. This is the approach used in some closed employee-owned stock companies in the West. SAP plans to refine its internal market rules once it has some experience.

[23] The communications program with SAP workers was intensive and took several forms. Managers at all levels received special training and discussed the issues with their subordinates. Extensive use was made of the factory newspaper to explain the impending change and its rationale. Finally, Yermishin started a weekly radio program in which workers could

185

call in and ask questions and he would discuss the answers over the radio. As a result of these efforts, worker support for the change grew rapidly. For example, by October 1992, about 90 percent of SAP employees had written in their share book that they intended to transfer the ownership of their shares in the collective to the new joint stock company. Additionally, there was a noticeable change in the employees as individuals: they were becoming very interested in the change, and no one was trying to sell shares.

[24] There was concern that inexperience could put SAP and its employees at a disadvantage if the company became partially owned by outside investors. Hence, in spite of the need for investment capital, SAP made the decision to stay closed so as to be better able to control its own destiny.

[25] Representatives from the CISAC team visited SAP in both October and February, participated in both conferences as observers, and provided consultations and training. In October, the principal issues of concern to SAP management focused on the mechanics of employee-ownership: the election of a board of directors, the distribution of property, the operations of an internal market. In February, SAP management asked for help on various aspects of corporate operations, and many of the issues discussed in earlier training sessions were revisited.

[26] Yermishin, author's interview, Saratov, January 1992. SAP faced all these issues while coping with an additional constraint: state price controls required SAP to sell aircraft below actual costs. This is no longer an issue.

[27] V. Gorbunov, author's interview, Saratov, April, 1992.

[28] Y. Kovshov, author's interviews, Saratov, January, 1992, and McLean, Virginia, April, 1992.

[29] SAP plans to create a family of fully integrated local area networks to handle all aspects of design, production, financial planning and monitoring, payroll, stock management and internal market operations, and personnel administration. It has a computer division of more than 200 people responsible for operations and system design and development, staffed by new computer science graduates of local universities.

[30] Decentralized financial operations, one of SAP's objectives, have not yet been adopted, because the necessary financial accounting, budgeting, and monitoring computer systems have not yet been developed. SAP's annual budgeting process is also still a holdover from the command-economic mode of operations. It must be adapted to meet the requirements of budgeting with market-driven demand.

[31] Three of the SAP collective farms were formed into a joint enterprise with U.S. agricultural companies. SAP will own a controlling interest in this joint enterprise, but the board of directors includes representatives of the Western partners. SAP is also working on a program to sell the housing complexes to individuals, and transfer ownership to the individual workers. The firm is promoting single-family dwellings, and has programs underway to finance their construction. At this time, SAP is one of the few enterprises in Saratov continuing to build houses.

[32] L. Hayes, "Russian Plant Weans Itself from the Military," *Wall Street Journal*, January 5, 1993: A10.

[33] The development of a new Yak–40 airplane, supported by Western European investment, is now a priority for SAP. SAP is also continuing to develop the flying plate, an economical flying machine capable of lifting very heavy loads.

[34] Yermishin attributed this distinction to general uncertainty about the future political and economic stability of Russia, and not to specific conditions at the firm. Author's interview, Saratov, October, 1992.

[35] The salary structure within SAP is still based on old standards established by the Soviet Ministry of Aviation. SAP intends to revise the salary structure soon to meet contemporary requirements.

[36] The Saratov Aviation Plant is in the Southern Saratov Industrial Zone, which suffers from air, water, and solid waste pollution. The Saratov region itself, including the Volga river, is a major region of environmental concern. The development of economically feasible methods to reduce SAP's environmental pollution is important for several reasons. First, pollution directly affects the health of SAP workers, most of whom live very near the plant. Second, environmentally clean operations will be cheaper than paying to clean up pollution, which SAP would be required to do under a new Russian law soon to take effect. Finally, in order to receive international certification for aircraft production, SAP production technology must meet strict environmental standards. Hence, solution of SAP's environmental problems is directly related to SAP's future economic viability. E.I. Pyrozhenko, author's interview, Saratov, October, 1992.

[37] In January 1992, a survey was taken of the workers to determine if they preferred to remain a collective enterprise or to transition to a joint-stock company. Of those sampled, 46 percent asked for more information about the differences.

[38] There are also underlying psychological issues that may need to be addressed. For example, one SAP manager argued that some workers are not prepared for transition to a joint-stock company because it is a major step toward the capitalism that they were taught to despise.

[39] For a detailed discussion of legal issues relating to SAP, see Kathryn Hendley, "Steps on the Road to Privatization: A Preliminary Report on the Saratov Aviation Plant," June 1992 Project Status Report of the Center for International Security and Arms Control (Stanford, CA: Stanford University, 1992).

[40] During 1992, several versions of draft Russian privatization laws appeared, each of which treated employee ownership somewhat differently. For example, one draft Russian privatization law provided for a maximum of 51 percent of employee ownership. For more details, see Chapter Two of *Can the Russian Military-Industrial Complex Be Privatized? Evaluating the Experiment in Employee Ownership at the Saratov Aviation Plant* (Stanford University: Center for International Security and Arms Control, 1993).

[41] This right means that if an employee-owner receives an offer to sell stock to someone outside the corporation, or if the employee leaves the corporation and decides to sell his or her stock, the corporation has the first right to repurchase the stock. This right is acknowledged by the employee as one of the conditions of employment or of stock ownership.

[42] During the first six months of 1992, there was also the question of the legal status of the debt that SAP incurred from the former Soviet government. SAP resolved this question by paying the Russian government in June 1992.

[43] This is the kind of "economic sense" that works in the Western context to prevent all of a bank's depositors from withdrawing their funds at the same time, although the bank guarantees each individual depositor the right to withdraw the full deposit on demand. If all depositors suddenly lost such a sense of the economy, the entire banking system would not be viable, and severe economic damage would occur, as it did in the United States in 1929.

10

Enterprise Strategies To Cope with Reduced Defense Spending: The Experience of the Perm Region

Tarja Cronberg

In terms of the absolute number of workers employed in military production and in the defense complex's share of total employment, the Perm region ranks as one of the ten top regions in the Former Soviet Union.[1] This paper examines defense conversion experiences in the Perm region from November 1991 to May 1993. In November 1991, March 1992, November 1992, and February 1993, I interviewed managers and chief engineers from 10 of the 30 military enterprises in the region. The paper is based on an analysis of the competitive advantage of military industries in the conversion process. Starting with Michael Porter's analysis, which has been adapted to military conversion by Hilton [2], I have attempted to identify enterprise strategies that bridge the gap between military and civil production, and to draw conclusions about the supply and demand factors which dominate the conversion process in the Perm region.

A Question of Assets

The absence of obvious civil applications does not mean that they do not exist, but to be developed they require an organization to play the role of translator to foresee possible applications for advanced technology in unlikely areas. Even to identify possible uses does not mean that a market exists or that it will yield an adequate level of profitability within the time horizon of private firms.[3]

Tarja Cronberg is an associate professor at the Technical University of Denmark.

The defense industry should not be viewed as a uniform entity, as Hilton points out, because it does not consist of enterprises using identical resources and operating at the same optimum output. Rather, defense enterprises vary both in size and in the technology they employ in production. Enterprises also have different organizational structures, from single-product small firms to large multi-product conglomerates.[4] Hilton prefers to define industrial groupings by the assets they deploy rather than the products they sell. These groupings can then be used to analyze the conversion potential of an enterprise and to aid in the selection of future strategies. Hilton's categories are competitive assets, efficiency assets, complementary assets, and specialist assets. Competitive assets provide enterprises with a competitive advantage on the demand side and a differentiated product, while efficiency assets provide enterprises a competitive advantage on the supply side to enable them to drive down costs. Complementary assets are not crucial for a business, but enable enterprises to deploy other assets effectively; i.e., they give access to economies of scope. Specialist assets, on the other hand, are a key part of a business, allowing the enterprise to exploit the division of labor to its fullest possible extent.

After defining these terms, Hilton refers to Gilmore and Coddington's 1966 analysis of a number of conversion case studies,[5] and lists a number of deficiencies in defense firms seeking to convert or diversify. In many enterprises, commercial marketing skills are absent (lack of an efficiency asset), while in others the cost base is too high (high use of complementary assets). An enterprise's technology may be too sophisticated (excessive emphasis on competitive assets), or its production may be overly oriented toward high technology as opposed to efficiency (the deployment of competitive assets given precedence over efficiency assets). Often, managers find adjusting to the different challenges of the commercial market unappealing (specialist assets are competitively, not efficiency, oriented), or are unfamiliar with commercial management practices such as cost allocation and control (low investment in efficiency assets and high investment in complementary assets).

Hilton points out that in command economies, market size and relative development cost are not an issue if the state has agreed that production should occur. The inadequacies of the Soviet distribution system and the resulting shortages, however, forced enterprises to build up a store of complementary assets to compensate for the deficiencies in the system. While this overloaded the cost base and assured the effectiveness of the military-industrial complex, it did not assure the efficiency of either the enterprises themselves, or of the economy as a whole.

Since defense enterprises in the Former Soviet Union produced higher quality consumer goods than enterprises outside the military-industrial complex, some argue that these enterprises have a high potential for conversion or diversification. Hilton, on the other hand, points out that "producing products such as washing machines, televisions or the apocryphal titanium alloy wheelbarrows at marginal cost from inefficiently deployed complementary assets hardly qualifies as realistic diversification."[6] This is particularly true if these consumer products are to compete on the future European market.

Hilton is generally critical of the hopes attached to conversion, particularly those that rely on high-technology R&D as a competitive advantage in the marketplace:

> What should be evident from the foregoing is that while [high-technology R&D] may produce a competitive asset, this can only be turned to competitive advantage with the right efficiency assets made effective by competitively priced effectively deployed complementary assets whether owned by the enterprise or

not. One should not presume that competitive advantage, and therefore possible diversification opportunities, are to be found solely through ownership of technologically competitive assets. The process that creates such concentrations of competitive assets also has a tendency, unless positive corrective action is taken, to accrete excesses of complementary assets and excrete sufficiencies of efficiency assets.[7]

I will examine the conversion strategies of Perm enterprises with Hilton's analysis in mind.

Opportunities in Dual-Use Technology

The most immediate conversion opportunities for military enterprises lie in dual-use applications, products and processes which are applicable to both the military and the civilian sectors. As technology and research in the Perm area is gradually declassified, military products, know-how, and even equipment should find civilian applications. The higher technological level of military production, combined with the distortion of prices of defense products (military products are often priced much lower than actual production costs), make the dual-use approach both feasible and immediately accessible.

In the Perm region, hopes for dual-use technologies were attached primarily to the area's numerous aircraft engine design bureaus and production enterprises. An immediate dual-use approach turned out to be difficult, however, due to differences between civil and military requirements for aircraft engines, as well as to the decreased demand for aircraft engines on the world market. Engines from the Former Soviet Union have also had difficulty meeting international environmental and safety requirements. Furthermore, many Russian aircraft producers now prefer the products of Western companies such as Pratt & Whitney to those of Russian enterprises. In an effort to establish itself in this field, in 1993 the Perm region began a long-term project to design and develop more competitive civilian aircraft engines.

Dual-use technologies faced a number of difficulties in the early phases of conversion in Russia. A materials research institute in Perm, for instance, experimented with the use of powder metallurgy in the production of toys. One resulting product was a durable toy rabbit made of titanium powder. When pressed, however, the institute's director admitted that the new toy would be expensive, costing in the vicinity of one thousand dollars.

To date, the dual-use strategy has been successful in only one enterprise interviewed whose production was evenly divided between military and civilian products before conversion. Today, the enterprise is working solely and successfully on civilian production. The enterprise produces active coal from coal or home-made charcoal, and uses this technology in household filters for water purification and respiratory protective devices for industries with dust problems. The young, well-educated managers of the enterprise have implemented conversion without outside financing or assistance; the enterprise has searched for new networks independently, without relying on former associations. The search for dual-use technologies was characterized by trial and error and a reliance on existing know-how. The enterprise's former military production was conducted under ministry orders and in cooperation with the Active Coal Institute; today, civilian production is completely in-house.

The Technology Gap

A second strategy for seeking new business opportunities is to bridge the gap between military and civilian technology. The disparity between the two is due primarily to the priority the Soviet state gave the military sector. The defense industry had greater access to raw materials and supplies, for instance, and military design bureaus had access to prototype production facilities, enabling them to make experimental models before production. Quality control also differed between the civil and the military sectors. In the latter, designs and prototypes were carefully finished and tested. The technical documentation was checked and chief engineers of design bureaus were held personally responsible for the products. To facilitate inter-enterprise collaboration, the government granted institutions authority to coordinate efforts and to set up special agencies for weapons development programs (e.g., ballistic missiles, nuclear weapons). Larger R&D institutes have, in fact, functioned as prime contractors do in the United States. Finally, achieving technological equality with the rest of the world created competitive pressures within the military-industrial complex that did not exist in civilian production.[8] Military production had to be on a par with world technology standards, standards the Russian government is trying to maintain.

The lack of supplies, priorities, and competition has made it difficult for enterprises in the civil sector not only to attain world standard production, but to introduce new technology as well. In 1988, Zaichenko wrote:

> The realization of scientific and technical achievements in our country [the Soviet Union] is complicated primarily by the fact that we do not have the necessary material conditions for the introduction of new technical equipment. The majority of enterprises do not have the necessary experimental and testing base and through their own forces cannot provide [a] high level of organization or work for introducing new technical equipment within short periods of time.[9]

It should be noted that this applies not only to civilian industries in general, but to civilian production in the military-industrial complex. Even within the same enterprise, the technological level and quality control of civilian production is lower than that of military production. Under these circumstances, it is not surprising that many scientists and engineers are trying to bridge the gap between military and civilian production. Using military technology, advanced composite materials, or military testing equipment should give the civilian sector greater advantages, and scientists and engineers are generally willing to lower the quality of military technology if at the same time they can improve the level of corresponding civilian technology.

A number of military enterprises in Perm are trying to reconcile the military and civilian sectors. Design bureaus that had previously worked on missile engines, artillery, or steering systems are now considering producing glass-fiber pipes for the chemical or food industries. Composite materials research institutes that worked in space technology are looking into consumer composite products that require sturdy materials, such as canoe paddles and crutches. Typically, the chief engineer or head scientist presents the technical details of a possible product in written form. In our interviews in March, 1992, we noted that these descriptions were devoid of any market-oriented information, and the general expectation was that demand would follow an increase in product quality. By November, however, enterprises were beginning to prepare market assessments for their products.

This "closing the gap" approach is best described by the director of a small new company emerging from the military industry that plans to produce machinery for manufacturing artificial surface materials. According to the director, the company was manufacturing a high-quality product. Indeed, the quality may be too high for the needs of the civil market. When confronted with the fact that customers may not need such a high-quality product, the director answered that "We know they need it, but they are not willing or able to pay."

Planned Conversion

Efforts to convert the Soviet military-industrial complex were initiated by Mikhail Gorbachev as early as 1989-1990. These first efforts, however, are generally considered failures. A number of enterprises were told to convert, shown what to produce, and then given the appropriate resources to initiate new production. The initiative was criticized for its lack of serious preparatory efforts and research prior to conversion, as well as for its lack of financial resources and legal basis.[10] Others have reported that only a fraction of defense firms to be converted (50 out of 500) were ordered to convert completely, and only five or six were converted successfully.[11]

In 1992 a number of military enterprises in Perm were familiar with Gorbachev's initiative, and one, a composite materials research institute, was among the 500 enterprises that received the conversion funds. The enterprise subsequently began producing medical syringes in facilities previously used for aerospace research. In reality, the enterprise produces only the needle itself, while the total system for injection is produced by others. The enterprise has since become a private company, and plans to produce 600 million needles over the next few years. It would also like to begin producing the whole injection system. Market assessments from November 1992 show that producers of the entire injection system have a larger profit margin. The company has some customer contact, and by the end of 1992 the technical characteristics of the company's product were no longer defined by the original conversion plans, but rather by clients. The company is now looking for international contacts, particularly in France and Italy, hoping to arrange a joint venture through which the company could acquire access to equipment in exchange for products. In spite of the fact that the company has both the technological know-how and an existing market for its products, it is having difficulty manufacturing a consumer good that is technically competitive with European equivalents.

The Search for Demand

Military-industrial enterprises in the Former Soviet Union did not have to define market needs or to study demand. Each enterprise had a planning department that worked with a central planning office in Moscow. Consequently, enterprises do not have any experience assessing markets. As early as March, 1992, however, a number of enterprises had estab-

193

lished marketing departments, often by simply renaming the planning department. Between March and November, 1992, there was also an increased awareness of the importance of marketing and of market assessment for conversion proposals.

The lack of marketing capabilities and experience, however, does not necessarily mean that enterprises are only approaching conversion from a technological standpoint. Some market demands are easily identifiable, such as health care, environmental protection, and food and housing. A number of enterprises are also starting production lines based on existing demand. The active coal company, for example, has started producing a variety of consumer goods such as deodorant, shampoo, and silverware. In one year, the enterprise produced and sold two million bottles of shampoo and an equal amount of deodorant. The enterprise's technical director pointed out that had they the necessary material resources, they would no doubt have produced and sold more. He also emphasized that under normal market conditions it might not have been possible for the enterprise to sell knives and forks, since specialists in this field could have produced better products.

One enterprise that previously manufactured aircraft engines and helicopter gear boxes is now producing tractors for the civil market. Anticipating an increase in sales of farming equipment, the enterprise started manufacturing mini-tractors, cultivators, and engine units for agriculture. To get its products to farmers, the enterprise established 18 shops in different communities around Perm. The enterprise is also looking for foreign partners for the production of small windmills for family farming. A few enterprises we interviewed even discussed producing luxury yachts, anticipating the emergence of a new wealthy class. One area in which markets already exist is raw materials and semi-finished goods. Since military enterprises have had priority access to these resources, several have decided to market semi-finished goods such as metal castings, sheets, and bars. One enterprise in particular was interested in acquiring new technology for the production of more precise titanium castings and cutting instruments.

Demand-oriented conversion faces two major problems, however. In the first place, consumer goods face competition from foreign products. As one economist in Moscow pointed out, "All those who need Russian products cannot afford them, and are buying only butter. Those who can afford Russian products are buying foreign-made ones." Secondly, there is a lack of state orders. Military industries have a tradition of working with the state sector. State demand would not only fit their organizational culture, but could offer other advantages for conversion as well, such as high-tech to high-tech conversion (which is both state policy and the goal of the enterprises). Potential for state demand does exist, particularly in the medical field, but currently no funds are available for its development. In our interviews, for instance, we came across a number of proposals for medical and environmental applications that were either not developed or not marketed due to a lack of funds.

New Networks

In the past, military enterprises had contacts with a ministry, research institutes, and design bureaus. Despite the fact that most military enterprises are regionally concentrated, there was little regional interaction such as sharing of resources or equipment. Since military enterprises are vertically integrated, the number of subcontractors is limited (compared with that of enterprises in the United States). In Perm, for instance, enterprises were partners only if they were both members of the same scientific production association.

Military enterprises are now trying to establish new business networks, and are running into a variety of problems. While military technology and production are global, for instance, civilian production is more locally and regionally rooted, and thus requires a change of focus. There are no stable market institutions that provide marketing and distribution to civilian markets, and most enterprises lack in-house capabilities for marketing and distribution.

Nonetheless, since old networks no longer exist, there are clear indications that Russian military-industrial enterprises are trying to establish new ones. In 1992, the League of Scientific and Industrial Associations of the USSR (now the Union of Entrepreneurs and Industrialists) took a survey of the economic ties of enterprises.[12] The survey covered a wide range of enterprises (not only military), of which 82 percent were state-owned, 7.7 percent had become shareholding companies, 6.3 percent belonged to workers' collectives and 1.4 percent to local councils. The results of the survey show that by mid-1992 the role of ministerial and departmental links was diminishing in the economic ties of enterprises. The same applied to concerns and associations that had been built on the foundations of the old ministries. These associations use their old ministerial contacts to establish links with new partners, both domestic and foreign. Our interviews in Perm, however, show that old links do not often lead to new contacts, and most enterprise managers use them only to make initial contact abroad. Most enterprises, therefore, prefer to establish networks and ties independently of the old structures, perhaps also reflecting the Russian managers' newly gained autonomy from a restrictive and secretive environment. Whether independently of old structures or not, however, most enterprises seem to have only vague ideas of how to establish new networks: one-third of the new contacts acquired by the enterprises we interviewed came to the enterprises themselves.

The trends reflected in the survey apply to enterprises in Perm as well. All the enterprises we interviewed are in the process of establishing new networks. The task seems to be more difficult for high technology production and design bureaus. Enterprises with previous civil networks, for instance, naturally have a marketing lead in relation to those that had only produced for the military. The latter enterprises have difficulty approaching clients on the market, and their orientation may easily become one of technology and supplies rather than customers and markets.

Joint Ventures

Between 1991 and 1992, Russian military enterprises were extremely eager to establish joint ventures with foreign companies. At a 1991 United Nations conference in Perm on "Conversion and the Environment," the general atmosphere was very optimistic. Since the two were no longer enemies, the West could help the Soviet Union in its conversion effort. Russian participants emphasized, however, that they did not want handouts, but rather wanted to be considered partners.

In March 1992, managers' hopes were focused on Western investment and technology. Enterprises had drawn up very technical proposals for potential Western investors, usually lacking any market information, that consisted only of technical characteristics and a sum total for the investments required. A number of enterprises were eager to establish contacts with foreign companies, but did not have concrete proposals. While many Russian enterprises saw Western technology as a solution, however, the West was providing only humanitarian aid to Russia. Despite a number of promises about international financing, funds from the West were not forthcoming.

The importance initially attached to Western technology is somewhat paradoxical. In interviews and discussions with Russian scientists and engineers on concrete projects for cooperation, the Russians always emphasize that their technology is up to world standards. At the same time, however, the Russians acknowledge that Western technology is more advanced, and that they need it for their business ventures.

Since Perm has fewer Western contacts than St. Petersburg and Moscow, the region's level of information has been more limited. Furthermore, until recently Perm was a closed city, completely cut off to foreigners. Knowledge of Western technological achievements was traditionally channeled through companies' internal KGB departments. By 1991, however, foreign delegations were visiting Perm. A delegation from Japan visited a number of the enterprises; the delegation's intent, however, was to compare the Japanese situation following World War Two with the Russian situation, rather than to invest. Delegations from American banks and military enterprises, as well as a Finnish industrial delegation, also visited Perm before the end of December.

Our second interviews in November 1992 revealed that the situation had radically changed. Although neither foreign nor national funds were materializing, enterprises were still interested in developing civilian production, and had worked out a variety of proposals. Managers were not looking for Western investment or technology, however, but were hoping now for Western marketing assistance, particularly assistance in entering Western markets. Many of the enterprises were eager to learn how to establish and develop a business plan, for instance.

The Perm region established a cooperation with the Danish region Frederiksborg Amt in Northern Zealand. The regional administrations of the two areas frequently visited one another, and cultural exchanges were initiated between teachers, schoolchildren, and artists. Today, exchanges extend to industrial cooperation. In February 1993, a delegation of military industries from Perm visited Frederiksborg Amt. Russian managers were still willing to establish joint ventures, but quickly learned that Western companies are slow to open their doors to other enterprises.

Perhaps one of the most serious disappointments for the Russian side was "Conversion '93," an exhibition of Russian military enterprises in Birmingham (UK) in May 1993. The Russian government invested a lot of resources in the exhibition, to which only journalists, peace activists, and defense officials came. Russian participants, who displayed their latest conversion products, were justifiably displeased. At an OECD seminar on conversion, the director of one Russian enterprise spoke up:

"I cannot understand it. I have a saw that can saw almost anything. And I want to sell this saw, but who comes to the exhibition, only defense people and journalists. I do not need investments, I have products to sell. I want you to buy our products. Please come and buy my products. ... I have no contact with the Ministry of Defense. Please come and see my products."

The representative of an aviation enterprise spoke more aggressively, emphasizing the capabilities of Russian high-technology: "You underestimate us; do not send us biscuits. We will enter the world market as a high-tech nation, no matter what Western partners think." Finally, the representative declared Russian firms would not start with "simple little things," as one American suggested.

The comments made at the exhibition stress Russia's desire to establish itself in the world market as a high-technology nation. The comments also indicate that the "technology push" is still alive in Russia, and that products proposed are based on technological capabilities rather than market challenges. Finally, the exhibition shows that the military is still in charge of marketing civilian products. Russian enterprises' attempts to cooperate with the West are becoming more frustrated, pleading and aggressive at the same time.

A fundamental problem is that enterprise managers do not understand the notion of a competitor. When attempting innovation, managers either look at their enterprise's technological capabilities or, on a very general level, at the obvious needs of the market. Often, they have only rudimentary knowledge of which other Russian enterprises manufacture the same product, and how their product compares with that of other enterprises. Many of the managers interviewed viewed their own clients with envy, and—assuming a higher profitability—were planning to begin competing production.

When looking for Western partners, Russian managers expect to be greeted with the same enthusiasm they offer Western visitors. Managers are astonished when potential partners are reserved, do not immediately see the potential for cooperation, and are not willing to make decisions on investments on the spot. If competitive advantages are analyzed and reveal that the Russian product proposal is superior in technical qualities and can be produced for a much lesser price, Russian managers expect immediate interest and action. It is difficult for them to understand that cooperation is the result of mutual, often long-term confidence and that there may be reasons other than technical performance and price that promote or inhibit partnership.

Technology Push and Demand Pull

Figure 1 looks at the Russian search for innovation within the military-industrial complex in terms of incremental versus radical innovations that are either technology-driven or market-led. Most innovations are incremental, and are driven either by enterprises' existing technological capabilities, or by domestic market demand. Even when they are reponses to demand, the consumer products that result cannot compete on the world market. Although many hopes are attached to radical innovation—in which the military's technological capabilities would meet the challenges of the future—it is currently nonexistent. Even though some successful joint ventures have been established with the West, they are few in number. In spite of this, hopes for Russia's integration into the world market are still attached to this approach. Radical market-oriented innovation that would identify industrial and societal needs and provide technical and organizational solutions is also scarce. The lack of state demand, particularly in fields such as health, housing, and the environment, is the main barrier to such innovation.

Figure 2, on the other hand, examines another dimension of conversion: whether the new products satisfy new demand or replace old products (processes), and whether these goods are aimed at consumption or at investment (production). Most of the products emerging from enterprises in Perm fall in the first category: they are consumption goods that satisfy a new demand. Market expansion is taking place in household appliances, television sets, video and computers. Unfortunately, this is also the sector in which Western products are competitive. If they can afford them, consumers prefer Western products to Russian ones. Consumers who cannot afford Western products usually cannot afford Russian-produced goods either. Some products emerging from the conversion process are replacing older ones, however, particularly in the fields of cosmetics and household goods.

For investment goods, practically all initiatives fall into the category of replacing old products or processes. Perm enterprises produce equipment for oil drilling and they propose to produce high-strength piping for chemical industry or machinery for production of artificial surface materials. Very few examples can be identified as investment goods that satisfy new demand. A possible exception is filters in the chemical industry; however, these have a hard time finding markets due to lack of financing available for investment in environmental protection.

Figure 1: Structuring innovation in conversion

	Technology-Driven Innovation	Market-Led Innovation
Incremental Innovation	Most examples from the enterprises	A few successful examples in consumer products
Radical Innovation	The expectation of the Russian conversion policy	Environmental problems, housing, etc.

Figure 2: Examples of product ideas from the Perm enterprises, structured after Edquist.[13]

	Satisfies new demand	Replaces old products
Consumption goods	household appliances, water purification filters	knives and forks, shampoo, etc.
Investment goods	production equipment for artificial surface materials	high-strength piping

Conclusions: The Need for New Policy Instruments

Military enterprises' assets on the supply side such as competitive technology have not been able to guarantee successful conversion of military production to the civilian sector. Even though enterprises have made great efforts to establish new networks both within Russia itself and with foreign companies, these networks have not been efficient or extensive enough to provide the necessary complementary assets and a competitive edge. Companies have been trying to build new ventures or product areas and diversify internally while simultaneously creating more independent business structures. These ventures, however, are still integrated parts of larger production enterprises or design bureaus. Problems associated with transition of the economy, the lack of state demand, and increased competition from Western products are all factors which make effective conversion on the enterprise level a difficult endeavor.

One of the main barriers to efficient conversion is the overall fixation with the high-technology capabilities of the military industries. The high-technology industrial base of the military-industrial complex is expected to become Russia's window to the world economy. The resulting desire to maintain the structure of military production, i.e. large, vertically integrated production units, adds to the inflexibility of resources both within and among enterprises. Enterprises that resist restructuring may temporarily avoid problems of social unrest and large-scale unemployment. For the conversion process, however, the failure to restructure is very detrimental.

The creation of new demand-oriented ventures, even in areas where product ideas exist such as environmental protection, is hampered by the lack of financing. In 1992 and 1993, banks in Perm would not finance conversion proposals, preferring short-term projects instead. There was no regional financing for conversion, and national funds did not materialize. Most of the support for conversion consisted of—and still consists of—credits to the military industries, primarily for salaries and infrastructure. These funds could instead have been used both to create an institutional structure for venture capital and/or to create state demand in sectors where potential high-technology R&D results are available, such as medical science and environmental protection.

Military conversion in the Perm area has been hampered additionally by the decline of demand within civil aviation. The Perm region could have concentrated its efforts toward innovation in the field of aerospace. The lack of market potential in this field, however, has critically impacted conversion efforts, not only for the military production associations, but also for the design bureaus. The energy sector also could have been a key regional specialization due to the oil production facilities in Perm. Even though both the energy and aerospace fields have been identified as priorities for the national industrial policy, Perm's energy sector has not yet received any special state financing.

Other regional focuses, such as environmental protection (the area is environmentally hazardous) and arms destruction, could emerge in the future. One advantage for the region is its frequent contacts with China. Another is the energy with which Russians are pursuing contacts with Westerners. Whether these advantages can work to transform potential projects into regional prosperity remains to be seen.

199

Notes

[1] J. Cooper, *The Soviet Defence Industry: Conversion and Reform* (London: Pinter Publishers, 1991).

[2] Michael Porter, *The Competitive Change of Nations* (New York: Free Press, 1990); B. Hilton, *Defence Conversion or Diversification, East and West: An Overview of the Literature and the Arguments* (Templeton College, Oxford: Management Research Papers, 1992).

[3] B. Udis, *From Guns to Butter: Technology Organizations and Reduced Military Spending in Western Europe* (Cambridge, MA: Ballinger Publishing Co., 1978).

[4] Hilton, 11.

[5] D.C. Coddington and J.S. Gilmore, *Defense Industry Diversification: An Analysis With 12 Case Studies* (U.S. Arms Control and Disarmament Agency, 1966).

[6] Hilton, 20.

[7] Hilton, 20.

[8] T. Cronberg, *The Price of Peace. Military Conversion on the Enterprise Level in Russia* (Technical University of Denmark, Copenhagen: Technology Assessment Text No. 10, 1992). S.W. Popper, *The Prospects for Modernizing Soviet Industry* (Santa Monica, CA: The RAND Corporation, 1990).

[9] A. Zaichenko, "Risk and Independence of Innovative Activity," *Voprosy Ekonomiki* 1, January 1988: 41-51. In *Soviet Union Economic Affairs*, May 12, 1988: 27-33.

[10] A. Izyumov, *The National Experience of the USSR*. Proceedings of the United Nations Conference on Conversion: "Economic Adjustments in an Era of Arms Reduction," Moscow, August 13-17, 1990.

[11] K. Ballentine, *Soviet Defence Industry Reform: The Problems of Conversion in an Unconverted Economy*. Canadian Institute for International Peace and Security: Background Paper, July 1991.

[12] *Conversion*, Rica (Moscow), June 11, 1992.

[13] C. Edquist, *Technological Unemployment and Innovation Policy in a Small Open Economy*. Report to the Conference on Technology Innovation Policy and Employment. Helsinki, October 7-9, 1993.

11

Spin-offs and Start-ups in Russia: A Key Element of Industrial Restructuring

David Bernstein

Introduction

Russian industry, and especially the defense industry, must be drastically restructured in order to revive the industrial sector of the economy. Defense conversion[1] in Russia is in many ways a misnomer. In particular, complete conversion, where the facilities, technology, and personnel of a defense production enterprise are converted to civilian production, rarely occurs. In the examples of successful partial conversion, and there are not very many, some portion of the assets of an enterprise is utilized in new civilian activity. Skilled personnel and technology are the most easily utilized assets, while the physical assets are far less convertible. Even successful cases usually require a significant reduction of staff, restructuring including organization of new management functions, and an influx of new equipment and/ or technology.

Conversion in Russia must be considered in the context of an economy with a disproportionate amount of heavy industry, centralized planning, overstaffing, obsolete equipment and methods, and a shortage of capital. The initial moves to industrialize the Soviet Union were planned and implemented centrally. This may have been the most efficient way to start the process of industrialization, but as the industrial sector grew in size, complexity, and diversity, the central planning bureaucracy was unable to gather and analyze all of the data, let alone to find optimum structures for the industrial sector of the economy. With too many

David Bernstein is a research associate at the Center for International Security and Arms Control at Stanford University.

large enterprises, monopolistic suppliers, and enterprise interfaces that were centrally dictated rather than market driven, industry, and particularly the military industry, consequently is now poorly structured to function in a market economy. Some transactions are now international, because the enterprises involved are located in what were formerly other republics of the USSR, but the modes of commerce between republics are not yet fully established.

If a reasonable fraction of the military industry is to convert successfully, it must undergo a transition to organizational structures and operating practices more characteristic of a market economy. As the military industry undergoes this transition, there are at least two approaches that enterprises are adopting. The first is the restructuring and conversion of large- and medium-sized enterprises without changing the basic organization. The second is the formation of new, small high-technology groups, leading to start-ups and spin-offs.[2] These groups may or may not involve formal organizational changes. While the second approach probably comprises a much smaller amount of economic activity in Russia at this time, it may be a key factor in future industrial growth, as it has been in the United States.

Small High-Technology Companies in the United States

The American industrial model, which is submitted here as illustrative and successful but not necessarily as optimum, involves a modest number of large companies and a very large number of small to medium-sized companies. As markets change, such as when defense spending is reduced, the strategies of many large companies are to restructure, downsize, buy and sell components, and merge in whatever way they see as in the best interests of their shareholders.[3] This market-driven fluidity of large companies pales in comparison to the fluidity of the population of small companies, particularly high-technology companies.

Entrepreneurship is part of the American business culture. Small companies appear and disappear at a high rate. They are born when larger companies spin off new ventures, or when groups of individuals start totally new companies. They disappear by failing, by being acquired and absorbed into larger companies, or by becoming larger companies themselves. There are several major reasons why this portion of industry is so important:

(1) Small companies can move more quickly to take advantage of technical innovations and to fill new niches in the market (frequently of modest dollar volume) because the link between management, marketing, and engineering is much more direct than in large companies.

(2) They generate the fastest growth and new employment, particularly high-income jobs. Some start-ups have grown rapidly into billion-dollar companies.

(3) They keep the country competitive in emerging technologies and markets. In this role they also serve as a feeder of new products and technologies into many larger companies.

(4) They frequently provide services for larger companies in a far more efficient way than the larger companies could provide for themselves.

Both economic and state institutions are structured by the society's recognition of the critical role of small, innovative entrepreneurs. Capital markets and tax laws facilitate the creation and development of new businesses. The venture capital industry is specifically geared to investment opportunities with high growth potential, albeit with higher risk, as opposed to investments in more mature, large companies.

The Role for Small High-Technology Companies in Russia

Small high-technology companies can eventually perform the above functions in Russia although at present they are limited by the inchoate nature of the market economy and its commercial infrastructure. They can also perform some important additional functions related to the general economic reform process:

(1) The translation of scientific discoveries into industrial technology has been bogged down in the bureaucratic processes of the Soviet command economy. New, more efficient transitional paths are badly needed.[4]

(2) The privatization process has vested an inordinate degree of ownership and control in the hands of enterprise insiders. Since privatization usually has not included sufficient capitalization, spin-offs will have to be externally financed. The generation of these small high-technology companies will result in a greater amount of industrial ownership gravitating to sources of capital and innovation.

(3) The large enterprises in Russia are far more lethargic than their American counterparts, which after all have to perform in a competitive market economy. Therefore there is all the more need to establish a more dynamic component of industry in Russia.

(4) New small companies can be formed with rational organization structures, efficient staffing levels, and a lesser burden of social services from the beginning. This allows them greater operational efficiency without major and costly restructuring. (This does not eliminate the need for such restructuring of the larger industrial enterprises.)

(5) By forming new companies engaged in civilian business, it will be easier to segregate the military and civilian components of industry. This will not only enable the civilian sector to function without the bureaucratic freight of the military sector but also create opportunities for foreign investment and assistance.

(6) Finally, this process (in conjunction with bankruptcy procedures and a social safety net) can separate out the viable components of oversized enterprises while allowing the remainder to atrophy. Such reduction is necessary in such an overindustrialized economy, and this is one of the best ways to allow the market to select the survivors.

The atmosphere for establishing these new small, high-technology companies is very different in Russia than in the United States. There are several barriers to their formation and operation. The lack of functioning markets, including capital, real estate, and labor markets as well as sales markets, militates against the development of a dynamic community of small, high-technology companies. Cultural traditions that did not tolerate, let alone encourage, entrepreneurship are another barrier. The extreme vertical integration within enterprises and close, monopolistic links with suppliers also make it difficult for small, high-technology companies to compete.[5] Customer-supplier interactions are frequently based on long-standing personal relationships, which are very important in Russia. Many suppliers also require prepayment since many interenterprise debts have not been settled. As enterprises privatize, suppliers are even being given equity positions to strengthen the linkage. The incomplete commercial and legal infrastructure, including inadequate protection of intellectual property, is another serious barrier.

As a result of these barriers, most restructuring thus far in Russia appears to have occurred within existing enterprises. There are, however, some signs of the development of a community of small, high-technology companies. What these barriers have done is to create different, sometimes awkward, paths, by which small companies are emerging. Transitional structures can include corporatization and/or privatization of the entire (parent) enterprise and/or of some of its subunits. Privatization has not generally involved significant capitalization; the limited funds traded for equity go to the state and there is little indigenous capital available to replace obsolete equipment and facilities or to develop new products.

Another transitional form involves contract work for Western customers. Notwithstanding the difficulties of doing business in Russia, many American companies see a net advantage to utilizing skilled labor, especially in fields such as software development that are not capital intensive and have limited risks. The wage disparity is stunning, and even with inflation, it should persist for some time to come.[6] This allows Russian entrepreneurial activity to begin with relatively lower risk, such as a single project for an American client, completed while still within the institutional structure of the parent.

During these transitional stages, the parent enterprise or institute (and hence the state in most cases) often opposes and obstructs the spin-off. The parent's reluctance to cooperate can work to block creation of a legally or operationally separate spin-off in the first place, or may simply make all of its activities more difficult following the initial split. Before the spin-off even occurs, the parent may resist because in Russia the parent has little legitimate claim on equity in the spin-off following capitalization. Many enterprises have approached conversion by putting the burden on their subunits to develop new products and markets. This, coupled with insufficient intellectual property protection, puts the parent enterprise in a weak technical position vis-a-vis the subunits. Therefore, in considering a spin-off, the parent is in a weak bargaining position relative to an outside investor. If the parent cannot provide capital, technology, modern equipment, or restructured management, it has little leverage to obtain equity that logically gravitates to the new source of capital and the innovative capacity of the spin-off's principals. As a result many enterprises try to keep a tight rein on their subunits during restructuring.

Once a subunit has begun to operate fairly independently, the parent may find that its own interests do not always coincide with those of the spin-off. The high degree of vertical integration in the Soviet economy, for example, makes it difficult for parent enterprises to find alternative suppliers. Another conflict can arise when the parent still seeks control over the spin-off's revenue to subsidize the survival of the parent rather than for the development

204

of the spin-off. This contrasts with the Western spin-off model, where the parent is usually quite viable and does not compete with the spin-off for its revenues. In Russia the parent enterprise is often not willing, even if it were able, to provide the spin-off with the business advice and help it needs after it is established.

I do not have data on the extent of such spin-off and start-up activity, and I question that reliable data is available. One reason that data on spin-offs is scanty, aside from such indirect indicators, is that often the most significant moves toward independence involve technical team activities that do not yet involve new legal structures. These may be decentralization of the future parent enterprise or external funding of technical research and development. Others involve moonlighting (and sunlighting) for foreign companies. By Russian law an employer cannot prevent an employee from working for a second firm.

One bit of information that may be relevant is that according to the chair of the GKI for the Sverdlovsk oblast, one out of three enterprises in the oblast that seek to privatize comes to the GKI with a conflict between the enterprise's overall management group and a subgroup that wishes to privatize separately.[7]

The purpose of this paper is to examine some of the structural and operational issues that have arisen in a few cases, and to speculate on the possible development of this industrial sector. The questions are, what paths are likely to evolve in the circumstances that obtain in Russia? And, which are likely to be most useful in building a civilian high-tech industry?

The objectives of the principals involved in any given start-up or spin-off may not serve the wider priorities/needs for building such an industry sector on a national scale. It is important to analyze the issue from both the micro-level and the overall economic perspective in order to see how the Russian government, and others, may facilitate or impede the process. The state does not have the resources to adequately support spin-offs, but it could refrain from obstructing them. On the other hand, if the parent can be motivated to provide constructive assistance, this may facilitate a successful transition. Ways to encourage this could include compensating the parent for explicit release of rights to technology previously developed in the parent and to be used by the spin-off; giving the parent a right of first refusal for subsequent financing; preferential utilization of the parent's labor as the spin-off grows; or giving the parent a right of first refusal on licensed production.

Case Studies

The following are some examples of small, high-tech operations in Russia. They include (1) a fully independent new company with a foreign investor; (2) a new company that still has operational and ownership ties to its parent institute, while performing contract research for an American company; (3) Russian research institutes, design bureaus, and universities that remain in undivided state ownership and provide work by contract to American companies; (4) decentralized subunits of some larger enterprises, and (5) other potential developments.

(1) ELVIS+

ELVIS+ is a spin-off from a much larger research and production organization, ELAS

(Electronic Equipment Production). ELVIS+ has more than 70 employees, primarily engineers, who work mainly on the design and development of wireless communication systems for both space and ground-based applications. This work covers the complete systems, including computer design, software, and antenna design, but not serial manufacturing. ELVIS+ works with Sun Microsystems, a California-based manufacturer of computer workstations.

A nucleus of the group that became ELVIS+, led by the company's director, Alexander Galitskiy, worked together for twenty years at ELAS. In the late 1980s, ELAS, which had 12,000 employees, suffered the same dual blow as most Russian military production enterprises: the drastic reduction of military orders for hardware and R&D and the lack of guidance and funding for conversion. In early 1989, ELAS started to disaggregate when Galitskiy and 250 employees split off to form a new entity called "Scientific-Industrial Center ELVIS," or SIC ELVIS. The motivation was not necessarily privatization, decentralization, or attracting foreign investment but to keep the technical team together, and to circumvent various salary and operational constraints of the command system. At this time SIC ELVIS was collectively owned by the employees, but all of the physical assets were still owned by the state. Effectively, it was still a state-owned company. In early 1990, SIC ELVIS took the first step toward privatization by paying the government one million rubles for some equipment while continuing to pay ten percent of its income to ELAS, which was still state owned. Further moves toward privatization were difficult at the time, so in 1991 ELVIS+ was founded as a new private company. The residual company, SIC ELVIS, is now proposing to privatize under Option 2 (see glossary for details on privatization options).

ELVIS+ is hampered by being resident in the ELAS facilities, and moving out is definitely part of the company's future strategy. The transfer of funds from Sun to ELVIS+ is not subject to many of the difficulties of banking in Russia because much of it is equity money, which is exempt from some of the most troublesome regulations.

(2) Moscow Center for SPARC Technology (MCST)

The Moscow Center for SPARC Technology is a potentially successful example of conversion and privatization by the spin-off of a small portion (approximately 100 people) of a much larger defense establishment, the Institute of Precision Mechanics and Computers, IPMC (approximately 1500 employees in late 1993). MCST is a new company formed in March 1992 by Boris Babaian, a leading figure in computer research and development in Russia. Babaian and his partner, Alexander Kim, founded MCST specifically for the purpose of entering into commercial hardware and software development contracts with Sun Microsystems. MCST is also the marketing agent for Sun workstations in Russia. While Babaian is the company's main technical expert, Kim is the chief operating officer of MCST and is responsible for marketing, managerial work, etc.

Babaian also manages a division of about 250 people in the Institute, which is headquartered in Moscow. Other MCST personnel also have residual responsibilities and technical interests in some of the Institute's development projects. The staff of MCST is drawn from the Institute, and MCST's work is done in the Institute's facilities, although primarily with Sun equipment. MCST also has personnel in St. Petersburg and Novosibirsk. The technical personnel of MCST have been working together for many years.

Babaian was motivated to form MCST at least as much by technical and humanitarian factors as by entrepreneurial impulses, and hence his various objectives sometimes conflict in his decision making. Initially Babaian investigated the option of privatizing portions of the Institute, instead of establishing a new company that would be founded as private from the beginning. This was not allowed, however, under the regulations concerning privatization of defense institutes. It is still not possible for a portion of a state-owned enterprise to petition the GKI to privatize when the enterprise as a whole does not seek to privatize. If the government allowed such partial privatization, it could foster new industrial development while maintaining control over the defense establishment. On the other hand, this would still be awkward if key personnel, such as Babaian and Kim, are to work in both spheres.

MCST is a spin-off, but it continues to be housed at the Institute, use its facilities, and contract with it for administrative services. The state owns 45 percent of the equity in MCST (25 percent by the Institute, and 20 percent by the parent ministry of the Institute, while the other 55 percent is owned by five founding individuals). Notwithstanding the minority ownership by the Institute, communications between MCST and the Institute about the operations of MCST are minimal. For example, Institute management does not know the salaries paid by MCST.

IPMC is in grave financial difficulty in the wake of government procurement cutbacks. In fact, MCST appears to be the only viable component, even though it is only a small fraction of the Institute. The Institute director appears to be more oriented toward the old centrally planned structure than toward the development of new civilian businesses. He is more concerned with retaining all employees than striving for higher efficiency. Given the close ties between the Institute and MCST, it is not at all clear that MCST can survive, let alone prosper, under these conditions.

At the same time, however, it is difficult for MCST to make a clean break from IPMC. MCST has resisted leaving the Institute in favor of their own facilities for several reasons:

(1) They feel that they have a right to the space; as the legal principles for ownership evolve, there is room for argument over such rights. Precedents in "spontaneous privatization" by many managers have set an example for appropriation of state-owned property. Rights to this space are particularly important in Moscow, where commercial real estate and office space prices are among the highest in the world.[8]

(2) Some MCST people, including the top managers, still have responsibilities for Institute projects that predate the formation of MCST. These projects are not receiving much funding, but still are apt to drag on for a long time.

(3) If MCST left, they would lose access to Institute equipment, which would not be easy to replace. It would also not be easy to find suitable facilities.

(4) Babaian and Kim feel a responsibility to assist the (non-MCST) Institute employees. They also feel that the Institute employs highly skilled technical people that can be utilized for the contract work.

(5) Babaian is concerned that if there is a return to the old political and economic system MCST would be in a vulnerable position, having relinquished their tie to the Institute and thus to the state. The fluid political situation makes this easy to understand.

Notwithstanding the logic of maintaining ties with the Institute, this transitional approach in Russia has inherent problems that will limit the growth and viability of MCST until they are overcome. One problem arises in attempting to determine reasonable reimbursement rates to the Institute for rent and services. In the absence of a good cost accounting system, there is no established basis for these charges. Given the dire financial condition of the Institute, its management wants to maximize the charges. (An American parent, by contrast, might want to minimize them to stimulate the growth of the spin-off.) MCST directors feel that the Institute's charges for administrative services are excessive. Another problem is that MCST frequently needs small administrative services quickly, but it is almost impossible to get rapid response from the Institute. MCST feels that eventually it needs to have its own administrative structure, which would provide better service and perform new functions, such as maintaining Western accounting records. MCST has not moved very far in this direction as yet.

Apart from issues related to its link with the Institute, MCST also has problems with the laws regarding currency transfers, taxes, and social support. Some of these problems are not specifically related to their spin-off status. Half of the money from Sun must be changed into rubles; the bank takes months to do this, however, and then makes the exchange at the old rate, disregarding inflation. (Large interenterprise debt and the lack of bank reserves partly explain the delays in implementing currency transfers.)[9] Sun transfers hard currency into the bank, but MCST cannot easily withdraw it. These are typical examples of how the inadequate banking system is discouraging potential foreign investors. Between the Institute's charges for administration, social services, and government tax, the employees get at most 30 percent of the Sun money that was intended for them. MCST management is looking at various options such as establishing a Western company, having the people be employees of Sun, etc., but they have yet to find a better alternative.

Intellectual property is an issue that could cause problems in the future. Both Sun and MCST have made trust, communication, and personal understanding the cornerstone of their relationship. They believe that this provides greater protection of their business interests than legal documents could. To this end, Sun has hosted major delegations of MCST personnel, and has stressed social interaction as much as technical communications. Looking toward the future, Sun expects that MCST will eventually develop their own products as well as receiving royalties from Sun. The Sun contract clearly grants intellectual property rights to Sun; there are still at least three potential areas of conflict over intellectual property rights, however.

First, since the employees have all been at the parent institute for many years, the Institute or the state could claim that some of their new developments have roots in proprietary technology developed earlier at the Institute. Second, the fact that some MCST employees are still working part time on Institute projects could lead to new ideas of mixed or unclear ownership. Finally, some employees will inevitably leave both MCST and the Institute as more competitive wages become available for less technically demanding positions, such as maintaining software and equipment in financial institutions. (This has recently been occurring at the rate of three employees leaving the Institute per week.) In these new jobs, they may use concepts developed at MCST, and the ownership of these ideas may not be clear.

Several other major problems have been caused by CoCom (Coordinating Committee for Multilateral Export Controls) regulations and delays in receiving export licenses from the U.S. government. Sun's comments on the work performed by MCST are considered to be technical data that is subject to export control. Sun is permitted to describe the technology and clarify it for the MCST employees, but not to have detailed technical discussions. Obtaining the necessary approval from the U.S. government has sometimes been possible, but it puts major delays in the process. MCST performed an analysis that showed that over a period of 22 months, the time lost awaiting export approvals was at least as long as the time to perform their technical work. Until September 1993, the U.S. government did not recognize the importance of time in bringing commercial products to market, nor the futility of restricting export of equipment available from other sources. In the fall the government announced a planned relaxation of the rules on computer exports, but it was not clear whether implementation would improve commensurately.[10] With the expiration of CoCom, the government removed restrictions on the export of all computers except large supercomputers.[11]

The support of Sun Microsystems is valued very highly by MCST, and a relationship of mutual loyalty has developed. For this reason MCST has been reluctant to take contracts from other customers. They are beginning to relax that restraint, partly at the urging of Sun, and partly because there are other American companies that are currently interested in negotiating software development contracts with MCST.

Babaian and his associates have had some other work with the former Compass Company in Florida (Compass has since been acquired by Octel). This work, which was to develop software for IBM machines, was more routine programming rather than innovation as in the work with Sun. In order to minimize any potential conflict, both sides agreed to form a separate company, Compass-Elbrus, with fifty employees, rather than contracting for this work through MCST.

Although MCST is still dependent on the Sun contract, there is potential for considerable growth beyond that. As the disparity between Russia and the West in the cost of highly skilled labor decreases, firms such as MCST should be able to compete based increasingly on their capabilities alone. In order to capitalize on this potential, MCST should consider some of the following changes in their business strategy:

(1) Severing their physical ties with the Institute. Further work with the Institute could be done on a contractual basis, and it will probably decline over the next year or two.

(2) It would be better to sever the ownership ties with the Institute as well, so that equity shares could better reflect contributions of capital or creative work. The state's equity could be bought out by foreign or domestic investors such as the strategic marketing partner mentioned above, and/or employees. It could also be utilized to implement an employee-ownership incentive program. There is understandable concern in Russia about selling off valuable resources to foreigners; however, deals can be structured that protect Russian interests. In any event, MCST's principals own a majority share. When the parent has an equity interest in a spin-off, it would assist the transition if the spin-off had an option to buy the state out either itself or through an outside investor.

(3) MCST will have to build more of a business infrastructure. MCST was formed as a technical project team. It has some business functions to deal with issues such as transfer of funds and interactions with the Institute, but lacks other administrative functions. It also lacks an accounting system compatible with Western standards and capable of providing acceptable financial reporting. At the present time, Sun helps MCST work

through many of its administrative problems, and has assisted in the negotiations for other software development contracts. Future customers cannot be expected to do this.

(4) Babaian's group, regardless of the formation of multiple companies, clearly has a structure, expertise, and access to highly skilled personnel that would enable it to expand its business in a manner similar to that of contract research organizations or software producers in the United States. Thus, MCST might consider working with a U.S. company in the contract research business. This could create an alliance that would market the Russian expertise and labor rates in the United States as well as, in the long term, market both companies' capabilities in Russia. Some of the funds that are now being used to pay wages of additional Institute personnel could be used to develop marketing capability in Russia and the West. This has advantages beyond simply expanding the business; if the products or services are sold for hard currency, this can be used as an offset for the contract funds from Western customers to obviate some bank transfers.

Although both ELVIS+ and MCST work with Sun, there is no relationship between them. The two companies differed in their approaches both before and after Sun's initial involvement. Sun has taken a minority equity position in ELVIS+, which was privatized prior to its relationship with Sun, whereas MCST was formed specifically to be able to work with Sun, but Sun did not take an equity position.

Other relevant differences between the two companies include the fact that the parent organization of ELVIS+ has been subdivided entirely into many separate small enterprises, whereas the parent of MCST is still a large undivided institute. MCST's parent institute has minority ownership, but none of ELVIS+'s equity is owned by the state/institute. ELVIS+ has a variety of technical and business interactions with other (spin-off) components of the old ELAS, whereas there are no analogous spin-offs of MCST's parent institute.

(3) The Boeing Company

The Boeing Company recently opened the Boeing Technical Research Center (BTRC) in Moscow to work on experimental and analytical problems in aviation and aerospace. The experimental work will be conducted in facilities of the Central Aerohydrodynamic Institute (TsAGI), as well as other state-owned research institutes, design bureaus, and universities with which Boeing has contracted.

Some of the analytical work will be performed by scientists and engineers from the contracted institutes in the BTRC facility using Boeing's sophisticated computers. Other analytical work, especially that which does not require these computers, may be done off-site in the contractors' own facilities.

Working with state-owned contractors is a new development for American companies, as in the United States private companies and national laboratories have not usually collaborated on commercial R&D activities.[12] None of the researchers are Boeing personnel, and all the work is performed under contracts between Boeing and the institutes. Hence this does not involve the establishment of a spin-off or any other form of Russian company, an equity position of Boeing in any of the institutes, or the direct employment of Russian engineers by Boeing.

This type of arrangement could evolve into a spin-off or start-up company. One of the institutes could establish a private spin-off with their researchers on the Boeing project, seek outside investors, and try to build up this type of contract business. Alternatively some of the researchers could simply resign from their institutes and start their own company. Boeing is apparently not promoting such a transition since it seems to favor the contractual arrangement with the institutes as the most direct way of achieving its technical objectives. If this were to evolve from a structure like Boeing's, the questions of intellectual property would be similar to those discussed in the MCST case but conceivably more complex since the start-up would be formed after the performance of considerable contract work.

(4) Saratov Aviation Plant

Another spin-off example can be seen in the experience of the Saratov Aviation Plant (SAP), which went through two parallel transitions: (1) They converted from a roughly equal mix of military and civilian aircraft and missile production to almost completely civilian production; and (2) they transformed from state ownership, to collective employee ownership, to an employee-owned joint-stock company.[13] During the period when SAP was collectively owned by the employees, the general director realized that some of their component fabrication shops had the potential to generate orders with outside customers in addition to manufacturing components for SAP's aircraft production. Partly as a managerial incentive and partly to facilitate conducting this additional business, some of these shops were set up in 1991 as separate legal entities to pursue these other business opportunities.

This approach was actually too successful in that these shops found it more profitable to devote their capacity to work for outside customers than to produce components essential for SAP's aircraft production. Vertical integration, as mentioned above, made it difficult for SAP to find alternative suppliers. Eventually the market will align supply with demand, but this process will take considerable time.

During the transformation of SAP into a joint-stock company, extensive negotiations were necessary to bring these small enterprises back into the main corporate structure. This problem could have been avoided for both parent and spin-off by negotiating a more detailed contractual relationship in advance, but at the time there was very little experience to guide the process.[14]

(5) Other possible models

Other military production enterprises have decentralized their organizations without establishing subsidiaries. NPO Impuls, for example, a medium-sized high technology enterprise in Moscow, is conducting a conscientious restructuring and training effort at both the enterprise and the divisional level.[15] Management has transferred economic responsibility to the enterprise's divisions and shops. In many ways this is an extension of the state's devolution of responsibility to the enterprises. The recipients of this responsibility were not very well prepared to manage their own businesses, knowing very little about the stimuli and demands of a market economy, but Impuls and other enterprises are working with their middle management to develop the skills necessary to function in a market economy. In the cases where divisions are successful, however, this does leave parent enterprises open to pressure to grant full independence to these divisions.[16]

Many enterprises are considering the spin-off of a promising division as a part of an investment deal. The spin-off could be a joint venture, or the investor could simply purchase all assets and ownership of the division from the parent (private or state-owned) enterprise. These approaches could be in the best interest of many companies, but they frequently have great reluctance to give up any equity of their most promising units. Usually, the parent does not contribute capital, has a tenuous hold on technology and intellectual property, and has outdated equipment and facilities. This means it does not contribute to the creative core of the new company, but often the parent does have much greater access to expensive and hard-to-obtain space, assistance (or lack of obstacles) from bureaucrats and local or state authorities, and other resources that are hard to value but especially crucial until the commercial infrastructure develops. Since the parent's bargaining power for equity in the spin-off depends almost entirely on these unquantifiable assets, and it is likely that their worth will decline as the market develops, managers' desire to make the most of the parent's control and retain ownership over innovative subunits is understandable. One positive contribution a parent can make is a record of successful restructuring and management during the transition, and this may be considered of significant value by an investor.

In spite of these concerns, some large enterprises including TsAGI and Soyuz have established subsidiary joint stock companies in preparation for separate privatization and/or joint ventures.[17] By providing autonomy to their subunits of their own accord, they may retain more goodwill, cooperation and eventual profit-sharing.

Conclusion

Most of the research, development, and production activity of the Soviet Union's military-industrial complex was carried out by large, centrally managed organizations. There is an enormous amount of technical talent and team synergy within the former military industrial complex. If this talent disperses, the process of reassembling it for civilian economic activities will be very slow and inefficient as it frequently is in the United States. Utilization of this talent is essential to the building of a new civilian industrial economy in Russia. If the utilization of this talent must depend on the economic viability of enterprises that now use it—institutes, design bureaus, or NPOs—the process will be far too slow. Furthermore, the talented technical teams may never be assigned to work on the most important or potentially profitable problems. Western resistance to technology transfer will also be stronger while civilian and military activities are commingled. Finally, privatization of the larger SOEs within which these teams are employed may be delayed or never occur at all.

With drastic reductions of the military procurement budget and the advent of privatization, there are strong reasons and pressures to break up some of these organizations into smaller, more specialized entities. This process has led to a variety of new ownership and operational structures. Some of the trajectories involve transitional forms that will undoubtedly evolve further; others may be fully developed. This is slowly leading to the emergence of a few small, high-technology companies.

As capital, real estate, and labor markets develop, this segment of industry can be expected to grow substantially in volume and diversity. As in the United States, small, high-technology companies can be expected to become a major factor in the industrial landscape, a healthy trend that will foster competitiveness and innovation; help redistribute equity to the sources of capital and entrepreneurship; improve efficiency and market orientation; and help break down the centrally controlled, vertically integrated, monopolistic elements of Russian industry.

The emergence of a segment of Russian industry comprising small high-technology companies can be a major factor in revitalizing Russian industry for several reasons:

(1) The size, organization, and business line of industrial units will be driven by the market rather than by central edict. New small organizations can be staffed and structured for much greater efficiency than many of the very large state-owned enterprises.

(2) Ownership of industrial assets will be redistributed along more reasonable lines than those of the initial privatizations. Ownership will coincide more with innovation, entrepreneurship, and capital investment than with traditional management.

(3) More and smaller corporate entities will result in greater competition, and the U.S. experience suggests that innovation will flourish better in smaller organizations.

(4) Smaller organizations will be more capable of responding quickly to business opportunities, partly because there will be a closer link between management and technical personnel.

(5) Larger enterprises will have access to many components, technologies, and services by working with these small firms whereas they may not be able to maintain the full array of capabilities in-house. This could also lead to more efficient operation of some of the larger enterprises.

(6) Despite the cultural and educational barriers inherited from the Soviet era, there are some talented young people with the predilections necessary to lead new businesses. While such initiative can be wasted within the large, old-style behemoths, the emergence of a small, high-tech sector will provide the environment for these people to put their talents to use.

In Russia, several steps could be taken in order to realize these benefits:

(1) The legal structure for the definition and protection of intellectual property rights must be completed. This should be a major focus of Western technical assistance.

(2) The privatization of defense enterprises should proceed. In particular, the state should allow the privatization of segments of an enterprise or institute in response to a petition by such segments. If the state allows privatization of segments of a defense plant or institute, it can foster the development of a civilian high-tech industry, and, at the same time, maintain the control it desires over the key residual military components of industry.

(3) When subunits do spin off from their parent enterprises to form new companies, they should establish more clear-cut ownership, operational, and substantive ties with the parent. This is all the more important when the parent is still state-owned because it will not be functioning as a profit-driven business and therefore will have different priorities.

(4) The infrastructural and legal disincentives to foreign investment should be reduced. (For more discussion of this issue, see Chapter 1, Alexander Radygin, "The Russian Model of Mass Privatization: Governmental Policy and First Results.")

(5) The state should continue to work to foster flexible real estate, capital, and labor markets.

Notes

[1] More appropriate terms are diversification and restructuring, but in this paper, I will stay with the more common term of conversion.

[2] By start-ups I mean the formation of wholly new companies by a group of individuals who may or may not have worked previously for the same organization. By spin-offs I mean the transformation of a portion of a larger enterprise into a separate legal entity, accomplished through cooperation between the larger (parent) enterprise and the principals of the new entity.

[3] "General Dynamics' Selling Strategy," *Fortune*, January 11, 1993: 56-57.

[4] David A. Dyker, "Restoring Technological Dynamism to the Economy," RFE/RL Research Report, Vol. 2, No. 30, 23 July, 1993.

[5] Katherina Pistor, discussion comment in Workshop on Economic Reform in Russia, Stanford University, November 22-23, 1993.

[6] On December 30, 1993 (UPI, Moscow), finance minister Fyodorov estimated 1993 inflation to be 900 percent. On January 19, 1994, *The New York Times* published data showing a decline of the ruble relative to the dollar by about 220 percent in 1993.

[7] Vladimir Ilyich Vaulin, chair of the Sverdlovsk oblast GKI, private communication to CISAC visiting team, Ekaterinburg, January 24, 1994.

[8] Leyla Boulton, "An Unpredictable Fledgling," *Financial Times*, March 12, 1993, special section.

[9] Barry W. Ickes and Randi Ryterman, "The Interenterprise Arrears Crisis in Russia," *Post Soviet Affairs*, October-December, 1992.

[10] *Federal Register*, Vol. 58, October 6, 1993: 52166-52168.

[11] "U.S. Ending Curbs on High-Tech Gear to Cold War Foes," *The New York Times*, March 31, 1994.

[12] There are cooperative development programs in the United States between national laboratories and private companies called CRADAs (Cooperative Research and Development Agreements), but these are R&D activities jointly funded by the labs and industry. See "Defense Conversion: Redirecting R&D," Office of Technology Assessment, May, 1993.

[13] For more information, see Chapter 9 of this volume, John Battilega, "A Case Study of Russian Defense Conversion an Employee Ownership: The Saratov Aviation Plant," or Michael McFaul, editor, "Can the Russian Military-Industrial Complex be Privatized? Evaluating the Experiment in Employee Ownership at the Saratov Aviation Plant," Stanford University, 1993.

[14] Kathryn Hendley, "Steps on the Road to Privatization: A Preliminary Report on the Saratov Aviation Plant," Stanford University, 1992.

[15] A case study on Impuls with more information on the privatization of the enterprise, etc., is forthcoming from CISAC.

[16] This issue was raised by the management at Impuls during meetings in April 1992.

[17] A case study on TsaGI is in preparation at CISAC, and interviews were conducted at Soyuz in November 1993.

Acronyms

CMEA		Council for Mutual Economic Assistance
FNPR	*Federatsiya Nezavisimykh Profsoyuzov*	Federation of Independent Trade Unions
GKI	*Goskomimuschestvo*	State Committee for the Administration of State Property
JSC		Joint-stock company
NPO	*Nauchno-Proisvodstvennoe Ob'edineniye*	Scientific-Production Association
OECD		Organization for Economic Cooperation and Development
SOE		State-owned enterprise
STK	*Sovet Trudovogo Kollektiva*	Workers' council
VPK	*Voenno-Promyshlenny Komitet*	Military-Industrial Committee

Glossary of Terms

Association
Voluntary associations of enterprises emerged in the late 1980s in the Soviet Union, comprised of enterprises engaged in similar types of production and bureaucrats from the ministries that controlled them. The 1991 Russian Law on Enterprises and Entrepreneurial Activity gave enterprises the right to create associations, or "concerns," on a voluntary and contractual basis, provided all member enterprises retain the status of independent legal entities, and associations have no supervisory power over the enterprises. Some associations have been successful in lobbying the state for credits and privileges, and politically inclined associations have wielded considerable influence in government policy and personnel.

All-Russian Association of Privatized and Privatizing Enterprises
The Association of Privatized and Privatizing Enterprises was founded in 1992 by Yegor Gaidar as a pro-reform rival to the powerful Russian Union of Industrialists and Entrepreneurs (RSPP). The organization has supported the Yeltsin government, and worked to speed economic reform and the privatization program.

Competitive Investment Tender
Enterprises that offer shares for sale at a voucher auction have the option of reserving some stock for an investment competition or tender following the voucher auction. To conduct such a competition, the workers' collective (usually strongly guided by the general director) decides on a set of conditions for investors; these conditions may include, for instance, the retention of a certain number of jobs, investment in certain priorities including social services, or a commitment not to change the basic profile of the enterprise. Investors submit bids detailing how much financing they can offer, which conditions they plan to fulfill and how, and how much stock they expect for their offer. The general director negotiates with the bidders, and recommends one of the offers for the approval of the workers' collective. The amount of stock that will go to the winning bidder includes not only the ten percent or more that was held back from the voucher auction for the tender, but also additional shares that can be issued by the state property agency specifically for this purpose. (This increases the total number of shares, and consequently the proportion of ownership belonging to the winner of a tender, who may end up with majority, or at least significant, ownership.)

Concern
See "Association," above.

Coordinating Committee for Multilateral Export Controls (CoCom)
CoCom was a regulatory organization that controlled exports from member nations of high-technology products of potential military or strategic importance. Members included all NATO countries except Iceland, as well as Australia and Japan. CoCom originally controlled exports to Communist bloc countries, but in recent years focused primarily on restricting sales that could aid terrorism and exports to countries that might be developing weapons of mass destruction. CoCom was disbanded on March 31, 1994; member nations may create an organization to replace it.

Corporatization

Corporatization is the legal procedure by which state-owned enterprises are transformed into joint-stock companies.

Golden Share

The "golden share" is a method of retaining state control over strategically important enterprises while still allowing them to privatize. Rather than allocate majority ownership to the state, the golden share accomplishes nearly equivalent control. The golden share is one symbolic share of an enterprise that remains in state ownership, and carries with it the power to veto any shareholders' decision that fundamentally changes the production profile or other policy of the enterprise.

Holding Company

Holding company structures are one method by which large Russian enterprises can retain control over their subdivisions. Before, during, or following privatization the enterprises set up separate joint-stock companies for each of their major subunits. The parent company keeps significant ownership shares in each of the daughter companies, usually majority ownership and sometimes 100 percent. One advantage to this structure is that it allows separation of profitable divisions from those that lose money, such as social assets, in order to attract new capital and keep funds in profitable areas.

Holding companies can also be used to maintain ties and establish ownership links between existing independent enterprises that work closely together.

Internalization

When an enterprise engages in production of components or other necessities within its own territory as a substitute for ties with outside suppliers, this movement is known as "internalization." Soviet enterprises developed many industrial activities not directly essential to their main production, in order to protect themselves against lags and shortages in supplies.

Khozrashchetnoe Predpriyatie

A *khozrashchetnoe predpriyatie* is an enterprise that is owned by the state, but is responsible for balancing its own budget. Under Gorbachev, this status was granted to certain enterprises as a step toward financial independence. While these enterprises could still receive state credits, subsidies, or payments for state orders, government funds were no longer given automatically at the end of each year to cover all losses.

Model Charter

As part of the process of corporatization, all enterprises are required to adopt a model charter specified in the commercialization statute attached to Presidential Decree No. 721. This charter mandates a two-tiered management structure, with a board of directors and a management council, both headed by the company's general director. The general director and the board of directors are to be elected at the first shareholders' meeting, while the management council is to be selected by the general director, subject to confirmation by the board of directors.

Option 4

The official government privatization program approved in June 1992 included three options for employee privileges (see "Summary of the Privatization Programs," page 228 below). A fourth option was debated in 1993, which would have allowed the employees and managers of large enterprises (those with a nominal value over 50 million rubles) to buy 90 percent of the shares of their enterprise on advantageous terms. According to representatives of the executive branch, who opposed Option 4, it would have benefited workers' collectives hugely at the expense of the rest of the Russian population, who would not be able to take advantage of these privileges. Option 4 was defeated.

Russian Union of Industrialists and Entrepreneurs/*Rossiiskiy Soyuz Promyshlennikov i Predprinimatelei* (RSPP)

The Union of Industrialists and Entrepreneurs, founded by industrialist Arkadiy Volskiy, lobbies for slower economic reform and greater state regulation of the economy. While the RSPP originally represented industrial interests, it now seeks to represent agrarian interests as well. In general, the organization has been associated with "centrist" forces in Russian politics, particularly the Civic Union political movement, in which Volskiy was also active.

Shareholders' Fund for Enterprise Employees/*Fond Aktsionnerov Rabochikh Predpriyatiy* (FARP)

The FARP is a reserve of stock that is set aside at the time an enterprise privatizes, for future distribution to employees. This fund may consist of up to five percent of the total stock for enterprises privatizing under Option Two, and up to ten percent for enterprises privatizing under Options One or Three. The FARP was created to serve two purposes: first, to keep some stock for later distribution so as to be fair to employees hired after initial privatization, and second, to give incentive to the workers to make sure privatization is carried all the way through to the end. The FARP increases the total percentage of stock for the workers' collective, and thus under managers' effective control.

The 1994 privatization program eliminates the FARP for enterprises submitting privatization plans after February 1, 1994, and provides guidelines for when and how stock in existing FARPs is to be distributed.

Social Assets

Under the Soviet system, some social services were administered by the state or local authorities, but many others were built by industrial enterprises, retained as assets on their balance sheets, and managed through their administrative structures. These included housing, primary and sometimes secondary education, health care, child care, and recreation facilities. With privatization, many enterprises are finding these programs too expensive to maintain. Municipalities are now supposed to accept the transfer of such social assets from enterprises, but with local budgets also strained, extensive negotiations are necessary to determine the fate of these facilities.

Spin-off

A spin-off is the transformation of part of a large enterprise into a separate, independent legal entity. While the term "spin-off" suggests an amicable separation, in Russia these relationships can often be complicated and antagonistic.

Spontaneous Privatization

The haphazard, ad hoc means by which Russian managers have established legal ownership of industrial assets they control has been called "spontaneous privatization." The first, least formal examples of this phenomenon date back to the early 1970s, but the term is still used to describe the transfer of property rights to managers when it occurs in a particularly lucrative way and not through the official privatization program.

"Trust"

The legislative framework for corporate governance allows for the possibility of delegating the state's ownership and voting rights that are initially assigned to the property funds. The property funds were first authorized to invite representatives of ministries to exercise these rights "in trust" for the state. Later, Decree 721 provided that property funds might make individuals or institutions trustees of blocks of shares. These trustees would presumably be potential investors, who would thus be able to exert some control over the enterprise even before buying shares. Although these arrangements are at the discretion of the property funds in theory, workers' collectives (and thus directors) have the right to veto these "trust" arrangements and may well have positive influence over such decisions as well. Holders of state shares in trust are likely to include workers' collectives, managers, and "concerns" or other industrial associations.

"Unbundling"

A reduction in size combined with structural reorganization of extremely large, vertically and horizontally integrated industrial enterprises is called "unbundling" by some economists. This process is supposed to be a rationalization of industry, as the new, smaller companies that emerge from the old enterprises are expected to be more efficient and responsive to market pressures.

Voucher Investment Funds

These funds are private companies that invest individuals' vouchers in enterprises. Although technically voucher investment funds are regulated by the GKI, which can suspend or take away their licenses, there is little legislation controlling their activities. The 1994 privatization program increased the number of shares investment funds may hold in a single enterprise from ten to 25 percent. This could potentially enable them to play a greater role in the management of joint-stock companies.

Workers' Collective

The workers' collective refers to all employees of an enterprise, both workers and managers. Despite the word "collective," these individuals do not own or manage anything as a single entity; when 25 percent of an enterprise's stock, for example, is given to the workers' collective, it is in fact distributed to each worker separately.

Workers' Council

Starting in 1988, workers' councils were established as a new institution that was supposed to give workers more input into enterprise management. Although the councils were intended to represent workers' interests vis-a-vis management, they have not consistently played that role. In some enterprises, they have been used by management to provide formal worker approval for management's policy decisions.

222

Summary of Privatization Programs

The State Program on Privatization of State and Municipally Owned Enterprises of the Russian Federation was passed by the Supreme Soviet on June 11, 1992. The program divided enterprises into a number of categories: enterprises that were forbidden to privatize, enterprises that had to obtain official permission to privatize (depending on their importance, some of these had to get approval only from the local GKI, while others had to get permission from the state-level GKI, or even from the Russian Federation Council of Ministers), and enterprises for whom privatization was mandatory.

According to the program, there were also three methods of privatization depending on the size of the enterprise to be privatized. Small enterprises, with no more than 200 employees and a total book value of less than one million rubles, were to be sold at auctions/ tenders. Enterprises with more than 1,000 employees or a total book value of more than 50 million rubles were to be privatized by transformation into open joint-stock companies. The remaining enterprises could be privatized by any method established in the state program.

Between 1992-93, enterprises were privatized in the following ways:

1) Sale of shares in a newly formed joint-stock company, by closed subscription to management and employees, and to the public through voucher and cash auctions.

2) Sale of enterprises at auctions.

3) Sale of enterprises through commercial tenders (including those with a limited number of bidders).

4) Sale of enterprises through non-commercial investment tenders (investment bidding).

5) Sale of assets of enterprises being liquidated or already liquidated.

6) Buy-out of leased assets (redemption by the workers' collective of property of enterprises that were previously partially or fully leased from the state).

The state program gives enterprises that are converting to open joint-stock companies three options for distributing stock preferentially to their workers' collectives (which include managers, workers, and, for this purpose, retired or laid-off employees). Under Option One, all employees receive as a one-time benefit, free of charge, inscribed preferred (non-voting) shares representing 25 percent of the charter capital.[1] With a 15 percent down payment, employees can also buy common (voting) shares representing up to 10 percent of the charter capital at a 30 percent discount from their nominal value, with payment deferred for a period of three years. Managers are entitled to purchase common shares representing up to 5 percent of the charter capital, but receive no discount.

Option Two allows all employees, including managers, to buy common shares representing 51 percent of the charter capital through closed subscription, at 1.7 times their nominal

---

[1] The percentage indicated is the *total* number of shares acquired by all employees put together; the allocation of these shares within the group is determined by complicated formulas established at each enterprise, usually assigning a minimum for each employee and then an additional amount based on factors that may include the employee's position, the number of years she or he has worked at the enterprise, etc. Similarly, other percentages established by the privatization options should also be read as *total* amounts of stock, to be distributed among the group indicated.

223

value. The remaining 49 percent of the shares are sold to the public.

Option Three provides that if a group of employees makes a commitment to carry out the privatization plan and avoid bankruptcy for a one-year period, the group will be granted the option to buy 20 percent of the charter capital in common shares at face value. For the duration of the agreement, the group is entitled to voting rights on 20 percent of the total shares, but the shares are held by the appropriate property fund. All employees, including the group that is party to the agreement, can buy 20 percent of the enterprise capital at a 30 percent discount and with a three-year deferred payment schedule. This option was available only to enterprises with less than 200 employees and a book value between one and 50 million rubles.

In 1992, the first year of the privatization program, nearly two-thirds of privatizing enterprises selected Option Two, while almost all the rest used Option One; fewer than two percent chose Option Three. In 1993, more than 75 percent of privatizing enterprises chose Option Two.

1994 Privatization Program

A revised privatization program was signed by Yeltsin on December 24, 1993, and took effect January 1, 1994. The 1994 program keeps most of the main features of the 1992 program, such as the three options for privatization; there are a number of changes, however, including the following:

1) The 1994 program includes revised enterprise lists for the categories for which privatization is mandatory, conditional, or prohibited. The new program increases the number of enterprises that may privatize but will have to get governmental approval to do so; many enterprises that were originally required to get special approval have privatized, but out of those that have not yet done so, the percentage that needs approval has increased from 30 percent in 1992 to 35 percent in the 1994 program. A related change is that under the 1992 program, the state GKI had the final decision on enterprises that needed government approval to privatize, while under the 1994 program, the local GKI makes the final decision. Local property committees therefore have greater control over the privatization process.

2) The 1994 program has added incentives for enterprises to choose Option Three. All enterprises, regardless of size, can now choose this option. Furthermore, the group that prevents the enterprise from going bankrupt is now entitled to up to 30 percent of the capital.

3) Approval from the Ministry of Finance is no longer necessary for foreigners to participate in voucher and money auctions; this essentially removes all restrictions for foreign investment.

4) Investment funds are now allowed to hold 25 percent of the stock in an enterprise, as opposed to a maximum of 10 percent under the old program.

5) The 1994 program has greater protection of shareholders' rights. All fundamental decisions now require the consent of three-fourths of an enterprise's shareholders rather than a two-thirds majority.

6) The new program makes the creation of holding companies more difficult. Previously, companies were prohibited from putting more than 20 percent of their shares into a holding company; now the limit has been tightened to 10 percent. Activity of unregistered financial-industrial groups is forbidden, and cross-ownership is also prohibited.

7) Certain regions no longer have any restrictions on privatization, including regions that have been particularly successful to date, or regions that have suffered natural disasters.

References

State Program for the Privatization of State and Municipal Enterprises in the Russian Federation for 1992, *Rossiyskaya Gazeta*, July 9, 1992: 4-6, in *FBIS Report. Central Eurasia, USR-92-098*, August 5, 1992: 21-37.

"The State Program of Privatization Approved by the President of the Russian Federation," *Privatization in Russia*, Information Bulletin of the State Committee of the Russian Federation for State Property Management and the Russian Information Agency Novosti, No. 1-2, 1994.

Bekker, Aleksandr, "State Privatization Program Basically Approved," *Segodnya*, December 21, 1993: 3 in *Current Digest of the Post-Soviet Press*, vol. XLV, no. 51 (1993): 19.

Karpenko, Igor. "New Privatization Program Is Adopted. But There Are Already Plans To Revise It," *Izvestiya*, January 13, 1994: 2 in *Current Digest of the Post-Soviet Press*, vol. XLVI, no. 2 (1994): 21-22.

Soviet and Russian Legislation Relevant to Enterprise Reform

The following are some of the main laws referred to in these papers. Many of the Russian sources can be found in translation in *Foreign Broadcast Information Service Daily Reports* of the U.S. government on Central Eurasia, cited below as FBIS-SOV, or in less frequent reports from the same service, cited below as *FBIS Report*.

Law on Enterprises and Entrepreneurial Activity
December 25, 1990
This law established forms of legitimate property in Russia. Property could be held by the state (both federal and municipal), by individuals and family members, by economic societies or partnerships, by joint-stock companies, by economic associations, and by labor collectives. The law also granted owners full rights to manage their property without state interference.
TASS 1951 GMT, December 25, 1990, in FBIS-SOV-90-248, December 26, 1990: 64-65.

Decree No. 601 of the Russian Council of Ministers On Regulations on Stock Associations
December 25, 1990
This decree established open and closed joint-stock companies, and outlined a three-level management structure with a general assembly of shareholders, a board of directors, and management council.
Sobranie Postanovlenii Pravitel'stva RSFSR No. 6, 1991, item 92.

Law on the Privatization of State-Owned and Municipal Enterprises
July 3, 1991
This law was the first Russian legislative outline for privatization. It authorized the GKI to develop a state privatization program, and to organize and supervise implementation.
The Law and Basic Documents on Privatization in Russia, Moscow, n.p., 1992, 3-23.

Basic Provisions of the Program for the Privatization of State and Municipal Enterprises in the Russian Federation in 1992
December 29, 1991
The Basic Provisions gave specific guidelines for privatization, and divided state property into four categories according to restrictions for privatization.
Rossiyskaya Gazeta, January 10, 1992, first edition: 3-4, in FBIS-SOV-92-010, January 15, 1992: 35-43.

State Program for the Privatization of State and Municipal Enterprises in the Russian Federation for 1992
June 11, 1992
This program outlined the three options for the privatization of enterprises. It did not cover the privatization of *sovkhozes*, land, or housing. See "Summary of Privatization Programs," page 223.
Rossiyskaya Gazeta, July 9, 1992: 4-6, in *FBIS Report. Central Eurasia*, USR-92-098, August 5, 1992: 21-37.

Presidential Decree No. 721 On the Organizational Measures To Transform State Enterprises and Voluntary Associations of State Enterprises into Joint-Stock Companies, with Accompanying Statute On the Commercialization of State Enterprises and Their Simultaneous Transformation into Publicly Held Joint-Stock Companies ("Commercialization Statute")
July 1, 1992
This decree instructed the GKI to convert all state-owned enterprises subject to privatization and closed joint-stock companies with more than 50 percent state ownership into open joint-stock companies by November 1, 1992.
Interfax 1750, July 9, 1992, in FBIS-SOV-92-133, July 10, 1992: 38-39.

Presidential Decree On Measures To Implement Industrial Policy During Privatization of State Enterprises
November 16, 1992
With this decree, the state retained its position in certain sectors of the economy (communications, electrical, oil and natural gas, precious metals and stones, radioactive and rare elements, weapons systems, liquor, and other areas) for up to three years through federal ownership of controlling blocks of shares in enterprises.
ITAR-TASS World Service, 1545 GMT November 16, 1992, in FBIS-SOV-92-222, November 17, 1992: 15.

Presidential Decree On Preventing Discrimination against Privatized Enterprises in the Allocation of State Financial Support
November 27, 1992
According to this decree, privatized enterprises would be granted state credits under the same conditions as state-owned enterprises.
Rossiyskiye Vesti, December 5, 1992: 4, in FBIS-SOV-92-237, December 9, 1992: 20-21.

Presidential Decree On the Use of the Social and Leisure Facilities and Public Utilities of Privatizing Enterprises
January 10, 1993
This decree defined the procedure for the privatization of enterprises' social assets, and listed facilities that could not be privatized.
Moscow Radio Rossii Network, January 11, 1993, in FBIS-SOV-93-006, January 11, 1993: 21.

Presidential Decree On State Guarantees of the Rights of Russian Citizens To Participate in Privatization
May 8, 1993
This decree required that 29 percent of the shares of privatizing state-owned enterprises be sold for vouchers at privatization auctions.
Moscow Radio Rossii Network, May 13, 1993, in FBIS-SOV-93-091, May 13, 1993: 33.

Presidential Decree On Additional Measures To Protect Russian Citizens' Rights to Participate in Privatization
July 26, 1993
This decree restored and reinforced the presidential edict of May 8 which had been overturned by the parliament.
Rossiyskiye Vesti, July 28, 1993: 4 , in FBIS-SOV-93-133, July 29, 1993: 30-31.

On Suspending the Edict of the President of the Russian Federation "On Additional Measures To Protect Russian Citizens' Rights To Participate in Privatization"
August 6, 1993
The Supreme Soviet issued this decree to counteract President Yelstin's edict of July 26.
ITAR-TASS 1050 GMT, August 6, 1993, in FBIS-SOV-93-150, August 6, 1993: 24.

Presidential Decree No. 1238 On Protecting the Right of Russian Federation Citizens To Participate in Privatization
August 10, 1993
The decree instructed the Council of Ministers to insure equitable conditions for all Russian citizens to acquire property, and established measures against infringements of privatization laws.
Rossiyskiye Vesti, August 12, 1993: 1, in FBIS-SOV-93-154, August 12, 1993: 25-26.

Presidential Decree On the State Program of Privatization of State and Municipal Enterprises in the Russian Federation
December 24, 1993
This decree put in effect new modifications to the 1992 privatization program (see "Summary of Privatization Programs," page 228).
Rossiyskaya Gazeta, January 4, 1994, in FBIS-SOV-94-003, January 5, 1994: 40-41.

The State Program of Privatisation of State and Municipal Enterprises in the Russian Federation.
January 1, 1994
See "Summary of Privatization Programs," page 223.
Privatisation in Russia, Information Bulletin of the State Committee of the Russian Federation for State Property Management and Russian Information Agency Novosti, No. 1-2, 1994, 3-56.